EISENHOWER'S
LEADERSHIP

Executive Lessons from West Point to the White House

BRIAN W. CLARK

For my children, Christopher and Jennifer

CONTENTS

INTRODUCTION

"The qualities of a great man are vision, integrity,
courage, understanding, the power of articulation,
and profundity of character."

On December 14, 1941, George C. Marshall, the Army chief of staff, reached down into his vast organization and summoned Dwight D. Eisenhower to Washington, DC, eleven days after Japan attacked Pearl Harbor. Marshall explained the current situation in the Pacific theater to Eisenhower and asked him to articulate a general response. Eisenhower asked for a few hours to develop a plan. He took a blank sheet of paper, wrote "Steps to be Taken," and began to outline America's strategic and tactical response to the recent events. After Eisenhower presented his plan, Marshall said he agreed, and wished Eisenhower all the best in its execution.

From that moment forward, through both his military career and his presidency, Eisenhower had to deal with some of the most complex issues imaginable. He led the nation through two of the most difficult periods in its history—World War II and the Cold War. The effective prosecution of the World War II campaigns in Africa and Europe required extraordinary leadership, from developing the mind-numbing logistical and battle plans, to ensuring collaboration with the multiple personalities of an international coalition, to effective communications, to mandating the proper allocation of an enormous amount of resources.

Guiding the nation through the unprecedented Cold War required a steady and stable hand in the Oval Office and someone who could endure the pressures of a volatile Soviet Union, while placating politicians and managing the military industrial complex. Eisenhower's international experience and reputation, along with his measured and calculated response to a number of hostile events, prevented situations from escalating into disasters.

Eisenhower's performance through these stages of history offers many lessons of leadership that can be applied to any leader in any organization. He personally believed that the qualities of a great person included creating a vision, acting with integrity, being able to communicate, and excellence in every endeavor. Eisenhower had all these traits, plus he was willing to take risks, he was decisive, and he was fortunate to be in the right place at the right time. This book is about applying the lessons learned from one of the greatest world leaders of the twentieth century.

Eisenhower achieved extraordinary results in his lifetime. He led the Allied forces to victory in World War II in North Africa, Italy, France, and Germany. As president, he ended the Korean War, he balanced the federal budget three times, he pushed through the Federal Aid Highway Act of 1956 (which built the interstate highway systems—one of his favorite projects), he sponsored and signed the Civil Rights Bill of 1957 (although he was upset about how much it was weakened by Congress), and most important of all, he kept America safe and at peace. Despite numerous hostile events during his presidency, Eisenhower refused to launch any military action, even as many of his closest advisors were advocating the use of power, including nuclear arms. He achieved peace through patient diplomacy, backdoor threats of force, and the power of his position. This man, who was a great leader in the military, became an even greater leader as a man of peace.

Eisenhower's character was also distinctly American. He was optimistic, honest, hardworking, and always respectful of others. He believed success was measured by the achievement of worthy goals and in having great personal relationships, rather than by achieving fame or fortune. He enjoyed just about every aspect of his military and political careers, and he enjoyed his personal life as well, including a long and loving marriage to his wife Mamie and an abundance of friends. Quick to give praise to others in success and just as quick to take personal responsibility for failures, he was liked by just about everyone who met him. Eisenhower once said he was grateful that his career brought him in contact with good and great men—he was one of them, and he had profundity of character.

There are many, many books about Eisenhower and about his leadership. What I believe makes this book different is that it strives to provide insights into leadership from Eisenhower's military and political careers, rather than just one or the other. Another difference is that some of the material presented has become available only recently, such as Eisenhower's role in promoting the development of spy satellites and new insights and views into his role in promoting civil rights.

This book doesn't have to be read sequentially. It can be read in any order, depending on the needs of the reader. Each chapter stands on its own and includes a summary of the lessons learned at the end. Every quote in the book is from Eisenhower except those that are noted.

When I told my family and friends I was writing this book, I would typically get asked "Why Eisenhower?" I have always been fascinated that many of America's greatest leaders of all time rose to levels of prominence during World War II—Eisenhower, George Marshall, Omar Bradley, George Patton, and Douglas MacArthur, to name a few. Maybe it's true that the times make the leader, and great leaders will always eventually appear during difficult times. Or maybe great leaders shape the times and history to bring about the desired results. Whichever it is, it can't be overlooked that they were some of the greatest leaders of our time, and there are lessons to be learned from all of them, especially Eisenhower.

CHAPTER 1

PRINCIPLES

---

*"A people that values its privileges above
its principles soon loses both."*

E ffective leadership is built on a foundation of an individual's core principles. These principles provide the basis for how a leader will behave when interacting with others, making decisions, and using authority. They guide a leader's daily behavior in good times and are especially relevant during difficult times. A person trying to lead without guiding principles will tend to behave randomly, and he or she will typically choose the most expeditious and self-serving path, rather than what's best for the organization and its constituents. Eisenhower believed that anyone, with the proper level of study and observation, could become an effective leader. That level of study needs to begin with defining the principles the person will live by, day after day, no matter what the circumstances.

While Eisenhower was born with many characteristics of a leader, over his lifetime he evolved into a great leader, and it was primarily because he always tried to act according to his principles. He never went through a period of soul searching about "who he was" or "what he believed in." His values were formed naturally. Like all of us, he made mistakes, and when he did, it was usually because he momentarily deviated from his core beliefs—integrity, honesty, loyalty, modesty, responsibility, discipline, and respect for individuals. His beliefs were formed early in his life and reinforced by continuous learning and life experiences.

Although Eisenhower wasn't very self-reflective, he did have his seminal moments. As his first day at West Point ended, Eisenhower and his freshman classmates were brought together to be sworn in. "The day had been one of confusion and a heroic brand of rapid adjustment," Eisenhower recalled. "But when we raised our right hands and repeated the official oath, there was no confusion. A feeling came over me that the expression 'The United States of America' would now and henceforth mean something different than it ever had before. From here on, it would be the nation I would be serving, not myself. Suddenly the flag itself meant something. I haven't heard other officers speak of their memories of that moment, but mine have never left me."[1]

Eisenhower's core beliefs were reinforced by a natural self confidence that was based on his ability to adapt and learn quickly, to focus intensely on the problem to be solved, his willingness to take responsibility and work hard at any assignment, and his capacity to get along with just about everyone. With those characteristics, a person can accomplish just about anything.

INTEGRITY

- -

"The supreme quality for leadership is unquestionably integrity. Without it, no real success is possible, no matter whether it is on a section gang, a football field, in an army, or in an office."

- -

Integrity is about saying what you will do and then doing what you said. Integrity also defines who we are and how we will be remembered. There is always a choice between acting with integrity or not. There are major and minor moments in our daily lives when we need to choose whether or not to behave in an honest and trustworthy manner. The behaviors of leaders at these critical moments are noticed by those following them.

One of the primary reasons Eisenhower was able to forge such an effective Allied coalition during World War II was because of his integrity. He said what he would do, and then he did it. People knew he kept his word, and they put their trust in him, even in the most difficult times. He would not engage in double-dealing or be deceptive with anyone because it would undermine his integrity, which was fundamental to who he was. Eisenhower and Field Marshal Bernard Law Montgomery (one of the premier generals in the British Army), would have many disagreements during World War II over everything from strategy and tactics to organization and supply, and some of them would be quite serious. While Montgomery "would not class Ike as a great soldier in the true sense of the word," he did believe that Eisenhower's "real strength lies in his human qualities...He has the power of drawing the hearts of men towards him as a magnet attracts the bits of metal. He merely has to smile at you, and you trust him at once. He is the very incarnation of sincerity."[2]

When Eisenhower arrived in North Africa after the invasion in November 1942, he "sensed that every individual was suspicious of everybody else—every man was sure all others were crooks and liars. The atmosphere tended to make difficult any progress in obtaining the concessions and cooperation desired." He was determined to create a collaborative environment, and he would show the way. "I immediately started a personal campaign to establish myself a reputation for the most straightforward, brutal talk that could be imagined," he wrote. "I refused to put anything in diplomatic or suave terminology, and carefully cultivated the manner and reputation of complete bluntness and honesty...I couldn't adopt any other attitude and act naturally."[3]

One of the Allies' objectives during the early stages of the North African campaign was to secure the ports and airfields of Dakar in French West Africa. Through negotiations with Francois Darlan, the Vichy French admiral who had assumed administrative authority for French North Africa, Dakar was soon in Allied hands. However, details on the use of the facilities and the future of the Vichy French Army still needed to be finalized. The governor of that area, Pierre Boisson, was a French World War I veteran who loved his country deeply and had little use for the Nazis. Boisson was fanatical in his primary mission of preserving Western Africa for the French Empire—he even battled with British and Free French invasion forces earlier in the war, with both sides taking prisoners in the process.

Although Eisenhower was busy with his own problems of fighting the campaign and Western Africa was outside of his theater, Eisenhower offered to negotiate a framework for future operations with Boisson, and a meeting was scheduled for late November 1942. As the meeting proceeded, things became extremely volatile, with many issues to be resolved. The British wanted their prisoners released immediately. Boisson countered they would be released when the British government released its French prisoners, including the crew of a submarine, and when they stopped the Free French radio from broadcasting propaganda aimed at him and his government. They were being charged with "every kind of crime," and it "was causing him trouble with the natives." Similar demands and counterdemands surfaced, none of which had anything to do with why Eisenhower was there—to secure an agreement on the use of Dakar. With emotions high and everyone speaking at once, the negotiations were in danger of collapse.

Eisenhower decided to take Boisson to a quiet corner of the room to have a private conversation. Eisenhower told him it could take weeks to finalize all the details before an agreement was reached, and they could not afford the time. He told him "if you sign the agreement…I assure you on my honor as a soldier that I will do everything humanly possible to see that the general arrangements between us are carried out."

Eisenhower gave his word to Boisson that as long as he was in his current role, "you may be certain that the spirit of our agreement will never be violated by the Allies." Without saying a word, Boisson walked to Eisenhower's desk "and, while the chatter was still going on in other parts of the room, sat down" and signed the agreement.[4] Boisson then told Eisenhower, "I will accept this because I believe you. I have found and all other French leaders here tell me that you will not lie or evade in any dealings with us, even when it appears you could easily do so."[5]

About a month after reaching the Dakar agreement, Boisson paid Eisenhower a visit. He expressed his concern that although he had held up his end of the bargain and had released his prisoners within two days of his return to French West Africa, the British had not. The French prisoners had not been released, and the propaganda broadcasts continued.

Eisenhower responded immediately by sending a cable to British Prime Minister Winston Churchill, which explained the situation and asked him to intervene in getting the broadcasts stopped and the prisoners released. Even though Eisenhower had no official role in French West Africa, he explained to Churchill that he felt compelled to bring this to his attention because "I engaged my personal word and honor that the commitments I made to Governor Boisson...would be faithfully carried out." Eisenhower added that "my whole strength in dealing with the French...has been based upon my refusal to quibble or to stoop to any kind of subterfuge or double dealing. I have been brutally frank and honest" with them. Churchill "promised to patch things up with Boisson" and soon ordered the release of the French prisoners and an end to the propaganda.[6]

- -

"One of the most difficult decisions the individual in a democracy faces is whether or not he should forgo an immediate personal gain or advantage for the good of his country."

- -

Having integrity also means being honest with yourself and others. The idea of being dishonest was completely foreign to Eisenhower. During World War II, from the troops in the field, to the commanders, to political leaders, everyone trusted Eisenhower. Even those who didn't believe in his capabilities or disagreed with his strategies trusted him. The main reason was because he was honest and forthcoming in all his interactions with others. A person is only as good as his or her word, and Eisenhower always kept his.

After the successful invasion of North Africa and Italy, the officers who served under Eisenhower in the Mediterranean held a dinner in his honor. At the dinner, they presented him with a silver platter, engraved with all their signatures, as a token of their esteem. In making the presentation, Admiral Sir Andrew Browne Cunningham, who had commanded the large fleet during the landings, recalled the days when many of them started working together in October 1942.

"At the time when we were all unknown to each other, I have no doubt most of us were posing the question: 'What sort of a man is this American General who has been entrusted with the command of this great enterprise?' It was not long before we discovered that our Commander was a man of outstanding integrity, transparent honesty, and frank almost to an embarrassing degree.... No one will dispute it when I say that no one man has done more to advance the Allied cause." Eisenhower was so moved he was at a loss for words, and sent a note to Cunningham the next day, thanking him for "the most magnificent present I have ever received...and I not only thank you for your share in its presentation but for the completely underserved personal tribute you paid me."[7]

During the planning of D-Day, the Allies spent considerable energy to keep the details of the date and location of the cross channel landing a secret, even going as far as establishing fake bases to make it appear as though the landing would occur at Calais. Any disclosure of the plans to the enemy could seriously compromise the entire operation.

In the spring of 1944, Major General Henry J. F. Miller, commander of the Ninth Air Force Service, was having cocktails and dinner with a number of friends. As the evening progressed, Miller was overheard complaining that he wouldn't get the supplies he needed in time for the invasion, which he said would definitely occur before June 15. Eventually the news of Miller's lack of discretion reached Eisenhower, and he became distressed over the incident. Miller vigorously claimed his innocence, but after careful consideration of the facts, including two witnesses of high character, Eisenhower promptly demoted him to the permanent rank of colonel and gave him twenty-four hours to return to the United States.

Eisenhower's reaction wouldn't seem that remarkable, except that Miller was a good friend and fellow West Point classmate. This wasn't easy for Eisenhower, but he had no choice. This was as much a message to all the Allied commanders and troops as it was to Miller — they were in Europe to win the war, and breaches of security were unacceptable. Eisenhower would do the right thing regardless of who the offender was.

RESPECT AND HUMILITY

- -

"There is no such thing as human superiority."

- -

On a crisp autumn day at West Point as Eisenhower was walking to one of his third-year classes, he collided with a plebe who was running to carry out an order. Although he wasn't prone to participate in the hazing that occurred there, this time he made an exception. Collecting himself, Eisenhower sarcastically asked the plebe, "Mr. Dungard, what is your previous condition of servitude? You look like a barber." The plebe responded meekly, "I was a barber, sir."

Eisenhower was embarrassed. He didn't say anything else to the plebe, and he went back to his room where he told his roommate, P. A. Hodgson, "I'm never going to crawl [haze] another plebe as long as I live. As a matter of fact, they'll have to run over and knock me out of the company street before I'll make any attempt again. I've just done something that was stupid and unforgivable. I managed to make a man ashamed of the work he did to earn a living." Decades later it still bothered him that he didn't apologize to the plebe for his rude behavior, but he learned a lesson that he took with him for the rest of his life — to respect each and every individual. "I learned the wickedness of arrogance and the embarrassment that can come about by the lack of consideration for others."[8]

Eisenhower At West Point

To get respect, you must give respect. Eisenhower was well known for not "engaging in personalities" — a phrase for his belief that it was always wrong to criticize a person's motives or personality regardless of the circumstances and the temptation to respond in kind. As president, Eisenhower once told a speech-writer to strike out the word "deliberate" in a public statement, because it amounted to an attack on a person. "When you said deliberate, what he had done, you were attacking his motives. Never, ever, attack a person's motives."[9]

Respect toward those who guide you and those who follow you is also a trait among the greatest leaders. As rumors swirled regarding who would be appointed supreme commander of the Allied Expeditionary Force for the invasion of Europe, Eisenhower was simply grateful to be in his existing role. Harry Butcher wrote, "I have heard Ike speak of his gratitude to General Marshall, to the President, and to the country for the opportunity he has been given" as Allied commander of the North African campaign. Eisenhower thought he "was the logical yet lucky choice" to lead the initiative. [10]

Eisenhower had deep respect for the American citizen soldier. He enjoyed his assignments to train the troops, and, as a commander, he went to visit them as often as possible. "The trained American possesses qualities that are almost unique. Because of his initiative and resourcefulness, his adaptability to change and his readiness to resort to expedient, he becomes, when he has attained a proficiency in all the normal techniques of battle, a most formidable soldier. Yet even he has his limits; the preservation of his individual and collective strength is one of the greatest responsibilities of leadership."[11]

Eisenhower's respect for others was also evident in his thoughtfulness. In December 1945, as Patton lay in a hospital trying to recover from injuries sustained in a car accident, Eisenhower wrote him a letter regarding the Battle of the Bulge that had taken place a year earlier. "Just a year ago this month we became engaged in one of our critical battles. It resulted in a splendid victory and one of the decisive factors was your indomitable will and flaming fighting spirit. Bradley has just come to my office to remind me that when we three met in Verdun to consider plans you and your army were given vital missions. From that moment on our worries with respect to the battle began to disappear. Nothing could stop you, including storms, cold, snow-blocked roads and a savagely fighting enemy."[12]

- -

"Humility must always be the portion of any man who receives acclaim earned in the blood of his followers and the sacrifices of his friends."

- -

Like the rest of us, Eisenhower liked to receive positive reinforcement for jobs well done. However, Eisenhower was genuinely modest and shunned the notoriety that came with his critical roles. He was almost embarrassed at being singled out, and, in times of success, he consistently asserted that others deserved the praise rather than him.

He would have accepted any assignment during World War II and given it his best. He was honored and humbled as he was promoted into positions of increasing levels of responsibility as the war progressed, yet he never let the power of his position influence who he was or how he acted—he was as unpretentious as a five-star general as he was when he entered West Point. He remained self-effacing even as he began to gain some recognition for his leadership in World War II, and despite his growing fame, he wanted to live a very normal life. He wrote a friend, "When this war is over I am going to find the deepest hole there is in the United States, crawl in and pull it in after me."[13]

He also had little patience for "grandstanding," or those who would take advantage of their positions to promote themselves. When his wife Mamie wrote that she thought Eisenhower should take a Hollywood firm up on its offer of a large financial payment for the film rights to his biography, he replied, "I can understand your feelings...But my own convictions as to the quality of a man that will make money out of a public position of trust are very strong! I couldn't touch it—and would never allow such a thing to occur. We don't need it anyway—it's fun to be poor."[14]

As supreme commander during World War II, although Eisenhower was under the constant attention of the press and part of his role was to communicate to them, he did his best to deflect any publicity. In a letter to his brother Edgar, he wrote, "To the extent possible in a position such as mine, I have constantly shunned the headlines. This has not been entirely due merely to a sense of modesty, but because of the nature of an Allied Command. Any 'glory grabbing' on the part of the top man would quickly wreck an institution such as this. Happily the official requirement has coincided exactly with my personal desire."[15]

Shortly after the successful completion of the Northern African campaign, Eisenhower received word from his chief of staff, Walter Bedell "Beetle" Smith, that President Franklin Roosevelt wanted to award him the Medal of Honor for his exceptional leadership. But Eisenhower wouldn't hear of it.

In his view, if there were any medals to give out, they were to go to the real heroes — the men fighting on the battlefront. Those junior officers and troops who put themselves in harm's way every day, under horrible weather conditions in strange lands, advancing under fire or vigorously defending a required position. Eisenhower told Smith that his response to Roosevelt would be, "I don't want it, and if it's awarded I won't wear it. I won't even keep it."[16]

In a letter written to General Albert Wedemeyer during the Italian campaign, Eisenhower wrote, "I have the earnest conviction that an Allied Command can be made to work only if the Chief is truly self-effacing so far as glory grabbing is concerned and succeeds in establishing among all the senior subordinates the honest belief that he is working for one cause only — winning the war. He must have a fund of patience and good humor and then when he necessarily drags out the big stick it is most effective."[17]

Some people mistook Eisenhower's modesty and tendency to deflect credit as evidence of weak leadership. When confronted with this by Henry Luce, who was drafting an editorial on Eisenhower's leadership style, Eisenhower explained that he believed in "maintaining a respectable image of American life before the world. Among the qualities the American government must exhibit is dignity. In turn the principal governmental spokesman must strive to display it. In war and in peace I've had no respect for the desk-pounder and have despised the loud and slick talker."[18]

RESPONSIBILITY

"When you are in any contest, you should work as if there were – to the very last minute – a chance to lose it. This is battle, this is politics, this is anything."

Responsibility cannot be given; it must be taken. Eisenhower was just as quick to take responsibility for failure as he was to give credit to others for success. He would always get out in front of an unfavorable situation, because he knew as a leader he was ultimately responsible for his organization and its actions. There is a noticeable pattern that surfaces from his voluminous correspondence during the war. In times of success, he would write, "We achieved our objectives." But in times of difficulty, he would write, "The decision was mine."

Eisenhower was often in command of vast resources, and certainly in the military he had the "power of his position." He didn't need to be empathetic, friendly, or considerate to those around him, especially subordinates, who would simply obey his orders based on the command and control structure imposed by the military. However, he was all of those things, and he worked relentlessly to foster teamwork and an atmosphere of mutual trust in all his relationships.

He believed "loyal and effective subordinates" were mandatory to achieving results, and effective leadership required building an "unbreakable bond" which required one rule—"Take full responsibility, promptly, for everything that remotely resembles failure —give extravagant and public praise to all subordinates for every success. The method is slow—but its results endure!"[19] His attitude and actions did not go unnoticed by those he led.

- -

"History does not long entrust the care of freedom to the weak or the timid."

- -

In September 1943, the Allies and Germans were locked in one of the fiercest battles of World War II. Eisenhower had taken a calculated risk in moving ahead with the plans to land and attack at Salerno, Italy. Allied troops were significantly outnumbered by the Germans, and they did not have the proper level of air and landing craft resources required to assure success. Repeated requests by Eisenhower for additional bombers and landing craft were turned down. At various points during the campaign, it seemed that the Germans would drive the Allies back into the Mediterranean, and the overall situation was quite tense for everyone. As what would be the last German counteroffensive was underway, Eisenhower wrote about the decisions and events that led to the current state of affairs.

He admitted that when the requests for the additional air and landing craft were refused, "doubts were frequently expressed in this headquarters as to the wisdom of going on with Avalanche [the code name for the attack of the Italian mainland]." Eisenhower weighed the pros and cons and "felt that the possible results were so great that even with the meager allotments in landing craft...and in air force, we should go ahead." He then accepted the responsibility that came with leading.

While his senior commanders supported the decision to move forward despite their prior misgivings, Eisenhower noted this "decision was solely my own, and if things go wrong there is no one to blame except myself." He emphasized that his officers have "striven in every possible way to make good these deficiencies through redoubled efforts in using what we have. I have no word of complaint concerning any officer or man in the execution of our plans."[20] Eventually Eisenhower received the additional resources he required, and the mission was a success, but it was close (more on Operation Avalanche later).

On June 5, 1944, after giving the order to launch the Normandy invasion, Eisenhower sat down at a desk and wrote a note to use in case the Allied efforts failed that day. "Our landings in the Cherbourg-Havre area have failed to gain a satisfactory foothold and I have withdrawn the troops. My decision to attack at this time and place was based upon the best information available. The troops, the Air Force and the Navy did all that bravery and devotion to duty could do. If any blame or fault attaches to the attempt it is mine alone."[21]

Eisenhower put the note in his wallet, preparing for the worst but hoping for the best. When he found the note and showed it to Butcher a month later, he said it was the kind of note he had written for every beach landing the Allies had conducted. Fortunately he never had to use this or any of the notes.

After World War II there were some concerns by the public and the government regarding the cause and effects of the Battle of the Bulge. It was a brutal campaign, and with more than eighty thousand American casualties (including nineteen thousand killed), some people wanted a better understanding of what occurred and why. As was typical, Eisenhower was honest in responding to these inquiries, and he accepted full responsibility for the decisions made prior and during this and every campaign during his command.

In a letter to Secretary of War Robert Patterson in December 1945, Eisenhower wrote, "From my standpoint, the German winter offensive of December, 1944, was the outcome of a policy for which I was solely responsible," and he viewed it as one of many episodes "in a long and bitter campaign which, starting from the most meager prospects in the minds of many doubters, ended in complete and unqualified victory."

His letter continued with the admission that "the German winter offensive was made possible because of my determination to remain on the strategic and tactical offensive from the date we landed on the beaches of Normandy until the German army should have been beaten to its knees. There were any number of times...at which I could have passed to the defensive, made the entire Allied position absolutely secure and waited for a laborious build-up which would have made cautious advances possible with a minimum of risk, but which would certainly have resulted in a material prolongation of the war. Every major tactical decision made during the campaigns of which I speak was made either upon my specific directive or with my full approval. The policy of unrelenting offensive during the fall and winter demanded concentration at the points selected for attack. This inevitably meant taking calculated risks at other places and one of these was the Ardennes region. I should like to repeat that I consider myself solely and exclusively responsible for this portion of the campaign just as I do for all other parts of the campaigns that were waged under my direction."[22]

- -

"The real satisfaction was for a man who did the best he could."

- -

Once Eisenhower took responsibility for an activity, he was relentless in achieving successful results. During the World War II years, beginning with the planning in late 1941 until September 1945, Eisenhower's workload and his work ethic were incredible — enough to tire anyone half his age (he was fifty-one in 1941). Almost every day for four years, he slept only five hours a night, working relentlessly to move the war effort forward. Eisenhower was blessed with a strong constitution and was rarely ill, which was fortunate, since whenever he was called upon to make a commitment, he felt "driven by the need to go at top speed, day after day, starting early and continuing past midnight."[23]

In the midst of the intense pre-war planning, Eisenhower wrote a friend who was joining the War Department: "Just to give you an inkling as to the kind of mad house you are getting into, it is now eight o'clock on New Year's Eve. I have a couple of hours' work ahead of me, and tomorrow will be no different from today. I have been here about three weeks and this noon I had my first luncheon outside of the office."[24]

Many people would consider Army life to be routine and boring. But Eisenhower viewed his profession as extremely interesting, since "it had brought me into contact with men of ability, honor, and a sense of high dedication to their country." He turned down lucrative offers from the private sector, because the positions were not interesting enough, and he had decided early in his career to not worry about promotions and to simply do the best job he could in every activity he was assigned. [25]

Eisenhower believed that work and life were connected, and it was important to find meaning in one's work. When his brother Milton asked for job advice, Eisenhower wrote, "Only a man that is happy in his work can be happy in his home and with his friends. Happiness in work means that its performer must know it to be worthwhile, suited to his temperament, and, finally, suited to his age, experience and capacity or performance of a high order."[26]

In November 1942 at Gibraltar, Butcher wrote "Now 7 pm… Ike still hard at it, and so are we satellites, but we don't have to make the decisions. He's iron. I've seen a lot of top-flight executives doing supposedly important things under considerable stress. Despite the pressure on Ike and the irritation caused by current confusion on political problems, he operates just as coolly as during the planning."[27]

"Discipline comes from the example and precepts of the commander day by day, hour by hour, minute by minute."

Leadership is a great responsibility, and great leaders know how to discipline themselves by focusing their thinking and efforts. In everyday life, there are actions and events that we can control, and those we can't. Being disciplined in how we conduct ourselves in those areas we can control can make the enormous difference in the ability to lead people.

Knowing your strengths and weaknesses as a leader is also essential. Leveraging one's strengths and working to improve one's weaknesses — or at least surrounding yourself with people who compensate for your shortfalls — will greatly improve your ability to deliver results. Eisenhower had a strong belief that "leaders are charged with responsibilities and must suppress personal impulse if duty so dictated."[28]

One of Eisenhower's weaknesses was his temper, and he had to forcefully restrain it throughout his life. Even in his later years as president, he didn't fully repress his anger, because he knew that there was no denying that people get angry. "Eisenhower's practice was suppression, not repression, and suppression for practical purposes. Public loss of temper was inconsistent, he felt, with a leader's duties. 'I learned a long time ago,' he told a CBS interviewer, 'that…anybody that aspired to a position of leadership of any kind…must learn to control his temper.'"[29]

While he would still show his temper, his anger was short-lived, and he did not hold grudges — he would simply not deal with people rather than get frustrated by them. He would accomplish this by either removing the person from his organization or working with others instead.

Time is a resource we cannot control, but we can manage it. Taking responsibility for rigorously prioritizing how and where one spends his or her time is essential to effective leadership. Shortly after receiving the assignment as the commander of the European Theater of Operations, invitations began arriving at Eisenhower's headquarters at 20 Grosvenor Square in London.

The British were thrilled that someone from the States was charged with the buildup of Allied forces (code-named Bolero), which would eventually bring the downfall of the Axis powers. As Geoffrey Perret recounts, "As the word spread that he was in London, invitations flooded in — to speak, to receive awards, to be feted and toasted, to open this or inaugurate that. He turned nearly all of them down, including a dinner hosted by the lord mayor of London. He also rejected, to Butcher's dismay, a chance to meet George Bernard Shaw. 'To hell with it,' said Ike. 'I've got work to do.'"[30]

Eisenhower's Leadership Lessons: Principles

1. As leader you're always being watched - do the right thing.
2. Say what you'll do and do what you say.
3. Give credit for success and take responsibility for failure.
4. If you want to be trusted, be trustworthy.
5. Show respect for everyone.
6. Be humble, and give credit where it's deserved.
7. Never speak poorly of others - don't engage in personalities.
8. If you want others to work hard for you, show them the way.

CHAPTER 2

LEARNING TO LEAD

EXPERIENCE AND STUDY

"The one quality that can be developed by studious reflection and practice is the leadership of men."

In studying Eisenhower's life, it would seem that every assignment he had and every lesson he learned through training, personal study, and interaction with others were vital to his development as a great leader. While it was true that Eisenhower grew and learned throughout his life, a lot of the foundation for his philosophy of leadership was formed during his various roles in the US Army and as a subordinate to a few excellent mentors and other leaders.

From an early age, Eisenhower was taught that hard work, self-sufficiency, and an ability to get things done were important aspects of life. He had a lot of energy, which in his early years he channeled into organizing sporting events and hunting trips.

He had a pragmatic curiosity, and he developed an interest in history, mathematics, and sports.

As he matured he developed a keen sense of his strengths and capabilities, and he began to cultivate a self-confidence that would serve him well in the future. He was a practical young man as he entered the West Point academy in 1911, and he had little self-doubt about his ability to learn and get along with others. He was determined to use his considerable powers of concentration for self-improvement—to learn how to make things work better and to grow as a leader through study, cultivating relationships, and observing people and situations.

Eisenhower enjoyed sports throughout his life. He found the competition, challenges, and camaraderie that came with organized sports to be directly relevant to succeeding in life, especially when it came to teamwork. "One of my reasons for going to West Point," he wrote, "was the hope that I could continue an athletic career. It would be difficult to overemphasize the importance that I attached to participation in sports." He was tenacious in pursuing a place on the football team, despite his relatively small size.

"Every moment I was allowed on the field I tried to take advantage of the opportunity. At the time my dimensions...were five-feet-eleven in height and 152 pounds in weight. I was muscular and strong but very spare. It was dismaying, then, to find that I was too light in comparison to men who were then on the team to be taken seriously. But the only thing to do was keep at it."[1] Eisenhower made sure his enthusiasm made up for his lack of size, and he told his friends, "I always played as hard as I knew how."[2]

After a serious knee injury prevented him from ever playing football again, Eisenhower became severely depressed, and his attitude and grades suffered. However, he wasn't down for long, and the events that followed showed an early example of his capability to turn challenges into opportunities. He eventually became a cheerleader, which gave him experience as a public speaker as he expressed his enthusiasm for the team in front of the entire school.

He continued to be involved around the game he loved, and he became an avid student of the strategies of applying resources effectively to win. Eventually he was asked to coach junior varsity. Eisenhower eagerly accepted, and he immersed himself into the task — an early indication of his approach to all his assignments. As Stephen Ambrose described it, "The act of coaching brought out his best traits — his organizational ability, his energy and competitiveness, his enthusiasm and optimism, his willingness to work hard at a task that intrigued him, his powers of concentration, his talent for working with material he had instead of hoping for what he did not have, and his gift for drawing the best out of his players."[3]

Although he would have rather been on the front during World War I, Eisenhower ultimately accepted and excelled at every assignment and used each experience to expand his portfolio of leadership skills. He was given large training assignments and always worked to improve instruction methods and the morale of the men. He would often ask for feedback from his subordinates, stressing the need to identify what was wrong rather than what was working well. On one occasion, when a subordinate was lavishing praise on Eisenhower's command, he told the young lieutenant, "I want you to figure out some things which are wrong with this camp. You make me uncomfortable by always agreeing with me. It can't be as good as you say it is. You either don't say what you think or you are as big a fool as I am!"[4]

- -

"Brainpower is always in far shorter supply than manpower."

- -

Eisenhower always enjoyed assignments that included working with soldiers. He respected his men and genuinely enjoyed their company, and the majority of the troops under his command felt the same way about him. However, in the military, just as in the public and private sectors, a person doesn't always get his or her choice of assignments. Key people within any organization may need to coordinate and complete initiatives that on the surface appear rather mundane or work on those that don't fit well with the perceived "fast track" of advancement for an ambitious leader. However, there are opportunities to learn and grow in every engagement, and aspiring leaders make the most of every experience.

Shortly after graduating from the Command and General Staff School in 1926, Eisenhower received orders to report to Fort Benning in Georgia to take command of the 24th Infantry's second battalion. He finally had an opportunity to realize one of his goals of commanding troops. But the assignment was brief. After six months, General John J. "Black Jack" Pershing requested that Eisenhower report for an assignment with the office of the American Battle Monuments Commission in Washington, DC.

The commission was chartered with establishing and maintaining monuments and cemeteries for the almost 120,000 Americans who died in Europe during World War I. Someone was needed to create a guidebook of the battlefields and burial sites within six months. Pershing asked Eisenhower to take on the project because of his reputation as an articulate, energetic, and well-organized officer, and Eisenhower agreed to take on the effort.

While this type of project was not exactly in line with Eisenhower's ambitions, he was determined to produce quality results on time and make the most of the assignment. "Always eager to learn, Eisenhower took full advantage of his posting. He immersed himself into the culture, politics and geography of France, and he studied the military history of World War One, both by reading and inspecting battle sites."

Eisenhower took advantage of being in Europe by organizing a seventeen-day, "carefully planned motor tour of France, Belgium, Germany, and Switzerland."[5] This assignment obviously had great benefits to Eisenhower during World War II in his role as supreme commander when he needed to understand the terrain of Europe and the attitudes of the French and Germans.

Traveling from southern France to the English Channel, Eisenhower and his driver (who doubled as an interpreter) surveyed the landscapes of World War I, where frontline trenches would barely move from 1914 to 1918. Eisenhower liked to join local workers in the countryside at lunchtime, and he began traveling with a bottle of Evian and *vin rouge* as a gesture of friendship as they shared stories.

Eisenhower worked hard to synthesize the large amount of data required for the guidebook, and it was completed on schedule, within six months. Pershing, who wasn't one to offer much positive reinforcement, praised Eisenhower for his "superior ability not only in visualizing his work as a whole but in executing its many tasks in an efficient and timely manner," and he said Eisenhower showed an "unusual intelligence and constant devotion to duty" in completing the project. [6]

"Knowledge...is a free people's surest strength."

Eisenhower was extremely ambitious and had a strong desire to succeed, but these traits were not readily apparent because he was also humble and a strong believer in teamwork. When he returned from his European guidebook assignment, Eisenhower was anxious once again to command troops or land some other challenging position. And once again he was assigned a role that would provide him with an excellent learning experience – one which would be vital in the future.

The mobilization of the economy and industry during World War I did not go well. The military had no industrial capacity of its own, it took too long to re-tool private-sector industry for war material, and inflation skyrocketed. The public had no appetite for military spending given the recent memory of a horrific war, especially during the Depression, and the military went through a decade of spending cuts. However, in the early 1930s, a small group of government and military people believed it was imperative to learn from the lessons of the past and to be prepared for the onset of another world conflict.

One of the strongest advocates for industrial mobilization was Brigadier General George Van Horn Mosely in the War

Department. Mosely had worked under Pershing and was responsible for logistics during World War I. Mosely believed the failures of world war planning would be repeated unless the army took the initiative to create industrial and economic plans for the production and procurement of ships, tanks, and aircraft from the private sector. Mosley was looking for an energetic young officer, and it wasn't long before Eisenhower was assigned to his staff.

Eisenhower was thrilled to be working on something new and exciting that would have an impact on future war planning. It would also give him an early look into what he would later call the military-industrial complex. Eisenhower enjoyed working under Mosely, who he described as "dynamic...always delving into new ideas, and an inspiration to the rest of us."[7]

Although Eisenhower had little experience with economics or industry, he characteristically immersed himself into the assignment. He went to work learning about manufacturing and industrial mobilization, and, along with a team of engineers, he traveled the country meeting with the leaders of factories. They would ask the industrialists what could be done to improve upon the production and procurement processes of the past, and how did they think their firms could ramp up rapidly to contribute to another war? Most of the time, the responses they got were not encouraging—many industrialists did not believe there would be another war, and they were too busy trying to hold things together during the Depression.

In 1930 Congress established a war policies commission to explore how to take the profit out of war. After World War I, the public had been outraged to learn how much businesses had profited from the conflict, calling the industrialists "merchants of death." Congress wanted to consider changing the Constitution to allow the president to seize factories in the event of another war.

Eisenhower was assigned to help create the report for Congress. In conducting his research, he wisely reached out to Bernard Baruch, a Wall Street executive who was chairman of the War Industries Board during World War I. This was the beginning of a lifelong friendship, and Baruch provided Eisenhower with many ideas, such as the freezing of prices, wages, and commodities at the outbreak of a conflict to avoid inflation.

Eisenhower worked for several weeks to create the "Plan for Industrial Mobilization, 1930" for Mosely and the commission. The twenty-page report included an observation that "a reasonable preparation for defense is one of the best guarantees of peace…the objective of any warring nation is victory, immediate and complete," as reiterated often by George Washington. The report covered all aspects of economic and industrial mobilization, including "price and trade controls, procurement of raw materials, labor, utilities, transportation, organization of the Executive Branch to coordinate efforts and even included draft legislation authorizing the creation of special agencies."[8]

In 1931, Eisenhower entered the newly formed Army Industrial College. Each student needed to generate a study, and Eisenhower submitted a seventeen-page report entitled "Brief History of Planning for Procurement and Industrial Mobilization Since the World War." The report provided context and justification for Mosely's ideas on industrialization, as did another article Eisenhower published for a military magazine, where he argued it was feasible to align military industrialization with sound economics.

Unfortunately, the Hoover administration largely ignored the commission report, indicating that the executive branch had no intention of thinking about a future war. But it was another excellent learning experience for Eisenhower. He knew little about industry, logistics, and economics when he started the assignment, but within a year, he had a very good working knowledge of the subject, and he sharpened his analytical and communication skills, especially in writing. In reading his reports, one would think he had been a subject matter expert in the field his entire life.

MENTORS

----

*"Always try to associate yourself closely with and learn as
much as you can from those who know more than you, who
do better than you, who see more clearly than you. Don't be
afraid to reach upward. Apart from the rewards of friendship,
the association might pay off at some unforeseen time – that is
only an accidental by product. The important thing is that the
learning will make you a better person."*

----

*"Nobody ever defended anything successfully, there is only
attack and attack and attack some more."*

- George S. Patton

He was larger than life, in stature, intensity, and ego. He lived
at the emotional extremes; he could be wildly enthusiastic one
day and despondent the next. Eisenhower called him the "finest
leader in military pursuit the U.S. Army had ever known," and
"from the beginning he and I got along famously."

Eisenhower first met George Patton in the summer of 1919
at Camp Meade in Maryland. Five years older than Eisenhower,
Patton shared Eisenhower's interests in horseback riding, pistol
shooting, and poker, as well as a passion for the military. They also
were both early advocates for the expanded use of tanks in battles.

At Camp Meade they were each responsible for their own tank
corps. Patton had been in Europe during the war, so Eisenhower
and others eagerly absorbed all of his tank stories, strategies, and
tactics from the conflict. The military doctrine at the time had
tanks supplementing infantry – they were to precede and accom-
pany the troops and destroy enemy machine gun locations.
These tanks had to go only as fast as the infantry, about three
miles an hour.

Eisenhower and Patton had other ideas. They believed if tanks were fast and reliable and had more firepower, they could be used collectively for surprise attacks, to break down defenses quickly, and spread confusion and fear within the enemy ranks. The two of them spent about a year working through their theories. They designed the ideal tank, describing material to defend against machine guns that wouldn't inhibit mobility. They learned what made tanks work by taking one apart completely and then putting it back together (and, to their surprise, there were no parts leftover).

They conducted field experiments by simulating battles, using the terrain to conceal and then surprise the imaginary enemy. One day they were working through an attack problem with a tank in a deep, muddy ditch. As the tank strained to come up the side of the ravine, a cable broke, whipping past both their heads at the speed of a bullet, missing both of them by about six inches. That night after dinner, Patton said, "Ike, were you as scared as I was?" Eisenhower responded, "I was afraid to bring the subject up. We were certainly no more than five or six inches from sudden death."

Another time they were testing how long the tank gun could fire before it lost its accuracy, caused by the barrel of the gun getting too hot. As they got out of the tank to have a look at the target, the gun started shooting on its own. They scrambled to safety and jammed the gun so it would stop. Embarrassed, they decided they had better not press their luck— they had taken their field experiments about as far as they could.

They documented all their successes and failures and described the exploitation of terrain and every other bit of information to add to World War I's lessons. They analyzed military problems from the Leavenworth Command and General Staff School, modifying the tactics, and in every scenario where tanks were included, the battle was won. They were evangelists, and they worked on converting others.[9]

They both published articles about tanks—Patton in *The Calvary* and Eisenhower in the widely read *Infantry Journal*. Eisenhower's article was titled "A Tank Discussion." It proposed a new tank doctrine for the next war, advocating for the redesign and redeployment of tanks so they could become integral to the attack plans. Newly designed tanks could maneuver as a group and, with supporting artillery, could either outflank the enemy or "tear gaping holes in the enemy line and precipitate the collapse of an entire front."

These ideas were creative, innovative, and extremely compelling. But change doesn't come easy, and some generals (and businessmen) are notorious for always fighting the last war. These ideas were new, they weren't aligned with existing military doctrines, and Major General Charles S. Farnsworth, the chief of the infantry, was not happy. He had no use for tanks or anyone who commanded them. He viewed Eisenhower and Patton as radicals who would change all the strategies related to ground warfare. Eisenhower was summoned to Farnsworths's office, where he was warned that his "ideas were not only wrong but dangerous," and that he should keep them to himself. If he "published anything incompatible with solid infantry doctrine," he would face a court martial. Patton got the same message.[10]

They were stunned. All they were trying to do was advance the use of new technology for the benefit of winning battles. It seemed obvious to them that this was the future. They would commiserate about this strange turn of events over the next few weeks, but they weren't down for long. They continued to drill at the camp, setting up teams and scenarios to sharpen their battle skills.

They were right about using the tank as a fierce and adaptable weapon, as the Germans proved during the Blitzkriegs of World War II. Eisenhower and Patton displayed admirable foresight into the future of mobile warfare, and Patton would go on to become one of the most celebrated tank commanders in military history. They supported and learned from each other throughout the entire experience, challenging each other to achieve more and working through adversity. The time and experiences at Camp Meade solidified a friendship that would survive through the best and worst of times during World War II.

"Always take your job seriously, never yourself."
- Fox Conner

On a Sunday afternoon in the fall of 1919, the Pattons invited the Eisenhowers over for dinner. George Patton also invited another guest: Brigadier General Fox Conner, an expert in military strategy and administration. Conner graduated from West Point in 1898 and had served as Pershing's chief of operations and trusted aide during World War I. Conner was an intellectual and an avid student of military history and operations, and he was well-respected throughout the military — Pershing believed him to be indispensable.

After dinner, Patton and Eisenhower took Conner for a tour of the base, and they discussed how tanks would influence the future of warfare. They conversed into the night with Conner taking a keen interest, questioning them intensely about their ideas about using tanks in war. Conner was impressed with Eisenhower, and when he received command of an infantry in Panama, he asked Eisenhower to join him as his executive officer.

Eisenhower learned from many of those around him, but he had a special mentoring relationship with Conner, who he described as "a natural leader and something of a philosopher." Conner believed that the lessons of the past could be applied to the future, and he was a shrewd judge of talent. In the 1920s, he predicted there would be another global conflict, telling Eisenhower, "We cannot escape another great war. When we go into that war it will be in the company of Allies…We must insist on individual and single responsibility — leaders will have to learn how to overcome nationalistic considerations in the conduct of campaigns. One man who can do it is [George] Marshall — he is close to being a genius."[11]

During his tenure under Conner, Eisenhower embarked on a learning experience that he later would call "the most interesting and constructive" tour of his life. Conner encouraged Eisenhower to read historical novels and military literature. Eisenhower read

Clausewitz's *On War* three times, as well as many books on the battles of the Civil War. Conner and Eisenhower would often reinforce this book knowledge by having long discussions about the books' contents and exploring alternatives to the way various battles had been fought. Conner would have Eisenhower write essays on the reading material, and he would edit them mercilessly to make them clear and concise.

In later years, Eisenhower wrote, "It is clear now that life with General Conner was a sort of graduate school in military affairs and the humanities, leavened by the comments and discourses of a man who was experienced in his knowledge of men and their conduct...In a lifetime of association of great and good men, he is the one more or less invisible figure to whom I owe an incalculable debt."[12]

In 1925, Conner enrolled Eisenhower in the Command and General Staff School at Leavenworth, Kansas. The course was extremely intense, and the competition among the attendees was fierce. But rather than shrink from the pressure, Eisenhower eagerly embraced it. He went into the school with every intention of being number one in his class.

Eisenhower excelled at solving the case studies with his teammate Leonard Gerow, which sharpened his strategic and analytical skills. He believed it was better to solve problems with a rested mind, so he would limit his study time. When he did study, it was with intense focus and concentration, which allowed him to accomplish more in less time. He was able to grasp critical details but not get overwhelmed by them. When establishing various strategies, he would turn ideas into actionable plans, emphasizing the need for teamwork and a smooth-running organization. His years of study on his own and with Conner paid off as he displayed a mastery of his profession. When the course was over, Eisenhower was ranked number one in the class, just as he had intended. It was a great accomplishment, and one that was noticed by Eisenhower's senior commanders.

"We are not retreating. We are advancing in another direction."
- Douglas MacArthur

Eisenhower worked for two of the most celebrated generals in history—Douglas MacArthur and George Marshall, and their leadership styles and personalities were at extreme opposites. MacArthur was smart, flamboyant, flattering, and he had an ego the size of the Philippines. George Marshall was also smart, but soft-spoken, modest, reserved, and not much on positive reinforcement. Both these leaders would have a profound influence on Eisenhower's career. Eisenhower had good and bad experiences with each of them, and he would go on to adopt some of their styles and methods as his own and reject those he disagreed with.

Poor leaders can sometimes be the best mentors. Although they can drive you crazy while you're with them, you can learn great lessons about what not to do. The experience can also reinforce your own leadership principles and sharpen your skills at "managing up" during the inevitable disagreements. While MacArthur obviously wasn't a poor leader, it's safe to say that he and Eisenhower had something of a "love-hate" relationship.

Eisenhower worked for Douglas MacArthur for most of the 1930s, first in Washington and then in the Philippines. His years with MacArthur were filled with learning experiences, but they were volatile. MacArthur was highly political and was not afraid to take on controversial issues. He seemed to thrive on collecting more enemies than friends. This sometimes made life difficult for MacArthur's staff.

When MacArthur was appointed chief of staff in 1930, he had Eisenhower assigned as an executive assistant under the assistant secretary of war, Frederick Payne. In this role Eisenhower would complete various staff work, mostly involving his exceptional writing skills. With the country in an economic depression and having no appetite for military spending, the war department needed people who could communicate what was going on. Eisenhower would write annual reports, official reports, speeches, memos, and letters in a clear and concise manner that anyone could understand.

MacArthur was so impressed with Eisenhower's work on the chief of staff's annual report that he wrote him a formal commendation letter, praising him for his "excellent work" and for "performing it in addition to your regular duties…This is not the first occasion when you have been called upon to perform a special task of this nature. In each case you have registered successful accomplishment in the highest degree."[13]

Eisenhower delivered quality results on time, every time. His goal was to have his writings proceed up the chain of command without any modification. As Eisenhower generated more results, more work came his way. He was working harder than ever—twelve-hour days, six days a week, and under constant stress, some of which he brought on himself. But his work was appreciated, and he was gaining invaluable experience.

Eisenhower's relationship with MacArthur in Washington was one of mutual respect. They were cordial but not friendly. MacArthur was both a genius and an enigma to Eisenhower. "He did have a hell of an intellect!" he would say. "My God, but he was smart. He had a *brain*."[14] He was impressed with MacArthur's speaking ability and his command of information, which he felt came from "his phenomenal memory," allowing him to repeat entire passages of a speech after reading it once. [15]

Eisenhower liked that MacArthur would never interfere in the details of an assignment once it was delegated, and he never cared what working hours people maintained as long as the work was getting done. However, MacArthur could be very stubborn once he took a position on an issue, and he could be close-minded. At times he would shut down debate when people disagreed with him, which would demoralize his team and sometimes lead to a suboptimal solution.

In 1934, Congress gave the Philippines commonwealth status, the first step in providing it complete independence in 1946. In a visit to Washington, its first president, Manuel Quezon, asked

MacArthur to come to the Philippines as an advisor to help the country build a military. MacArthur eagerly accepted and used his considerable charm to persuade Eisenhower to come with him. Although Eisenhower wanted a troop assignment, "he was in no position to argue with the Chief of Staff." Eisenhower had trouble saying no to MacArthur, but that was about to change.[16]

From the beginning, the Philippine assignment was a huge challenge. The Philippines weren't a priority for the US government because it wasn't strategic, and a buildout of the military couldn't be funded given the weak economy. And even though Quezon wanted MacArthur there as his military aide, it didn't mean he was going to allocate money for the military instead of funding other domestic programs for the fledging nation. These constraints put pressure on both MacArthur and Eisenhower, and their relationship deteriorated over time.

MacArthur ordered Eisenhower to develop plans to create a military within a budget of $11 million. When Eisenhower presented the detailed plan, MacArthur said they couldn't spend more than $8 million. So Eisenhower eliminated line items including artillery and engineering corps and trucks. When MacArthur subsequently tripled the amount of troops that had to be trained by 1946 without providing additional funding, Eisenhower was shocked and angry.

"We have no officer corps to supervise organization on such a scale, and officers cannot be produced out of thin air," Eisenhower protested. "We have no comprehensive supply system," and they needed places to train these troops, which meant construction projects with "water, roads, lights, etc." Eisenhower argued forcefully, but MacArthur pushed back just as hard, reverting to his position of authority when he couldn't argue the facts.[17]

They argued over everything, from forecasting the winner of the presidential elections in the States to how often MacArthur should be meeting with Quezon. When Quezon offered MacArthur the rank of field marshal in the Philippine Army, he was thrilled, but Eisenhower was appalled and strongly advised him to decline the offer. He thought it was ridiculous to accept a high rank in an army that didn't exist, and when Quezon offered a higher rank to Eisenhower, he rejected it immediately. Initially

MacArthur violently disagreed with Eisenhower, but over time he understood, although he still accepted the appointment because he didn't want to offend Quezon.

Eisenhower grew so concerned about MacArthur's increasing "habit of damning everybody who disagrees with him over any detail, in extravagant, sometimes hysterical fashion" that he began keeping a diary on a regular basis. He was also growing tired of MacArthur's "refusal to permit the presentation of opposing opinion" and silencing his subordinates. Whenever a tirade would start, Eisenhower usually found himself bearing the brunt of MacArthur's displeasure. Eisenhower supposed he "could be the fair-haired boy if only he'd say yes, yes, yes!!" to MacArthur's points of view.[18]

Eisenhower also kept notes to keep track of changes in direction. "Changes are not bad in themselves," Eisenhower wrote, but when there was a "flat denial that the original plan ever existed it is best to keep in written form, some record of the…orders and directives a subordinate is" to follow. Eisenhower thought it was a terrible way to work. "Such a practice carries an implication that someone is crazy," he continued. "Maybe keeping notes will reveal whether or not it is I."[19]

To showcase the progress of their military plans, MacArthur thought a military parade was in order. What could be better than forty thousand troops marching through the streets to patriotic cheers and salutes to the new president? Eisenhower told MacArthur there was no way to pay for this within the existing budget, but he started planning for it. MacArthur neglected to tell Quezon about the parade, and when the president found out about it through back channels, he was stunned. They didn't have the funds to transport, house, and feed forty thousand troops for a parade.

Quezon summoned for MacArthur and told him having a military parade was a dumb idea, and it needed to be called off immediately. MacArthur agreed, saying that Eisenhower had gone too far and that he would stop the nonsense. When Eisenhower met with MacArthur, they were both outraged. MacArthur insisted that he never gave the order. Eisenhower told MacArthur he was calling him a liar. It was the most heated exchange of their relationship, which would never be the same afterward. The trust was gone. MacArthur tried to smooth things over, telling Eisenhower it was just a misunderstanding and to let it go at that.[20] But to Eisenhower, the "misunderstanding caused considerable resentment — and never again were we on the same warm and cordial terms."[21]

With Germany invading Poland and Britain declaring war, Eisenhower knew it was just a matter of time before the United States would be involved. He was going back to the States, but the lessons he learned from his time with MacArthur were invaluable.

He had learned to persevere under a demanding, argumentative boss, which certainly helped him later as the supreme commander. "Probably no one has had more, tougher fights with a senior man than I had with MacArthur. I told him time, and time again, 'Why in hell don't you fire me? Goddammit, you do things I don't agree with and you know damn well I don't.'"[22] Despite the intensity of their arguments, MacArthur would never fire Eisenhower because he delivered. Eisenhower was probably the best staff officer in the Army at that time, and MacArthur needed him.

The assignment also reinforced Eisenhower's own beliefs about how to lead an organization and people, such as the importance of consistency in command, the free flow of information, keeping an open mind, and treating people with respect. These were all counter to MacArthur's behavior.

The most valuable lesson was the challenge that came with building an armed force from the ground up. This experience alone was what kept Eisenhower in the Philippines through all of MacArthur's theatrics. The knowledge gained in creating and executing the plans for recruitment, training, procurement, and other logistics was invaluable and certainly were lessons he would carry forward in the near future.

MacArthur was highly political with ambitions to be president of the United States. As Eisenhower observed MacArthur, he became determined to stay above politics. That didn't mean that Eisenhower couldn't survive or even thrive in political organizations—no one becomes a supreme commander or president of the United States without being political. He just would never let himself get so close to an issue that it became personal, and he knew how to work within organizations and with people to obtain the desired results.

In an interview in the early 1960s, Eisenhower said, "I have been in politics, the most active sort of politics, most of my adult life. There's no more active political organization in the world than the armed services of the U.S. As a matter of fact, I think I am a better politician than most so called politicians...because I don't get emotionally involved. I can accept a fact for what it is, and I can also accept the fact that when you're hopelessly outgunned and outmanned, you don't go out and pick a fight."[23]

- -

"Don't fight the problem, decide it."
- George C. Marshall

- -

"Eisenhower," Marshall said, "the [War Planning] Department is filled with able men who analyze their problems well but feel compelled always to bring them to me for final solution. I must have assistants who will solve their own problems and tell me later what they have done."[24] Marshall said this to Eisenhower when they met in Washington on December 14, 1941, just after assigning him to head the Pacific and Far East section of the War Planning Department. Eisenhower got the message—he was there to make decisions.

Eisenhower was fifty-one years old by the time he worked with Marshall on a regular basis. Clearly Eisenhower was his own man by that time. His years of service and experience provided him with a comprehensive body of knowledge about leadership, but his work with Marshall would sharpen and reinforce his skills. Eisenhower had unlimited admiration and respect for Marshall. He inspired affection in Eisenhower and others on his team, because he carried his burden of leadership without ever complaining. He was also highly confident that the Allies would win, despite the inevitable setbacks that were sure to come.

The demands on Marshall's time were too great for him to micromanage anyone. He needed people who could produce results on their own. Even as the inevitable disputes surfaced between subordinates, he would not intervene. "Fight the problem and not each other," he would tell them. This was fine with Eisenhower — he had a rather unique ability to understand events and problems from Marshall's point of view, along with an intuition on when to escalate issues to his senior officers.

They combined to form one of the closest, most successful wartime partnerships in history, but they were never friends. Everyone in the Army called Eisenhower "Ike" except Marshall — he always called him Eisenhower. Marshall was the consummate professional with all his colleagues. He was usually all business and showed little emotion regardless of the circumstances. He was extremely self-confident and cared little about what others thought of him, relying solely on his own intellect. "I have no feelings except those I reserve for Mrs. Marshall," he once said.[25]

When Eisenhower was working in the operations division for Marshall in 1942, they would meet every day. One morning, the topic turned to officer promotions. Marshall thought the promotion process used during World War I was wrong, because staff officers were favored and received more promotions than field officers. "The men who are going to get promotions in this war are the commanders in the field, not the staff officers who clutter up all the administrative machinery in the War Department and in higher tactical headquarters," he told Eisenhower. "The field commanders carry the responsibility and I'm going to see to it that they're properly rewarded."

Realizing that he had brought Eisenhower in from the field to be a staff officer, Marshall made it personal. "Take your case," he told Eisenhower. "I know that you were recommended by one general for division command and by another for corps command. That's all very well. I'm glad they have that opinion of you, but you are going to stay right here and fill your position, and that's that. While this may seem a sacrifice to you, that's the way it must be."

This was not good news to Eisenhower. He was already frustrated that he missed out on a field command during World War I, and now he was being told he was "condemned to a desk job in Washington for the duration" of the war. "General, I'm interested in what you say," Eisenhower responded, "but I don't give a damn about your promotion plans as far as I'm concerned. I came to this office from the field and I am trying to do my duty. I expect to do so as long as you want me here. If that locks me to a desk for the rest of the war, so be it!" Eisenhower rose abruptly to leave the office but started to feel bad about his outburst. As he reached the door, he turned to Marshall and smiled sheepishly to defuse the situation. Marshall smiled back at him as Eisenhower left the office.

Three days later Eisenhower received a copy of a letter Marshall had sent to the president, recommending him for promotion to major general. In the letter Marshall explained that Eisenhower wasn't really a staff officer. He was actually Marshall's subordinate commander, responsible for global strategy and deployment of all armed forces.

Eisenhower was both stunned and thrilled. For years he had conditioned himself to believe that promotions were inconsequential and that they didn't reflect the value of a person's worth in the Army. This was especially true during the Army's lean years, given his age and grade level. This attitude gave him a sense of freedom. He did not hold his superiors in awe—he worked with them as peers and felt free to challenge them when necessary. Eisenhower always wondered if Marshall's comments about promotions had actually been a test, to see how he would react. Eisenhower's passionate response about serving his country first, regardless of the role, was probably a good thing.[26]

After receiving command positions during World War II, Eisenhower would sometimes seek out Marshall's advice on key strategies and tactics, and he would always be open to Marshall's advice regardless of the content (many described in later chapters). During the North African campaign, Marshall would occasionally visit the command posts, primarily to see how the battles were going, but also to gauge how Eisenhower was holding up. "General Marshall gave me orders to take care of Ike," Butcher wrote of one of Marshall's visits. "You must look after him. He is too valuable an officer to overwork himself."[27] Marshall would often insist that Eisenhower take time off, saying that if he couldn't leave things to his subordinates, then he didn't have the right organization in place.

Eisenhower owed much of his extraordinary rise to Marshall, and he always appreciated it. In the next few years, Marshall would make Eisenhower responsible for the European Theater of Operations and the campaign in North Africa, which paved the way for Roosevelt to promote him to supreme commander. Eisenhower was already a seasoned, experienced soldier when he began working for Marshall in 1941. Even so, Eisenhower continued to learn and grow under Marshall, because Marshall empowered him to make decisions, large and small. This enabled Eisenhower to gain increasing self-confidence in his leadership and in his organizational and decision-making capabilities throughout World War II and beyond.

CONTINUOUS LEARNING

- -
"Don't join the book burners. Don't think you are going to conceal faults by concealing evidence that they ever existed. Don't be afraid to go to the library and read every book."
- -

Effective leaders always try to get the best people around them, because they know they cannot succeed on their own. However, there are times when leaders need to work with people who they don't know or who are already in place, and measure their performance to understand their capabilities and ensure success.

If people don't perform, they need to be removed immediately. Eisenhower learned this the hard way.

Major General Lloyd R. Fredenhall was an Eisenhower commander leading the Second Corps during the North African campaign (code-named Torch) in November 1942. Eisenhower had told Marshall he was satisfied with Fredenhall, but he had reservations. Fredenhall had made critical comments about the British, which was strictly against Eisenhower's policy of collaboration and mutual respect between the Allies, and he told Fredenhall so. Fredenhall also seemed to be overly concerned for his own safety, staying in his fortified command post most of the time.

Just prior to the major German attacks at Sidi-Bou-Zid and Kasserine Pass in Tunisia, Eisenhower took a trip to visit Second Corps headquarters. As Eisenhower tells the story, when he arrived he heard "the din of hammers and drills. Upon inquiring as to the cause, I learned that the corps engineers were engaged in tunneling into the side of the ravine to provide safe quarters for the staff. I quietly asked whether the engineers had first assisted in preparing front-line defenses but a young officer, apparently astonished at my ignorance, said, 'Oh, the divisions have their own engineers for that!' It was the only time, during the war, that I ever saw a divisional or higher headquarters so concerned over its own safety that it dug itself underground shelters."[28] Eisenhower tried to change Fredenhall's behavior by dropping general hints about the need to be near the front to gauge the situation and the terrain, saying, "Generals are expendable just as is any other item in an army." But it didn't work, and Eisenhower let it go.[29]

Eisenhower's hesitation in relieving Fredenhall was a mistake. After leaving Fredenhall, Eisenhower went to the front to review the situation firsthand, and he didn't like what he saw. There was a "certain complacency, illustrated by an unconscionable delay in perfecting defensive positions in the passes. Lack of training and experience was responsible."[30] He also felt the 1st Armored Division wasn't deployed correctly — it was split in two and wasn't able to operate as a unit.

After arriving back at his own headquarters, Eisenhower learned that the German attack had started, and it was a major one. Fredenhall's troops were "surrounded, attacked, and eventually overrun."[31] The Americans were taking heavy losses in terms of both lives and equipment. Eisenhower redeployed personnel and equipment to the front in order to reinforce the lines. As the battle raged for several days, serious issues between Fredenhall and his commanders were surfacing, especially with the 1st Armored Division commander Major General Orlando Ward and Brigadier General Paul M. Robinett, who was commanding an armored unit near Fondouk.

Ward was angry at Fredenhall for splitting his division in two. "Robinett charged that no one at Second Corps was coordinating the units in the field, no one knew what boundaries had been assigned, no one knew who was on the flanks or in support, no one was coordinating defensive fire, and the piecemeal commitment of small units was causing great confusion."[32]

Fortunately for the Allies, the Germans weren't completely organized either. It took a few days longer than necessary for a Panzer division to get to German Field Marshal Erwin Rommel for his attack at Kasserine Pass. Eisenhower was sure Rommel was driving toward the large Allied supply base at Le Kef, but he was also fairly certain that the Allies could hold a defensive line and ultimately push the enemy back, because the Germans would have to supply their lines through a narrow gap in the mountains. Eisenhower needed a trusted pair of eyes on the front, and he sent Major General Ernest N. Harmon to assess Fredenhall's performance and the battle situation and report back to him.

Eventually the German attack diminished due to their lack of supplies and the defensive stance and artillery attacks from the Americans. It was clear to Eisenhower that Rommel's attack was done. As was his nature, Eisenhower now wanted to take advantage of the situation and go on the offensive. He told Fredenhall, "The enemy is no longer capable of offensive action." He thought that Fredenhall should "take any reasonable risk in launching local counterattacks that could be properly supported by his artillery." Eisenhower was so sure of the situation that he said he "would accept full responsibility for any disadvantage that might result from vigorous action on his part."[33]

But Fredenhall disagreed with Eisenhower's analysis, believing that the enemy would initiate at least one more offensive attack, so he simply reinforced his defenses. Unfortunately, Eisenhower did not order his men into action because the Germans were indeed in full retreat, and the Allies missed a great opportunity to hand the Germans a major defeat early in the war.

Meanwhile, as Harmon arrived at the command post, Fredenhall was trying to decide whether he should move his headquarters further away from the front, to protect himself and his staff. He asked Harmon if he thought they should move to the rear. Since Harmon just arrived, he thought it was a strange question, and he responded, "Hell no." Fredenhall turned to his staff and said, "That settles it, we stay." Fredenhall then handed Harmon an envelope containing orders placing him in command of the "battle in process." Having turned everything over to Harmon, "Fredenhall went to bed and slept for twenty-four hours."[34]

Overall, it was a poor performance for Fredenhall and the Americans. However, there were some positive outcomes. It did have the effect of causing Hitler to redeploy resources from his Eastern front to the battles in North Africa, and it did give the Americans some much-needed battle experience. During the battle, Eisenhower wrote to Marshall, "Our soldiers are learning rapidly and while I still believe that many of the lessons we are forced to learn at the cost of lives could be learned at home, I assure you that the troops that come out of this campaign are going to be battle wise and tactically efficient."[35]

Eisenhower knew he made mistakes in his first real battle of World War II. "Several others, including myself, shared responsibility for our week of reverses."[36] Fredenhall showed himself to be unpredictable and uncertain, and even though Eisenhower's intuition and his principles (regarding Allied unity and having generals close to the action) told him he should remove Fredenhall from command, he didn't act. But he would not let that happen again — he had learned a valuable lesson. As the war continued, Eisenhower would remove commanders immediately if they showed any signs of incompetence or complacency. He told Butcher that "troops had a right to good leadership and it was up to top commanders to relieve any officer who failed to provide it."[37]

When he replaced Fredenhall with Patton, Eisenhower told him, "You must not retain for one instant any man in a responsible position where you have become doubtful of his ability to do the job...This matter frequently calls for more courage than any other thing you will have to do, but I expect you to be perfectly cold-blooded about it." To his old friend, Leonard Gerow, he said, "Officers that fail must be ruthlessly weeded out. Considerations of friendship, family, kindness, and nice personality have nothing whatsoever to do with the problem...you must be tough," and he stressed that the "lazy, slothful, the indifferent or the complacent" must be relieved.[38] Eisenhower had learned his lesson.

As supreme commander, Eisenhower was driven to succeed against the Axis powers. He used every resource at his disposal to destroy the enemy, including the coordinated use of air, sea, and land-based powers. Eisenhower did what had to be done. But throughout the war, he would visit the battlefield to witness and observe the effects of modern warfare for himself. He always considered war to be a tragic waste of lives and resources, and he learned firsthand how devastating war was to humanity.

Describing the scene after the battle of Falaise in France, Eisenhower wrote, "Roads, highways, and fields were so choked with destroyed equipment and with dead men and animals that passage through the area was extremely difficult. Forty-eight hours after the closing of the gap I was conducted through it on foot, to encounter scenes that could be described only by Dante. It was literally possible to walk for hundreds of yards at a time, stepping on nothing but dead and decaying flesh."[39]

Eisenhower's experiences and observations during and immediately after the war had a profound effect on him. As he traveled to German cities and concentration camps and saw all the devastation caused by war, he swore to himself, "Never again."[40] He would carry these memories and lessons with him into his presidency, where he would use politics, diplomacy, and negotiations — just about any tactic rather than military means — to avoid amed conflict.

Eisenhower's Leadership Lessons: Learning to Lead

1. When you experience a setback, get over it, and find a way to turn it around to your advantage.
2. Focus and concentrate on the matter at hand.
3. Embrace and excel at every assignment.
4. Seek out and learn from those who know more than you.
5. Learn to manage up.
6. Partner with innovators.
7. Read, watch, and learn from history.
8. Work with a rested mind.
9. There are lessons to be learned from both good and bad leaders.
10 Learn from your mistakes.

CHAPTER 3.

PEOPLE

"I liked Eisenhower at once. He struck me as being completely sincere, straightforward and very modest."
- Admiral Sir Andrew Browne Cunningham

E isenhower believed if you treated people with respect and gave them the training and the tools they needed to get the job done, then they would perform at the best of their abilities. He also knew that all the strategic and logistical planning required for a major battle didn't mean anything if the troops didn't have the courage and the desire to fight.

"The idea is to get people to work together," Eisenhower wrote to his son at West Point, "not only because you tell them to do so and enforce your orders but because they instinctively want to do it for you. Essentially, you must be devoted to duty, sincere, fair and cheerful. You do not need to be a glad-hander nor a salesman, but your men must trust you."[1]

Eisenhower was trusted and well-liked by a broad range of people, from Charles de Gaulle (the French general and statesman) to Montgomery to George Marshall. Indeed, almost everyone who met Eisenhower liked him, and Richard Nixon once said that he couldn't understand how that was possible. But it was possible because of Eisenhower's ability to connect with people. He was an excellent listener and very empathetic to anyone he spoke to, whether it was Prime Minister Winston Churchill or an infantryman from Kansas. He also reached out to his peers and subordinates for solutions, and although he would ultimately make the decision, he always tried to reach consensus, taking into account the views and perspectives of others. But the biggest reason he was so well-liked was because he worked at it.

TEAMWORK

"Leadership is the art of getting someone else to do something you want done because he wants to do it."

As both a general and president, Eisenhower always emphasized teamwork—putting aside one's ego for the benefit of team and working toward the desired goal in a cooperative, collaborative manner. Eisenhower played football at West Point until he was injured. Football suited Eisenhower's strong emphasis on teamwork. "I believe that football, perhaps more than any other sport, tends to instill in men the feeling that victory comes through hard work, team play, self-confidence, and an enthusiasm that amounts to dedication."[2] Indeed, many of his subordinates and colleagues believed his style was much like a football coach encouraging his team to reach the goal and win the game.

Though years of experience, Eisenhower knew how to build teams and keep everyone motivated as they moved forward. Eisenhower was a talented strategist and an exceptional mediator, patiently listening to different views from strong-willed generals of different countries, pushing and prodding them to consensus, and persuading them to work together as a team.

His leadership style was understated and unpretentious, and nearly everyone underestimated his abilities, which actually contributed to achieving results, as he quietly guided the debate in the direction he wanted. This doesn't mean there weren't disagreements among the Allies. There were many, many heated arguments and discussions over strategy and policy. Eisenhower was at the center of many of these debates, and he often encouraged them, believing that some of the best decisions were made through differences of opinions. But in the end, he held the Allies together in a common cause to defeat a common enemy.

Eisenhower's desire for teamwork and cooperation was almost fanatical. To be successful the Allies needed to be fighting the enemy and not each other, and they needed to stay together, no matter what. Eisenhower's leadership played a crucial role in holding the alliance together—it was one of the most successful aspects of his leadership. He would quickly replace people who could or would not work well with others, placing the objective above all, including egos, nationalities, and the personal ambitions of others.

In June 1942, Eisenhower was appointed commander of all American armed forces in Britain. From the beginning Eisenhower insisted on building a collaborative, cooperative environment, with an integrated organization in terms of nationalities and armed forces. He reached out to the British in an effort to build mutual trust and built strong bonds with key personnel, such as Churchill, Lord Louis Mountbatten, and General Hastings Ismay.

Eisenhower sought Ismay's advice on what could be done to create a collaborative, productive relationship between the British and Americans. Ismay found Eisenhower to be "tremendously alert" and confident, but without any "trace of conceit or pomposity. Frankness, sincerity, and friendliness were written all over him…but he could be firm to the point of ruthlessness if the occasion demanded it."

One day Ismay told Eisenhower of an American officer who, after a few drinks, would boast in front of a mixed crowd that his

American troops "would show the British how to fight." Ismay had told the story believing that the accused officer would simply be reprimanded, but instead, Eisenhower "went white with rage." Eisenhower ordered an aide to have the officer report to him the next morning, and he told Ismay, "I'll make the son of a bitch swim back to America."

Ismay was surprised by Eisenhower's reaction, and he expressed second thoughts about telling him, since it seemed that the discipline was going to be rather harsh. But Eisenhower dismissed Ismay's concerns. "If we are not going to be frank with each other, however delicate the topic we will never win this war." The officer was sent home by ship. "From the outset he regarded Anglo-American friendship almost as a religion," Ismay wrote. [3]

In his roles as an Allied commander in North Africa and Europe, Eisenhower would strive to be "country agnostic" in order to hold the coalition together and bring a balanced perspective to the war effort. Eisenhower didn't want problems solved on an "American vs. British basis" — he wanted them solved as a team. He wrote to General Thomas T. Handy, his successor at the Operations Planning Division (OPD) in Washington DC, that "I do not allow, ever, an expression to be used in this headquarters in my presence that even insinuates a British vs. American problem exists. So far as I am concerned, it doesn't. The job of winning this war is difficult, even with all of us pulling together as one complete team." [4]

He did this because he was certain that a united front in perception and a united force in reality would ultimately lead to the downfall of the Axis powers. The Allies were stronger together than they were apart. Even in the midst of the debates over battle priorities, Churchill was generous in his praise of Eisenhower. In a speech to the House of Commons in February 1944 on the progress of the war, Churchill "praised General Eisenhower's efforts to build up a unified Allied command." Such unity, Churchill emphasized, "will be found most serviceable, and unique also in all the history of alliances." [5]

Eisenhower and Hitler both knew it would be impossible for the Nazis to prevail as long as the Allies remained together. Hitler's entire strategy near the end of the war was to take action that would wear the coalition down, so he could deal with each country individually. In ordering the attack that became known as the Battle of the Bulge, Hitler wrote that "never in history was there a coalition like that of our enemies, composed of such heterogeneous elements with such diverse aims...Even now these states are at loggerheads...and if we can deliver a few more heavy blows, then this artificially bolstered common front may suddenly collapse with a gigantic clap of thunder." Hitler clearly misjudged the amount of disagreement between the Allies and the tenacity of Eisenhower and others in maintaining the coalition.[6]

"The best morale exists when you never hear the word mentioned. When you hear a lot of talk about it, it's usually lousy."

In his book *Supreme Command*, Forrest Pogue wrote that "the strength of coalitions is tested by controversies and trials," and the Allied coalition was tested numerous times through World War II.[7] As General Omar Bradley explained, while confrontational episodes were infrequent, there was "a sensitivity that can result in bitter misunderstandings under the most trivial of circumstances" between Allied commanders — small things could sometimes get blown out of proportion.[8]

Eisenhower worked hard and fast to reduce the inevitable tension that surfaced during disagreements between various parties. He confessed to a friend that "circumstances bring about odd situations, and I sometimes think that one of oddest of all is the picture of a western Kansan, with all his profanity and outspokenness, being in command on an Allied organization, where tact, suavity and diplomacy are all supposed to be essential weapons."[9] However, most people, including the British, liked Eisenhower, because he was completely candid and honest.

Eisenhower had to deal with many conflicts and debates during the war. Some of these were expected and welcomed. But there were also unproductive controversies that required his attention. The intensity and stress of the war caused many heated conversations and accusations that did little to contribute to Allied unity. He worked relentlessly to resolve these destructive disputes quickly by dragging "all these matters squarely into the open, discussing them frankly, and insisting upon positive rather than negative action in furthering the purpose of Allied unity."[10] He constantly worked to create an atmosphere of cooperation, which he accomplished at his headquarters, but his challenge was to have this spirit of cooperation propagated throughout the entire armed forces.

One dispute between the Allies occurred in April 1943. During the campaign in North Africa, Patton submitted a report to headquarters stating, "Forward troops have been continuously bombed all morning. Total lack of air cover for our units has allowed German air force to operate almost at will." The British commander of the tactical air force, Arthur Coningham, took offense at the charge, and he sent a communication to Patton, essentially accusing him of using the "air force as an alibi for lack of success on the ground," adding, "it can only be assumed that Second Corps personnel concerned are not battle-worthy in terms of present operations…it is requested that such inaccurate and exaggerated reports should cease."[11] Adding fuel to the fire, Coningham had the message distributed to all senior commanders in the Mediterranean.

Air Chief Arthur Tedder described this exchange as "dynamite with a short, fast-burning fuse, and the situation could well have led to a major crisis in Anglo-American relations." [12] Eisenhower was so beside himself about the incident that he drafted a memo to Marshall saying that "since it was obvious he could not control his Allied commanders, he asked to be relieved," but Smith convinced him to hold off on sending it. Tedder intervened and instructed Coningham to apologize, but all Coningham did was withdraw and cancel the message. That was not nearly good enough for Patton. He found it an "altogether inadequate apology to the United States troops, many of who have marched and fought over hostile country since the 17th [of March]." [13]

Eisenhower agreed with Patton, and he ordered Coningham to make a personal apology to Patton and to explain his mistake to those commanders who had received the original message. Looking to calm Patton about the "unjust criticism," Eisenhower wrote to Patton, "I realize how chagrined you were and why you felt that some public retraction or apology was indicated. However, I realize also that *the greatest purpose of complete Allied teamwork must be achieved in this theater* and it is my conviction that this purpose will not be furthered by demanding the last pound of flesh for every error, when other measures should suffice. Moreover, I am certain that the officer concerned quickly appreciated the gravity of the incident and has already taken steps to alleviate the effect...true cooperation and unification of effort will come about only through frank, free, and friendly understanding amongst all. This, once accomplished, will insure that every subordinate throughout the hierarchy of command will execute the orders he receives without even pausing to consider whether that order emanated from a British or American source.... Please do not look on this as a lecture. I am simply trying to present for your consideration, views that I deem to be of the highest importance in the further prosecution of this campaign and in the ultimate winning of the war." [14]

- -

"You do not lead by hitting people over the head – that's assault, not leadership."

- -

Eisenhower believed discipline and morale were key ingredients to effective teamwork. Colonel William Lee was a friend of Eisenhower's and was responsible for training B-26 air teams in Tampa, Florida. In March 1943, the Allies under Eisenhower's command were chasing Rommel across the desert in North Africa, but he took some time to give some advice to his friend. "Never be satisfied with the state of discipline of your organization," he wrote to Lee. "It is never high enough and this applies to officers as well as to the men. Discipline means dependability, and modern war is such a teamwork proposition that everybody must know that he can depend upon everyone else in the team. Discipline is the only answer—we must look for every possible way of increasing our standards of discipline...it is impossible to exaggerate the importance of this subject. I would venture a guess that if we had had proper standards of discipline in every unit, our initial battle losses would be sixty six percent less."[15]

Eisenhower believed that discipline started at the top. According to one of his subordinates, Claude J. Harris, "Eisenhower was a strict disciplinarian, an inborn soldier, but most human, considerate, and his decisions affecting the welfare of his officers and men were always well tempered...This principle built for him high admiration and loyalty from his officers perhaps unequaled by few commanding officers."[16]

He was also keenly aware of the importance of morale, calling it "the greatest single factor in a successful war." He thought leadership techniques to maintain morale could vary widely, but that in "any long and bitter campaign morale will suffer unless all ranks thoroughly believe that their commanders are concerned first and always with the welfare of the troops who do the fighting."[17]

Before Eisenhower left Manila in August 1940, Manuel Quezon asked that he submit a memorandum stating his "personal observations and convictions with respect to the Philippine Army and the Defense Plan." Eisenhower wrote that "Morale is born of loyalty...discipline and efficiency, all of which breed confidence in self and in comrades. Most of all morale is promoted by unity—unity in service to the country and in the determination to attain the objective of national security. Morale is at one and the same time the strongest, and the most delicate of growths. It withstands shocks, even disasters of the battlefield, but can be destroyed utterly by favoritism, neglect or injustice."[18]

One way Eisenhower worked to improve morale was to visit his troops. "Soldiers like to see the men who are directing operations," he wrote in his war memoir. "They properly resent any indication of neglect or indifference to them on the part of their commanders and invariably interpret a visit, even a brief one, as evidence of the commander's concern for them. Diffidence or modesty must never blind the commander to his duty of showing himself to his men, of speaking to them, of mingling with them to the extent of physical limitations. It pays big dividends in terms of morale, and morale, given rough equality in other things, is supreme in the battlefield."[19]

Providing positive reinforcement and showing sincere gratitude are other ways to improve morale—these actions show respect for individuals for their efforts on a leader's behalf. A simple thank-you or a note of congratulations for a job well done can be more rewarding to most people than money. On the first anniversary of the Allied landing in North Africa, Eisenhower sent a note to all the men and women in the theater, noting their accomplishments and thanking them for their efforts.

"During the year just past, you have written a memorable chapter in the history of American arms, a chapter in which are recorded deeds of value, of sacrifice, of endurance and of unswerving loyalty. You have worked effectively and in friendly cooperation with the Armies, Navies and Air Forces of our Allies and have established in a foreign land a reputation for decency and dignity in conduct. Hour by hour your efforts are contributing toward the ultimate defeat of mighty military machines that hoped to conquer the world. You are just as surely the protectors and supporters of American democracy as your fore fathers were its founders. From my heart I thank each of you for the services you have so well performed in the air, on the sea, in the front lines and in our ports and bases."[20]

RELATIONSHIPS

- -

"My ambition in the Army was to make everybody I worked for regretful when I was ordered to other duty."

- -

In Geoffrey Perret's excellent biography, he says Eisenhower "had not risen to the top by accident. Eisenhower had chosen not to try to please everyone he dealt with. He concentrated his efforts of pleasing whoever happened to be his boss, hoping to make that person feel he was virtually irreplaceable. In this, he nearly always succeeded."

On many occasions Eisenhower adopted one of MacArthur's techniques of "initially criticizing proposals that he actually agreed with and sounding enthusiastic about ideas he didn't agree with at all. It was when Eisenhower's mind seemed made up that he was probably still open to new ideas, and when he sounded undecided, there was a good chance he had already made a decision. Many people found this confusing and, like [British Field Marshal] Alan Brooke, concluded that Eisenhower was hopelessly indecisive. The effect, however, was that it reserved him his freedom on action while he went about picking other people's brains with the cold-blooded detachment of a professional burglar."[21]

The challenge as supreme commander was that Eisenhower essentially had many bosses, including Marshall, Roosevelt, Churchill, and the Allied Chiefs of Staffs. He also had to maintain effective relationships with Stalin and de Gaulle. Any one of these leaders would keep a commander on edge, never mind trying to satisfy all of them. But Eisenhower had excellent relationships with each of them, by engaging with them at both professional and human levels, by always being honest, and by working extremely hard to deliver results.

During the war Eisenhower acted more as a chief executive officer than a military dictator, laying out the overall strategy, defining his organization, and allocating resources effectively.

He had to work that way — the operation was obviously too large to have one person making all decisions, and there were too many national interests involved. So instead of micromanaging the effort, he did what he always did when leading teams — he provided the conditions and resources to make sure his commanders could execute his strategy. And the Allies functioned as a team, because Eisenhower was inclusive and flexible when considering multinational interests in making decisions.[22]

"In the Army, whenever I became fed up with meetings, protocol, and paperwork, I could rehabilitate myself by a visit with the troops."

Perhaps the most important relationship Eisenhower had during his military career was with his troops. "A human understanding and a natural ability to mingle with all men on a basis of equality are more important than any degree of technical skill," he wrote.[23]

Eisenhower practiced management by "walking around" — long before it was a trendy management term. He would make many trips to visit the troops, which always lifted his spirits. Among the troops, "talking to each other as individuals, and listening to each other's stories," Eisenhower wrote, "I was refreshed and could return to headquarters reassured that, hidden behind administrative entanglements, the military was an enterprise manned by human beings."[24]

Eisenhower visiting the troops

His easygoing style allowed him to socialize with the men in an informal manner, and he was able to converse with many of the soldiers as they discussed their lives back home and winning the war. Eisenhower sincerely enjoyed being with his troops. He told Mamie, "Our soldiers are wonderful. It always seems to me that the closer to the front the better the morale and the less grumbling. No one knows how I like to roam around among them—I'm always cheered up by a day with the actual fighters."

Eisenhower felt he had a special relationship with his troops. Despite numerous informal visits to the field, he always had something new to say to the men—he rarely repeated himself. He had an easy ability to communicate with any soldier and an intuitive ability to ask just the right questions to create immediate trust and respect, regardless of what they did in the service or in civilian life.[25]

D-day training began in December 1943 with "a series of exercises...held at brigade, divisional, and corps level. Final rehearsals were held in late April and early May [of 1944] in the south of England. Activities included the concentration, marshaling, and embarkation of troops, a short movement by water, disembarkation, variation with naval and air support, each assault using service ammunition, the securing of a beachhead, and a rapid advance inland." The exercises were meant to closely simulate the beach landings, and Eisenhower would often travel to the training facilities because it gave him an "excellent opportunity to see his troops in action and to find errors which would need elimination before D Day."[26]

- -

"There is no substitute for a succession of great victories in building morale."

- -

Aside from engaging with the troops firsthand, Eisenhower would also visit supply areas to review how resources were being deployed and utilized and various battlefields to see how the terrain may be affecting war plans. Eisenhower traveled a great deal for three months beginning in September 1944. As the front broadened across France, many of his advisors and friends recommended he discontinue or lessen his visits. It was taking more time, he could reach only a small percentage, and it was wearing him down.

Eisenhower discounted these arguments. He thought it was essential to continue visits with his commanders and all the troops to resolve problems quickly and to measure everyone's state of mind. He knew that word would get out of his visits and believed "it would encourage men to talk to their superiors," which would "promote efficiency." He believed many of the troops possessed "a great amount of ingenuity and initiative." If they could communicate to their officers without restraint, "the products of their resourcefulness become available to all." This would also lead to "mutual confidence, a feeling of partnership that is the essence of *esprit de corps*. An army fearful of its officers is never as good as one that trusts and confides in its leaders."

In March 1945, the Allies were on the move to cross the Rhine River on their way to encircle the Ruhr, which would destroy one of Hitler's last manufacturing centers. Eisenhower had joined the troops on the front as they prepared to cross the river. He found them to be eager to get the job done and the war over with. But as he was walking, he came across a soldier who seemed distressed.

"How are you feeling, son?" Eisenhower asked the young man.

"General," he said, "I'm awful nervous. I was wounded two months ago and just got back from the hospital yesterday. I don't feel so good!"

"Well," Eisenhower replied, "you and I are a good pair then, because I'm nervous too. But we've planned this attack for a long time and we've got all the planes, the guns, and the airborne troops we can use to smash the Germans. Maybe if we just walk together to the river we'll be good for each other."

"Oh," he said. "I meant I *was* nervous; I'm not anymore. I guess it's not so bad around here."[27]

Eisenhower knew what he meant. The Allies had not made any secret of their plans to cross the Rhine, and they expected some fierce resistance. But the attacks never came, and by the end of the day, all the troops had made it across the river safely.

Eisenhower's conversation with the young soldier was like many he had during the war — friendly, casual, and concerned. He wanted to reassure him that everything was put in place to succeed, and he even offered to stand by him as they moved forward. His relationship with the troops was excellent because he respected and admired them, and the feelings were almost always mutual.

MANAGING CONFLICT

"The world must learn to work together, or finally it will not work at all."

But not all relationships are frictionless. Field Marshal Bernard Law Montgomery and Eisenhower were polar opposites in their personalities and leadership styles. Montgomery was a loner; he would develop plans on his own and would communicate with his commanders only to tell them what to do. He had limited social skills and no desire to persuade people. Once he reached a decision, he would communicate it forcefully, believing that the facts and his conclusion would be enough to convince others of the validity of his solution.

Eisenhower had a genuine interest in others, was engaging in social situations, and his preferred leadership style was collaborative. He would actively seek the counsel of his superiors, peers, and subordinates to augment his own knowledge and beliefs, and then synthesize the information to reach a decision. Eisenhower preferred to use his formidable influencing skills to persuade others, but he also wasn't shy about using the power of his position. Eisenhower's collaborative style was crucial in his role as supreme commander because "in both the U.S. and British armies it was understood that proposed plans might be debated and various viewpoints developed. General Eisenhower encouraged this type of discussion and often invited criticism of his plans."[28]

As D-day approached, Montgomery went out of his way to show his admiration for Eisenhower. With his troops he would note that "General Eisenhower is the captain of the team and I am proud to serve under him."[29] After a dinner with Eisenhower just prior to D-day, Montgomery wrote in his diary, "Eisenhower is just the right man for the job...he is a really 'big' man and is in every way an Allied Commander—holding the balance between Allied contingents. I like him immensely; he has a generous and lovable character and I would trust him to the last grasp."[30] This admiration would change dramatically as the European campaign evolved.

For his part, Eisenhower felt that "Field Marshal Montgomery, like General Patton, conformed to no type. He deliberately pursued certain eccentricities of behavior, one of which was to separate himself habitually from his staff. He lived in a trailer, surrounded by a few aides. This created difficulties in the staff work that must be performed in timely and effective fashion if any battle is to result in victory. He consistently refused to deal with a staff officer from any headquarters other than his own, and, in argument, was persistent up to the point of decision."[31]

After the Allied armies were able to breakout from the Cherbourg Peninsula, and certainly after the envelopment of the enemy at Falaise in the summer of 1944, the defeat of the Nazis was assured — it was just a question of time. With their armies chasing the enemy across France, some arguments developed between the Allies about who should receive credit for the victories.

Eisenhower continued to stress that there was enough credit to go around and also that they hadn't won anything yet. The Nazi army would continue to fight hard, especially as it began to defend its homeland. Each commander also insisted that if he were only given the proper amount of resources, he could end the war in a matter of months. Montgomery was particularly insistent — he didn't like the battle strategy, and he didn't like the pending command structure.

Months before the D-day invasion started, Churchill and Roosevelt had agreed to reorganize the Allied Expeditionary Force (AEF) structure to have equality in British and American army group commanders, once the breakout from the Cherbourg Peninsula was accomplished. The plan called for the creation of the US 12th Army Group, which would include the First Army, formerly under British command, and the newly activated 3rd Army under General Patton. The British 21st Army Group would include the British 2nd Army and the Canadian 1st Army. Eisenhower was to assume direct responsibility for the command

and coordination of these two army groups, in addition to his other responsibilities as supreme commander. Eisenhower assigned Bradley to command the US 12th Army Group, and Montgomery continued commanding the British 21st Army Group. This was both political and practical.

Politically, many Americans believed that British commanders dominated key positions in the AEF as it landed in Normandy, and they thought it was only fair that Americans have proper representation, since the United States was providing two-thirds of the AEF ground forces and a majority of the supplies. On the practical side, the purpose of establishing an army group commander was to "assure direct, day-by-day battlefield direction in a specific portion of the front."

Similar to any leader of any large organization today, it was virtually impossible for the supreme commander to control every aspect of the campaign at every given time, at every location. However, as Eisenhower explained, the supreme commander was "the one person in the organization with the authority to assign principal objectives to major formations. He is also the only one who has...the power to allot strength to the various major commands in accordance with their missions, to arrange for the distribution of incoming supply, and to direct the operations of the entire air forces in support of any portion of the line."[32] Any intermediary between the supreme commander and all ground forces would be ineffective and inefficient, since it would essentially add another layer of communications, and that person wouldn't have the power to allocate resources or command air or naval forces.

Montgomery strongly disagreed with Eisenhower taking control of the ground forces. Eisenhower tended to welcome an open and honest debate with his team — to a point. Montgomery argued that commanding the ground troops was a full-time job for one person, and changing the system of command "after having won a great victory, would be to prolong the war effort."[33]

On August 23, Montgomery invited Eisenhower to lunch at his headquarters to discuss future operations. Eisenhower's chief of staff Bedell Smith joined him for the trip from London, but Montgomery said he wanted to speak one-on-one with Eisenhower. Smith had to leave, which didn't set a very positive tone for the discussion to come.

Montgomery tried to be diplomatic, but Eisenhower was already annoyed at excluding Smith from the conversation. To make matters worse, Montgomery started giving Eisenhower a patronizing lecture, as if he was a young recruit. Montgomery told Eisenhower he believed it was a mistake for him to assume command of all ground forces, because "the supreme commander must sit on a very lofty perch in order to be able to take a detached view of the whole intricate problem."

Montgomery felt so strongly about one person being in charge of just the army that he said he'd be willing to serve under Bradley. Eisenhower explained that the politics of the situation required that he take control of the battle, and he had no intention of placing anyone other than himself in control. The British were already upset about the perception of Montgomery being demoted. Having him report to Bradley would cause even more political problems.

Montgomery knew he couldn't persuade Eisenhower to change his view regarding the command structure, so he proceeded to criticize the overall battle strategy, and the debate went to fundamental differences in the American and British approach to the campaign. Ever since Ulysses S. Grant's relentless campaign during the Civil War, American military doctrine had been to deploy an overwhelming force and launch a constant, aggressive offensive to destroy the enemy and their resources. Rapid mobility and maneuvers, along with unyielding pressure along a broad front, would enable the capture of valuable terrain and confuse and demoralize the enemy. Using a stationary front was completely foreign to Eisenhower and his colleagues.

The British, having suffered enormous causalities in World War I and having been engaged in World War II for more than four years, wanted a more focused and conservative approach to avoid as much bloodshed as possible. Montgomery had nearly died in World War I, and he believed that attacking along a broad front would prolong the war and waste lives. Montgomery subscribed to British military theorist Basil Liddell Hart's view that a focused attack along a narrow front was better — it would unbalance the enemy, force them to commit additional resources, and expose them to vulnerabilities which could be exploited by additional attacks.[34]

Eisenhower with Montgomery (far left)

Rather than strike along a broad front, Montgomery wanted to be given control of the US First Army and the First Allied Airborne resources for a hard thrust northward to "clear the coast as far as Antwerp, establish a powerful air force in Belgium, and in advance of the Ruhr." Montgomery also wanted Patton's advance to stop, so all his supplies could be diverted to Montgomery's armies.

After arguing for an hour, Eisenhower agreed to support some of Montgomery's plans. Eisenhower gave Montgomery operational control over one corps from the First Army and priority in supplies, primarily because his objectives were key to the overall strategy — the capture of Antwerp and the Ruhr. But Eisenhower would not stop the advance of the 12th Army Group, including Patton, so the attack along a broad front would continue. "Both Bradley and Montgomery were dissatisfied — Bradley because

[Montgomery's] 21st Army group received preference in supplies, Montgomery because [Bradley's] 12th Army Group was allowed to move east from Paris. Both complained that Eisenhower had adopted the other's plan."[35]

With the strategy settled (at least for the moment), Bradley and Montgomery's armies began advancing eastward, and they both made incredible progress. Patton raced towards the Meuse, and he was soon one hundred miles east of Paris, which was also about the distance to the Rhine. Although he would continue, he was running out of gas because Montgomery was receiving additional supplies for his initiative, which was also going very well.

By September 4, Montgomery's team had liberated Brussels and taken the city of Antwerp, although the outer waterways remained in control of the Nazis, so the ports were still unusable. They had gone two hundred miles in less than a week — an extraordinary accomplishment that provided the Allies with new opportunities and difficulties.

With the enemy showing signs of collapsing all along the front, Eisenhower wrote to Marshall that "we have advanced so rapidly that further movement in large parts of the front even against very weak opposition is almost impossible…the potential danger is that while we are temporarily stalled the enemy will be able to pick up bits and pieces of his forces everywhere and reorganize them swiftly for defending the Siegfried Line [a 390-mile defensive line in western Germany] or the Rhine." So despite the administrative and logistical challenges of long communication and supply lines, Eisenhower intended to keep the pressure on. "It's obvious from an overall viewpoint," he wrote to Marshall, " that we must now as never before keep the enemy stretched everywhere" to prevent him from regrouping.[36]

However, fresh from his brilliant success, Montgomery thought he could do even more to end the war early. Once again he presented his case to Eisenhower. He told Eisenhower they had "reached the stage where one really powerful and full-blooded thrust to Berlin is likely to get there and thus end the German war." He didn't believe there were enough resources to support the broad front approach, and it would be best to allocate all of them to a single effort, and that "other operations must do the best it can with what is left over.... If we attempt a compromise solution and split out resources so that neither thrust is full-blooded we will prolong the war."

He thought the best single effort was the one he was responsible for, which was "the northern one via the Ruhr." He ended by saying that time was of the essence and "the matter is of such vital importance that I feel sure you will agree that a decision on the above lines is required at once. If you are coming this way perhaps you would look in and discuss it. If so, delighted to see you lunch tomorrow. Do *not* feel I can leave this battle just at the present."[37]

Eisenhower thought Montgomery's enthusiasm was fueled by the rapid advances of the preceding week and, since he was convinced that "the enemy was completely demoralized, he vehemently declared all he needed was adequate supply in order to go directly to Berlin."[38] Eisenhower responded that while he appreciated Montgomery's idea of a forceful move toward Berlin, he didn't agree that it should be done to the "exclusion of all other maneuver." And even if he were to reallocate all the resources to Montgomery, there weren't enough to support a drive all the way to Berlin.

He felt that the "bulk of the German army that was in the west has now been destroyed." He intended to quickly "exploit our success by promptly breaching the Siegfried Line, crossing the Rhine on a wide front and seizing the Saar and Ruhr." Capturing these two industrial cities would eliminate the enemy's "capacity to wage war," while giving the Allies options to move in any direction along the front. He expected that by the time he held the cities, the ports of Antwerp and Havre would be opened to provide additional support for the campaign. He would continue to give supply priority to the Ruhr (Montgomery's) campaign, since he did believe the northern thrust was the most critical.[39]

Eisenhower's policy was clear—the broad front strategy would continue. He saw "no reason to change this conception. The defeat of the German armies is complete, and the only thing now needed to realize the whole conception is speed."[40] There were also political reasons to maintain the original strategy. There was no way Eisenhower was going to stop Patton's advance or provide Montgomery with all the available resources for a single campaign to Berlin, since it would subordinate American forces to a support role—something that was unacceptable at home.

While Montgomery was probably aware of these factors, he was still unhappy with Eisenhower's reply, and he still believed he could change his mind. Montgomery knew Eisenhower's note authorized Patton to continue his advance eastward, and when he discovered that Bradley was receiving supplies for his drive east even though his campaign had been given priority, he requested that Eisenhower come to meet him in Brussels. Montgomery's request was somewhat disrespectful—he never seemed to understand that he worked for Eisenhower. It was also somewhat insensitive, since Eisenhower had badly injured his knee, making travel difficult.

Despite the inconvenience, Eisenhower preferred that his commanders remain near their battlefronts and troops, and he agreed to go to make certain that Montgomery understood the plans. Eisenhower traveled to Brussels with Arthur Tedder, commander of the Allied air force, and Lieutenant General Sir Humfrey Gale, Eisenhower's chief administrative officer. Montgomery asked that Gale leave (although his own administrative officer was with him).

As soon as Gale left, Montgomery pulled from his pocket Eisenhower's letter of September 4. In angry, agitated tones, he asked if Eisenhower had really dictated these messages, essentially rejecting his plan for a single-thrust attack toward Berlin. Eisenhower said he had. "Well they're nothing but balls!" Montgomery yelled. "Sheer balls! Rubbish!" Eisenhower listened silently as Montgomery's tirade continued to become more aggressive. But soon he'd had enough—Eisenhower leaned forward and touched Montgomery's knee. "Steady, Monty. You can't speak to me like that. I'm your boss." Monty quietly said he was sorry.[41]

"What you're proposing is this," Eisenhower said. "If I give you all the supplies you want, you could go straight to Berlin.

Right straight to Berlin? Monty you're nuts. You can't do it! What the hell! If you try a long column like that in a single thrust, you'd have to throw off division after division to protect your flanks from attack." Besides, a study conducted on a drive to Berlin by personnel at supreme headquarters in London had indicated "the beachhead can't supply a thrust into Germany," Eisenhower added.[42]

Montgomery again made his pitch to receive all the supplies to support a single thrust to Berlin. But Eisenhower was adamant and refused to even consider it. "Monty's suggestion is simple," Eisenhower wrote in his diary, "give him everything, which is crazy."[43] Eisenhower did reluctantly agree to support Montgomery's Market-Garden Operation (intended to accelerate entry into Germany by seizing bridges over the Rhine, which would ultimately fail despite its daring and ingenuity). Eisenhower's position was clear, yet he was having difficulty closing the debate with Montgomery.

Within a few days, Montgomery once again asked Eisenhower to stop the advance of the other armies and divert their supplies to him. Montgomery essentially made the same arguments as before—that the broad front strategy was flawed because an operation "in which all the available land armies move forward into Germany is not possible" to accomplish in an expedited manner. He wanted the First US Army and his army combined for a drive along the north to Berlin. "Such a force must have *everything it needs in the maintenance line;* other armies would do their best with what remained," he wrote Eisenhower. "As time is so important, we have got to decide what is necessary to go to Berlin and finish the war; the remainder must play a secondary role." He then called for an immediate decision.[44]

Eisenhower reiterated his decision, but he tried a different approach. He reached for common ground. "Specifically I agree with you on the following: My choice of routes for making the all out offensive into Germany is from the Ruhr to Berlin," he wrote. "A prerequisite from the maintenance viewpoint is the early capture of the approaches to Antwerp so that the flank may be adequately supplied."

He also did not expect all the armies to advance into Germany simultaneously—supplies and maintenance support would require balance across the front. But, "there is one point...on which we do not agree...you imply that all the divisions that we have except those of the 21st Army Group and approximately none of the 12th Army Group, can stop in place *where they are* and that we can strip all these additional divisions from their transport and everything else to support one single knife-like drive toward Berlin. This may not be exactly what you mean but it is certainly not possible."

Montgomery summarily dismissed the notion that they agreed at all, and he was sure Eisenhower "would wish me to be quite frank and open in the matter."[45] A few days later, Montgomery told Bedell Smith "the command organization was unsatisfactory. To achieve success, the tactical battle will require very tight control and very careful handling. I recommend that the Supreme Commander hands the job over to me, and gives me powers of operational control over First U.S. Army."

On September 22, 1944, Eisenhower held a meeting with his commanders at Versailles to review the overall strategy and command and resource requirements. Montgomery didn't attend, but he sent his representative, General Francis "Freddy" de Guingand. Eisenhower asked for "general acceptance of the fact that the possession of an additional major deep-water port on our north flank was an indispensable prerequisite for a final drive to Germany."[46]

He said the current priority was the capture of the Antwerp ports and the drive to the Ruhr by Montgomery's 21st Army. He wanted Bradley's US First Army to support Montgomery by holding some of the British sectors and continuing to protect Montgomery's flank by attacking toward Cologne and Bonn as resources permitted. Eisenhower also wanted Bradley to exploit any opportunities to attack the Ruhr from the south. Eisenhower wanted Patton's army to suspend any aggressive actions until Antwerp was captured.

Upon his return to the 21st Army headquarters, General de Guingand told Montgomery that Eisenhower fully supported his plan, which was not true. Montgomery had wanted control of all the ground forces, but especially the US First Army. What he got was permission to communicate directly with the First Army, and only in an emergency.

Also, while Eisenhower wanted Patton's army to stand down, he turned a blind eye to Patton's advances. Patton had expected Eisenhower to favor Montgomery at Versailles, so prior to the conference, he had organized his attacks so they would have to continue even after the directive. It's highly likely Eisenhower knew about Patton's plans, but he did nothing to stop them, which just added to Montgomery's frustrations. So the arguments would continue, especially as the prospects for a successful Market-Garden campaign began to fade.

Many of Eisenhower's commanders felt that Montgomery's absence made the conference ineffective, and his absence was another example of disrespect to the supreme commander. Eisenhower didn't show any annoyance at Montgomery's absence, but he did send a note to Montgomery, writing, "Do not hesitate for a second to let me know at any time that anything seems to you to go wrong, particularly where I, my staff, or any forces not directly under your control can be of help. If we can gain our present objective, then even if the enemy attempts to prolong the contest we will rapidly get into position to go right squarely to his heart and crush him utterly. Of course, we need Antwerp."[47]

Montgomery tried to salvage Market-Garden, but the enemy was resisting furiously, reinforcing its troops on the front. In response, Eisenhower directed Bradley to take over additional sectors from Montgomery to free up additional troops, and he asked that Bradley give Montgomery temporary operational support of two divisions. Both Montgomery and Bradley agreed.

Despite Eisenhower's repeated emphasis on obtaining the ports of Antwerp, Montgomery continued to press at the Market-Garden objectives and did little to strengthen the support of the Canadian Army, which was assigned to capture Antwerp. On October 9, the British navy reported to Eisenhower "that the Canadian First Army would be unable to move until November

1 unless supplied with ammunition." Eisenhower was beginning to lose patience.

Eisenhower wrote to Montgomery about "the supreme importance of Antwerp.... You know best where the emphasis lies within your army group, but I must repeat that we are now squarely up against the situation which has been anticipated for months and our intake into the Continent will not support our battle. Unless we have Antwerp producing [supplies] by the middle of November our entire operation will come to a stand-still. I must emphasize that, of all our operations on our entire front from Switzerland to the Channel, I consider Antwerp for first importance, and I believe that the operations designed to clear up the entrance require your personal attention."

It's hard to see how Eisenhower's direction could have been any clearer. Montgomery, assuming that British Admiral Bertram Ramsay notified Eisenhower of the shortages, responded testily, "Request you will ask Ramsay from me by what authority he makes wild statements to you concerning my operations about which he can know nothing." He said there was "no shortage of ammunition" and that "the operations are receiving my personal attention."

Montgomery then reminded Eisenhower that at the con-ference at Versailles on September 22, he had made the attack against the Ruhr the main priority. Nevertheless, Montgomery said he had stopped other operations for "various reasons, one of which was the need to get Antwerp."[48] This is certainly a case of hearing what you want, since Eisenhower specifically empha-sized the need to capture the Antwerp ports coming out of the Versailles conference, and in reality, Montgomery wouldn't give Antwerp "unequivocal priority" until October 16.[49]

Relieved that the report on the ammunition was false, Eisenhower essentially looked beyond Montgomery's selective listening. He noted that "in everything that we try to do or to plan our intake of supplies into the Continent looms up as the limit-ing factor and it is for this reason that no matter how we adjust mission and objectives for both groups in their offensive action toward the east, the possession of the approaches to Antwerp remains with us an objective of vital importance. Let me assure you that nothing I may ever say or write with respect to future plans in our advance eastward is meant to indicate any lessening of the need for Antwerp."[50]

More than a month had been lost in the capturing of Antwerp, and any hope of ending the war by the end of 1944 was gone. Even Montgomery's fiercest supporter, Brooke, knew an opportunity had been lost. On October 5 he noted, "I feel that Monty's strategy for once is at fault. Instead of carrying out the advance on Arnhem [the Market-Garden Operation] he ought to have made certain of Antwerp in the first place. Ike nobly took all the blame on himself as he had approved Monty's suggestion to operate on Arnhem."[51]

Montgomery blamed Eisenhower for the failure of both Market-Garden and Antwerp. Eisenhower's staff blamed Montgomery. As usual, Eisenhower took responsibility for the decisions, and in hindsight, believed he should have done more to finalize his orders and end the debate. The accusations and animosity might have died down, but Montgomery couldn't help but send one more inflammatory note.

On October 10, Montgomery wrote another letter to Bedell Smith, blaming Eisenhower for the lack of coordination between his army and Bradley's and for causing command confusion. He felt the armies had "been separated on a national basis and not on a geographical basis." He questioned the wisdom of having both him and Bradley having the same objective of capturing the Ruhr, and Eisenhower's style of reaching for consensus. Negotiation was essential in politics, Montgomery noted, "when the answer to most problems is a compromise between conflicting interests." But "in battle very direct and quick action is required; a compromise will never produce good results and may often produce very bad results; delays are dangerous and may lead to the initiative passing to the enemy."[52] Montgomery once again suggested that he receive operational control of the entire 12th Army Group, and by default become ground commander for most of the theater.

Montgomery suggested that Bedell show the letter to Eisenhower, who had now reached his tolerance threshold. He was furious and knew it was time to have it out with Montgomery, and he knew his response had to be an ultimatum. He asked an aide to draft a letter, which was reviewed by Smith and Marshall (who happened to be in Europe) and approved by Eisenhower.

Eisenhower started by acknowledging Montgomery's decision to make Antwerp the priority and agreeing with him on stopping further movement toward the Rhine until the ports were secured. In terms of the supplies, he noted that while he didn't know exactly what Montgomery's situation was, he believed that compared to the rest of Europe, he was well off. Eisenhower went on to explain "why I keep reverting again and again to the matter of getting Antwerp into a workable solution. I have been informed, both by the Chief of the Imperial General Staff and by the Chief of Staff of the United States Army that they seriously considered giving me a flat order that until the capture of Antwerp and its approaches was fully assured, this operation should take precedence over all others.

"You and I agreed that the great chance to seize the bridges to the northward and the opportunity for crossing the Rhine and outflanking the Siegfried Line before the enemy forces could collect themselves was well worth the risk, and, as you know, I was a strong supporter of that operation [Market-Garden]. Moreover, I consider that, while it was not completely successful, it was worthwhile, and that we did get a substantial advantage. However, all this serves merely to re-emphasize *now* the importance of that port to our future operations, and, as you know, I have been for some weeks ready to furnish additional troops from the U.S. sources for the purpose, provided only that you desired them, and that they could be gotten up to you and supplied."

Eisenhower knew Montgomery was familiar with all the above, but "the reason for re-stating it…is that the Antwerp operation does not involve the question of command in any slightest degree. Everything that can be brought in to help, no matter what nationality, belongs to you. "In order that we may continue to operate in the same close and friendly association…I will again state, as clearly as is possible, my conceptions of logical command arrangements for the future. If, after having read these, you feel that you must still class them as 'unsatisfactory', then indeed we have an issue that must be settled soon in the interests of an Allied Command, and if you, as the senior Commander in this Theater of one of the great Allies, feel that my conception and directives as such endanger the success of operations, it is our duty to refer the matter to higher authority for any action they may choose to take, however drastic."

Eisenhower went on to say he strongly agreed with Montgomery "that for any one major task on the battlefield there must be a single *battlefield* commander, a man who can devote his entire attention to that particular operation. This is the reason we have Armies and Army Groups. When, however, we have a battlefront extending from Switzerland to the North Sea, I do not agree that one man can stay so close to the day to day movement of divisions and corps that he can keep a 'battle grip' upon the *overall* situation and direct it intelligently. This is no longer a Normandy beachhead! Operations along such a *wide* front break themselves into more or less clearly defined areas of operation, one of which is usually the most important and best supported operation, the others secondary and supporting in character. The overall commander, in this case myself, has the function of adjusting the larger boundaries to tasks commensurate to the several groups operating in these several areas, assigning additional support by air or reinforcements by ground and airborne troops, when he has a general pool, and shifting the emphasis in maintenance."

Eisenhower also agreed that there should be one commander responsible for attacking the Ruhr, but given the circumstances, "it has been impossible to foretell with exactitude which particular commander would be in position to provide the strength, or major portion of the strength, necessary for the task." As it stood now, he expected Montgomery's army to continue pressing to gain the Antwerp ports, which would inevitably diminish his resources. Subsequently, his current plan called for "assigning the capture of the Ruhr to [Bradley's] 12th Army Group with [Montgomery's] 21st Army Group operating in a supporting role on the north," and then on to Berlin when its strength would be consolidated.

Eisenhower had hoped Montgomery's forces would have taken care of Antwerp and the surrounding areas so they could take the lead role in attacking the Ruhr, and he had offered additional resources to make this happen, but Montgomery had concluded that his 21st Group didn't have the required resources to attack the Ruhr. "I have never hesitated to place under your command U.S. divisions, corps, or anything else that was need for immediate requirements of the battle," Eisenhower continued. "I have no interest in this subject other than the quick winning of the war. As an example, for the immediate task you have, we turned over to you the 7th U.S. Armored Division, and are bringing up another which is available to you if necessary."

As far as allocating resources based on national versus military considerations, Eisenhower wrote "it would be quite futile to deny that questions of nationalism often enter our problems. It is nations that make war, and when they find themselves associated as Allies, it is quite often necessary to make concessions that recognize the existence of inescapable national differences." For example, equipment differences required separate lines of communication for the British and American forces. Also, "wherever we can, we keep people of the same nations serving under their own commanders."

Eisenhower tended to welcome debate, but he needed Montgomery to start acting as part of the team. He told Montgomery that he believed his job and the job of his commanders was to "meet their military problems sanely, sensibly, and logically, and, while not shutting our eyes to the fact that we are two different nations, produce solutions that permit effective cooperation, mutual support and effective results." Eisenhower concluded by saying these were his plans, stated as clearly as possible. As with any plans, they were subject to change as events unfolded, but he was certain they provided a framework for operating "effectively and with full cooperation."

Montgomery got the message, and he took it to heart. "You will hear *no* more on the subject of command from me," he wrote to Eisenhower. "I have given you my views and you have given your answer.... I and all of us here will weigh in 100 percent to do what you want and we will pull it through without a doubt. I have given Antwerp top priority in all operations in 21st Army Group and all energies and efforts will be now devoted towards opening up that place." Montgomery signed it, "Your very devoted and loyal subordinate." Eisenhower thanked Montgomery for his "fine message."[53]

On the battlefield, the fighting continued with "a series of bitterly contested battles, usually conducted under the most trying conditions of weather and terrain," Eisenhower wrote in his war memoirs. "Walcheren Island, Aachen, the Hurtgen Forest, the Roer dams, the Saar Basin, and the Vosges Mountains were all to give their names during the fall months of 1944 to battles, that...greatly hastened the end of the war in Europe. In addition to the handicap of weather there was the difficulty of shortages in ammunition and supplies. The hardihood, courage, and resourcefulness of the Allied soldier were never tested more thoroughly and with more brilliant results than during this period."[54]

Although the Allies were making progress, it was a grinding affair, and the pace of progress was making both Montgomery and Brooke anxious. Britain had been at war now for more than four years, and the human and financial stresses were taking their toll. They wanted the war over quickly, and they didn't believe the current command structure or overall strategy was the most effective means of ending the conflict.

Despite his commitment not to do so, Montgomery again raised his concerns about command and strategy. On November 17 he wrote to Brooke that Eisenhower "has never commanded anything in his whole career.... Now, for the first time, he has elected to take direct command of very large-scale operations and he does not know how to do it." Brooke agreed, and said he believed that "Ike was no commander" and was "incapable of running a land battle and it is all dependent on how well Monty can handle him."[55]

Montgomery and Brooke met in England on November 26 to discuss various proposals for presentation to Eisenhower. They determined they had three objectives: to stop the destructive broad front strategy; to reduce the number of army groups from three to two, with Montgomery taking control of one army north of the Ardennes and Bradley taking control of the other south of the Ardennes; and to get a ground commander appointed, which could be either Montgomery or Bradley. These are essentially the same discussion points that Montgomery had been lobbying for since Eisenhower took control of the ground forces in August. But this time Montgomery was leveraging his relationship with Brooke as commander of the Imperial General Staff (CIGS) to persuade Eisenhower to make the changes, and the debate was about to escalate because on November 28, Brooke took their case to the prime minister.

Brooke told Churchill he was "worried about the course operations were taking on the Western Front," specifically, the "American strategy" and "American organization." He felt the strategy of "always attacking all along the front, irrespective of strength available, was sheer madness." As far as the organization, Brooke "did not consider that Eisenhower could command both as Supreme Commander and Commander of the Land Force at the same time" and told Churchill of his and Montgomery's proposed command structure and Army group reduction from three to two.[56] When Brooke had finished, the prime minister was noncommittal.

On the same day, Eisenhower was visited by Montgomery at his headquarters for what turned out to be a three-hour meeting. Eisenhower once again listened patiently and quietly as Montgomery repeated his criticism of the current strategy and organization. In reporting the conversation to Brooke, Montgomery said that Eisenhower had agreed with all their positions—that the current strategy and organization were flawed and that changes were required, similar to what Brooke and Montgomery had suggested.

Two days later, he sent a note to Eisenhower to confirm the key discussion points. "He opened by saying, 'We have failed; and we have suffered a strategic reverse. We now require a new plan. And this time *we must not fail.*'" Montgomery said the Allies had to "get away from the doctrine of attacking in so many places that nowhere are we strong enough to get decisive results. We must concentrate such strength on the main selected thrust that success will be certain."

Montgomery repeated his contention that the front should be divided along natural lines with two sectors: one north of the Ardennes, the other south, and that each should have one commander with full control. He continued, saying that he and Bradley had made a "good team," but that things had not gone well "since you separated us. I believe to be certain of success you want to bring us together again." Montgomery added that he would be agreeable to having full operational control north of the Ardennes. Montgomery wanted to have a follow-up meeting the following week with Eisenhower and Bradley and "no one else," except the Chiefs of Staff, "who must not speak."

Montgomery had apparently misinterpreted Eisenhower's passivity at their November meeting as agreement, and even at this stage, was still making demands that were counterproductive. The reality was that Eisenhower would never suddenly do a 180-degree turn and agree with a change in strategy or in command. He would also never tell anyone on his team to stay silent on key issues, or else Montgomery would have been told to keep quiet long ago.

Montgomery's letter angered Eisenhower. He responded quickly, telling Montgomery that his letter merely stated his "conception and opinions as presented to me the other evening." He hadn't agreed to all of Monty's points at the meeting, and he didn't agree to all of them now. "I am not sure I know exactly what you mean by strategic reverse," Eisenhower wrote. While "certainly to date we have failed to achieve all that we had hoped to by this time…I do not agree that things have gone badly since Normandy, merely because we have not gained all we had hoped to gain." While the Ruhr was an "important place," Eisenhower reminded Montgomery that "our primary objective is to defeat the German forces that are barring our way to Germany."

Since Normandy, Eisenhower had adopted Napoleon's principle that the destruction of the enemy, and not territorial capture, was the primary objective of battle. "We gained a great victory in Normandy," he continued. "Bradley's brilliant break through made possible the great exploitation by all forces, which blasted through France and Belgium and almost carried us across the Rhine. Had we not advanced on a relatively broad front, we would now have the spectacle of a long narrow line of communication, constantly threatened on the right flank and weakened by detachments of large fighting formations.... As it is now, we have a rear that is cleared of the enemy. We can look to the front."

Accordingly, Eisenhower had "no intention of stopping [General Jacob L.] Devers's and Patton's operations as long as they are cleaning up our right flank and giving us *capability of concentration*. On the other hand I do not intend to push those attacks senselessly." Eisenhower also rejected Montgomery's demand of silencing others at the next meeting. "Bedell is my chief of staff because I trust and respect his judgment," Eisenhower wrote. "I will not by any means insult him by telling him that he should remain mute at any conference he and I both attend."

Eisenhower ended by telling Monty, "I most definitely appreciate the frankness of your statements, and the usual friendly way in which they are stated, but I beg of you not to continue to look upon the past performances of this great fighting force as a failure merely because we have not achieved all that we could have hoped. I am quite sure that you, Bradley, and I can remain masters of the situation and the victory we want will certainly be achieved. But we must look at this whole great affair stretching from Marseilles to the lower Rhine as one great theater."[57]

The meeting that Montgomery requested was held on December 7, 1944, in Maastricht, where Eisenhower reviewed the current situation and said he believed things were going as well as they could. The German army was taking large causalities, and with the Russian winter offensive to start soon, it was clear that the enemy couldn't last much longer. He asked for Montgomery's views, who essentially repeated the same old arguments. He called for a concentrated effort north of the Ruhr and for a change in command, requests that were again rejected by Eisenhower.

After the meeting, Montgomery reported that he had had a "very cheery lunch" with Eisenhower. "Before he left I made it clear to Eisenhower that it was for him to command and for me to obey; but I was the Commander of the armed forces of one of the principal allies, and as such he must know what I thought about things. I said that in this case we differed widely and on fundamental issues. He said he quite understood and we parted great friends."[58]

Despite the cordial lunch, Montgomery was still upset about the events of the meeting and his inability to persuade Eisenhower. He realized he had taken the argument as far as he could, and that it was now up to Brooke to try to influence the Americans. He told Brooke he believed that Bradley, Tedder, and Smith had reinforced Eisenhower's resolve to stay the course in attacking all along the front.

"We shall split our resources, and our strength, and we shall fail," Montgomery wrote to Brooke. "I think now that if we want the war to end within any reasonable period you will have to get Eisenhower's hand taken off the land battle. I regret to say that in my opinion he just doesn't know what he's doing."[59]

In a bit of political maneuvering, Eisenhower knew the best way to end this ongoing debate and criticism from the British was to make a subtle appeal directly to Churchill. "Weather permitting," Eisenhower wrote to Churchill, "I hope to make a short visit to London early next week.... If you and the British Chiefs of Staff might like to have a personal and very informal presentation of our situation and general plans, Tedder and I will be happy to come anywhere you say." Churchill agreed, and on December 12, Brooke asked Eisenhower to present his plan over dinner.

Eisenhower described the broad double advance north of the Rhine and south by Frankfurt to penetrate into Germany. While flooding conditions in the southern region prevented movements at the moment, the northern thrust was receiving full support, including new resources. Once conditions in the south improved,

Eisenhower expected Bradley to move aggressively toward the Rhine.

Afterward, Brooke noted in his diary, "I disagreed flatly with it, accused Ike of violating principles of concentration of force, which had resulted in current failures. I criticized his future plans and pointed out impossibility of double invasion with limited forces he has got. I stressed the importance of concentrating on one thrust.... I got no further in getting either Winston or Ike to see that their strategy is fundamentally wrong."[60]

Churchill told Brooke the next day that he felt compelled to support Ike, since there were many British against just Ike and Tedder. But by this time, it was clear that Eisenhower's arguments would prevail. He had the full support of the president and Marshall, and most importantly, he had gained credibility and had the self-confidence to withstand any pressures from those who would disagree.

Eisenhower was supreme commander for a reason. He knew how to play politics to hold the alliance together while still getting what he wanted for his primary objective — winning the war. Eisenhower's briefing to Churchill was successful, and, for the first time, Brooke seemed to understand that Eisenhower was in control and in command.

Meanwhile, on the battlefield, supplies were lacking and the troops were stretched thin all along the front. To execute the dual thrust, forces had to be concentrated near the Roer dams in the north and close to the Saar in the south, which weakened the defensive lines in the Ardennes region. Bradley and Eisenhower discussed this and concluded "that in the Ardennes region we were running a definite risk," but they both believed "that nothing could be so expensive to us as to allow the front to stagnate, going into a defensive winter quarters while we waited for additional reinforcements from the homeland."[61]

There were other reasons to continue the offensive. Even with a lack of resources, the Allies were inflicting heavy losses to German troop levels. The only weak portion along the front was in the Ardennes, and even if there were an attack, Bradley doubted it could be sustained because of an inability of the

Germans to supply their lines. It seemed that Bradley almost dared the Germans to launch a counteroffensive. When intelligence officer Kenneth Strong warned Bradley of a potential spoiling attack around the Ardennes, Bradley said "the danger was exaggerated" and added, "let them come."[62]

Well, they did come. On December 16, 1944, Hitler initiated his Autumn Fog counteroffensive in the Ardennes, commonly known as the Battle of the Bulge. The Allies worked quickly to respond to the situation, and many, including Eisenhower, saw this as an opportunity rather than a problem. Eisenhower ordered reinforcements and concentrated strength at critical points along the attack.

The splitting of the battlefield by the Germans also made it more efficient to make a temporary change in the command structure—Eisenhower was not about to put prior organizational debates or national loyalties above the need to respond quickly to the current situation. He wanted the enemy stopped and the Allied armies on the offensive again as soon as the German armies had expended themselves. He placed Montgomery in command of the northern flank and Bradley in the southern flank of the penetration, which moved command of the US First and Ninth Armies from Bradley to Montgomery.

Through flexibility and courageous fighting, the Allied front held, and, after about a week, the major thrust of the German counteroffensive was finished. Eisenhower sensed that the Germans were spent. Their forces were seriously weakened all along the lines of the bulge and, in many cases, supplies were nonexistent. Eisenhower was anxious to hit the Germans hard as soon as possible.

With a temporary respite on the battlefront, Eisenhower visited Montgomery's headquarters on December 28 to discuss next steps. Based on intelligence information, Montgomery was certain the Germans intended to initiate one more major offensive against the northern front. He was highly confident that he could absorb the attack and then launch an offensive against the weakened German front. Eisenhower wasn't so sure, but Montgomery insisted it was "a practical certainty. If the enemy should renew the assault," Montgomery said, he could "use the time in reorganizing, re-equipping, and refreshing his troops."

Eisenhower and Montgomery agreed to use the time to "get ready for a strong counterblow" against the Germans, while "constantly preparing to beat off any German attack that might be launched."[63] However, if the enemy didn't attack, then Eisenhower "wanted Montgomery to begin his counteroffensive as soon as possible, by January 1 at the latest." Eisenhower did not want to waste too much time. He didn't want to give the Germans an opportunity to maintain their current positions and redeploy resources elsewhere. Eisenhower wrote to Montgomery the next day that "we must not allow this to happen," and it was critical to destroy the enemy while they were "out in the open."[64]

Meanwhile, the British media were having a field day, implying that Montgomery had come to the rescue of the failed Americans. "The rumblings in the press, particularly in London, have now grown to a roar of demand that there be a British deputy commander for all of General Ike's ground forces." Butcher wrote in his diary, "The implication is clearly given that General Ike, as much as he is respected, has undertaken too much of a task himself."[65]

General Francis "Freddy" de Guingand, Montgomery's chief of staff, was well-liked and respected by both the British and American staffs. Possessing the proper balance between professionalism and camaraderie, over time Eisenhower had developed a friendship with de Guingand and felt he "lived the code of the Allies and his tremendous capacity, ability, and energy were always devoted to the coordination of plan and detail that was absolutely essential to victory."[66]

On December 30, de Guingand went to supreme headquarters in London to let everyone know that Montgomery was planning to attack the northern front on January 3, not January 1. Eisenhower's senior staff reacted angrily. Besides going back on the agreement, Montgomery didn't even communicate directly. De Guingand said there must have been some misunderstanding, because Montgomery didn't commit to a January 1 date. Eisenhower said there was no misunderstanding, and that

Montgomery had promised him he would attack by January 1, and he wanted them committed, now. The problem with the delay was that the offensive was to be coordinated with Bradley attacking along the south. Without a northern attack by Montgomery, the Germans would be able to redeploy their tanks to the south to stop Bradley.[67]

In the midst of the heated discussions over the timing of the northern attack, Eisenhower received a letter from Montgomery resurrecting the old debate on command structure and the overall strategy. "We want to be careful," Montgomery wrote, "because we have had one very definite failure when we tried to produce a formula that would meet this case." Montgomery already had two of Bradley's armies under his command, but he wanted control over all of the ground forces, and he "informed Eisenhower that any statement giving him only coordination would not be strong enough."

Montgomery urged Eisenhower to issue a new directive outlining the objectives of the two armies prior to joining his and Bradley's armies. "It is then that one commander must have the powers to direct and control the operations; you cannot possibly do it yourself, and so you would have to nominate someone else." Of course, Montgomery wanted to be the nominee.

Montgomery went so far as to write the end of the proposed directive for Eisenhower: "From now onwards full operational direction, control, and coordination of these operations is vested in C.-in-C. 21 Army Group [Montgomery], subject to such instructions as may be issued by the Supreme Commander from time to time." Montgomery told Eisenhower he was compelled to suggest this "because I am so anxious not to have another failure." Montgomery wanted all offensive power allocated to the northern advance, and he wanted to command all the offensive power. "I am certain that if we do not comply with these two basic conditions," Montgomery wrote, "then we will fail again."

Meanwhile, Marshall had read the British papers and wired Eisenhower "that it would be unacceptable to give a British general command of any substantial American force," adding that "Eisenhower had the full confidence of the president, himself, and the American people."[68] Marshall told Eisenhower, "You're doing a grand job and go on and give them hell."[69] Eisenhower's staff also gave him words of encouragement, advising him to have a final confrontation with Montgomery.

But Montgomery, Marshall, and even his own staff had underestimated Eisenhower's resolve. Eisenhower had not risen to his current position by accident. He understood the balancing act between politics and warfare. He was his own man, and he was not about to let Montgomery or anyone else undermine the role of supreme commander, or of the Allied coalition. Eisenhower knew the subtleties of leadership, including when to yield to others, when to push back hard, and when to end the discussion, which was now. Already disturbed by Montgomery's failure to attack, he saw this last message as an ultimatum, something he would not tolerate. His patience had run out, and he was ready to make a change.

De Guingand, back at Montgomery's headquarters, had telephoned his counterpart Smith, who told him that someone had to go, and it wouldn't be Eisenhower. De Guingand immediately left Brussels, traveling by plane through a major storm to get to Versailles in an attempt to resolve the crisis. Eisenhower was in his office meeting with his staff when de Guingand arrived. Eisenhower liked de Guingand, but now he was all business. "Does Monty realize the effects of the line taken by the British press? And I wonder if he recognizes the effects of his continual pressing for the establishment of a land commander? I am tired of the whole business and have come to the conclusion that it is now a matter for the decision of the Combined Chiefs of Staff."

Eisenhower handed de Guingand the message he planned to send to Marshall, which was unequivocal — either Eisenhower or Montgomery had to go. De Guingand was devastated. He was sure that Montgomery didn't realize he had overplayed his hand, and he pleaded with Eisenhower, Tedder, and Smith to give him a chance to solve the crisis. Eisenhower and Tedder were reluctant, but Smith was supportive of de Guingand. After much discussion, Eisenhower relented and gave de Guingand twenty-four hours to turn things around.

As de Guingand left, Eisenhower issued his own directive to Bradley and Montgomery, essentially restating his original plans, this time with specific tasks. He wanted immediate attacks from both the north and south. To reinforce his attack, Montgomery would retain control of US Ninth Army, but Bradley was to resume control of US First Army. "The one thing that must now be prevented is the stabilization of the enemy...permitting him opportunity to use his Panzers at will on any part of the front. We must regain the initiative, and speed and energy are essential."[70]

Eisenhower then dictated a cover letter to Montgomery, summarizing his plan and responding to his prior message. "The immediate thing is to give the enemy in the salient a good beating, destroying everything we can. In the matter of command," Eisenhower did not agree with Montgomery's assertion that there should be one single ground commander. "You know how greatly I've appreciated and depended upon your frank and friendly counsel, but in your latest letter you disturb me by predictions of 'failure' unless your exact opinions in the matter of giving you command over Bradley are met in detail. I assure you that in this matter I can go no further. Please read this document carefully.... For my part I would deplore the development of such an unbridgeable gulf of convictions between us that we would have to present our differences to the Combined Chiefs of Staff. The confusion and debate that would follow would certainly damage the good will and devotion to a common cause that have made this Allied Force unique in history."[71]

Traveling back to Brussels, de Guingand immediately went to Montgomery's headquarters. Putting aside any formalities, de Guingand told Montgomery, "I've just come from SHAEF [Supreme Headquarters Allied Expeditionary Force] and seen Ike, and it's on the cards that you might have to go." As de Guingand expected, Monty was surprised, but he derided any notion of dismissal. Even if it were possible, "Who will take my place?" Montgomery asked, "Who?"

"Alexander," replied de Guingand.

Montgomery quickly turned pale. He hadn't thought about British General Harold Alexander, a highly regarded military leader who was popular with both his colleagues and U.S. officers. Montgomery realized he had pushed Eisenhower too far. De Guingand said it looked "as if a cloak of loneliness had descended upon him." Montgomery turned to de Guingand, saying "What shall I do Freddy?" De Guingand produced a message he had prepared on the trip back and told Montgomery, "Sign this." After a quick read, Montgomery signed.

"Dear Ike," the message read. "Have seen Freddie and understand you are greatly worried by many considerations in these very difficult days. I have given you my frank views because I have felt you like this. I am sure there are many factors which have a bearing quite beyond anything I realize. Whatever your decision may be you can rely on me one hundred per cent to make it work, and I know Brad will do the same. Very distressed that my letter may have upset you and I would ask you to tear it up. Your very devoted subordinate, Monty."[72]

What does all this drama with Monty tell us about Eisenhower's leadership? He showed enormous patience while trying to manage conflicting priorities in a highly political and volatile setting. He was absolutely determined to hold the alliance together, he wanted to maintain the overall strategy of a broad front (until some event convinced him otherwise), and he also respected the opinions and views of one of his major commanders. Maybe he should have cut off the debate sooner, but in the end he got everything he wanted by tenaciously holding firm in his beliefs while finessing the discussions and debates with Monty. He also preferred to resolve these conflicts internally and offered to escalate the disagreements to his seniors only when he knew he couldn't debate the issue any longer.

POLITICS

- -

"I am always ready to learn although I do not always like being taught."
-Winston Churchill

- -

Eisenhower had a warm and friendly relationship with Winston Churchill, built upon mutual respect and common interests. Eisenhower liked and admired Churchill, and thought he was an "inspirational leader" with "extraordinarily strong convictions and a master in argument and debate." Most of the time, Churchill and Eisenhower were in agreement on strategies and tactics. But when there was disagreement, Churchill could be relentless in arguing his case, injecting emotion and rhetoric into the discussion. "He used humor and pathos with equal facility," Eisenhower wrote, "and drew on everything from the Greek classics to Donald Duck for quotation, cliché, and forceful slang to support his position."[73]

Knowing how to "manage up" is critical for anyone working in any organization. This includes having the courage of your convictions and the determination to stand up for what you believe in. Eisenhower always respected the chain of command and his seniors, but he was not afraid to use his considerable intellect and leverage when the stakes were high and he truly believed in a course of action.

In early 1944, Eisenhower threatened to resign if he did not get total control of Allied air forces so he could direct the bombing campaign of France prior to the invasion. Eisenhower didn't do this to gain more power. He did it because over his years of service in the military, he believed there was a right way to do things, and if he wasn't empowered to establish the proper organizational structure and given the authority along with the responsibility, then he would leave. Because he stood up for his beliefs, he was given the responsibility he asked for, which certainly played a key role in the success of the invasion.

When Eisenhower and Churchill didn't agree, their debates were always civil and courteous. They were both students of politics and military history, and they both had deep respect for the troops (Churchill once became upset when an administrative officer referred to soldiers killed as "bodies," launching into a passionate speech condemning the very idea of talking about soldiers in such cold terms).

If Churchill didn't like a position, he would return to it again and again, trying various methods of persuasion, right up until the end. But once the battle plans were executed, he got behind them completely, always looking at ways to bring success to the campaigns. While the discussions could be exhausting, Eisenhower always appreciated Churchill's ultimate support, intellect, and singular focus on winning the war.

One such disagreement came at the end of the war in March 1945. At the Yalta Conference in February 1945, the Allies agreed to occupation zones once the troops began to overrun Germany. At the time the boundaries were defined, it was assumed the Soviets would occupy most of Germany, but as the Western Allies advanced rapidly, it soon became obvious that they would be further east than originally planned.

As the Western Allied troops penetrated Germany, Eisenhower made the decision to stop at the Elbe River rather than continuing on to attack Berlin. Eisenhower had two reasons to meet the Soviets at a major geographic demarcation. He didn't want to stretch his resources thin with a campaign to capture Berlin, and he was afraid the Soviets and Western Allies would end up killing each other as they converged on the city.

He certainly understood the emotions and pride that would come with defeating the enemy in their capital, but he also knew the Soviets had lost more than twenty million in the war and were more passionate about seizing Berlin. He was also aware of the occupation zone created by the Yalta agreement—even after he stopped at the Elbe River, he would have to pull his troops back as the Soviets entered from the east. In the end, his decision to stop was based purely on military rationale. As he was instructed to do, Eisenhower sent a message to Stalin about his plans through the American Military Mission in Moscow. Stalin happily acknowledged and agreed to the plan.

When Churchill heard about the message to Stalin, he protested on two grounds. First, Churchill and many in the British military wanted to drive straight to Berlin, and they had argued the case for many, many months. Unlike Roosevelt, Churchill always viewed the Yalta Agreement as negotiable, and he now wanted to take advantage of the situation on the ground. Second, he believed Eisenhower was overstepping his authority as supreme commander in communicating directly to Stalin. In Churchill's view, this was a political matter, and Eisenhower hadn't even informed the British Chiefs of Staff (BCOS) or Montgomery of his plans.

Eisenhower strongly disagreed. He argued that Stalin was effectively the head of the military for the Soviets, and he had no choice but to communicate directly to him. Churchill continued to protest, this time directly to Roosevelt and the American Joint Chiefs, but they agreed with Eisenhower. After a number of exchanges arguing their mutual positions, Churchill relented. "I still think it was a pity that Eisenhower's telegram was sent to Stalin without anything being said" to the senior British commanders, Churchill wrote to Roosevelt. However, "my personal relations with General Eisenhower are of the most friendly character. I regard this matter as closed."[74]

"Here in America we are descended in blood and in spirit from revolutionists and rebels — men and women who dare to dissent from accepted doctrine. As their heirs, may we never confuse honest dissent with disloyal subversion."

On June 14, 1951, Joseph McCarthy took to the floor of the Senate to deliver an angry speech about the failures of George Marshall (who at the time was Defense Secretary under President Truman), especially for "losing China" to the Communists. "This must be the product of a great conspiracy, a conspiracy on a scale so immense as to dwarf any previous such venture in the history of man. A conspiracy of infamy so black that...its principals shall be forever deserving of the maledictions of all honest men." McCarthy criticized Marshall of everything from giving up Eastern Europe to the Russians in World War II, to being a little too friendly with Stalin, to the failure to take Berlin at the end of World War II (which was actually a not-too-subtle criticism of Eisenhower).[75]

Eisenhower considered McCarthy to be "a disciple of hate" who would make general accusations, which were often extreme, unsupported, and unjustified. As he was campaigning for president in 1952, Eisenhower was scheduled to give a speech in McCarthy's home state of Wisconsin. Included in the speech was a paragraph praising Marshall's "outstanding character and achievements," which Eisenhower had given just a short time earlier at a Denver news conference. But his staff and other conservative Republicans urged Eisenhower to delete the paragraph, because it was an unnecessarily criticism of McCarthy and "out of context" in a local campaign speech. Thinking that he had covered the subject in Denver, Eisenhower agreed with little protest.

The reaction to the deletion was fast and furious. The press accused Eisenhower of capitulating to the McCarthy crowd, and saying that he would subdue his personal convictions for political gain. Eisenhower and his staff deeply regretted removing the paragraph, and it became the low point of the campaign. "If I could have foreseen this distortion of the facts...that even led some to question my loyalty to General Marshall," Eisenhower wrote in his memoirs, "I would never have acceded to the staff's arguments." The next day at a campaign train stop, Eisenhower made it clear that while he was as concerned as anyone about Communists within the government, he did not approve of "making baseless accusations against people who had not been proved guilty of wrongdoing, " and that as president he would "fight against such practices."[76]

From that time forward, the relationship between Eisenhower and McCarthy was extremely strained. As he began his presidency, Eisenhower made it clear that he despised McCarthy's tactics. He realized that McCarthy's methods required constant attacks and publicity, so Eisenhower began working his "invisible hand" to diminish the Senator's power and influence.

Eisenhower was receiving almost daily requests to attack McCarthy, to use his power to "fire" McCarthy. Although instinctively that's what Eisenhower wanted to do, he refused. He was not going to engage in personalities. By attacking McCarthy, he would only "enhance his publicity value without achieving any constructive purpose." Eisenhower believed that the newspapers, television and the radio were all stirring a dark public interest and inciting McCarthy to do even more harm. He strongly believed that McCarthy would eventually self destruct, and that's exactly how it was about to play out.

Eisenhower was determined to continue to speak out against "all unfair, unjust and un-American practices in trials, investigations, and inquiries," and to ignore McCarthy, believing "that the only person who could destroy McCarthy as a political figure was he himself."[77] When McCarthy wanted the government to eliminate books which were subversive or un-American, Eisenhower gave an impromptu talk during a speech at Dartmouth.

"Don't join the book burners," Eisenhower urged. "Don't think you are going to conceal faults by concealing evidence that they ever existed. Don't be afraid to go in your library and read every book, as long as that document does not offend our own ideas of decency. How will we defeat communism unless we know what it is, and what it teaches, and why does it have such an appeal for men, why are so many people swearing allegiance to it? It is almost a religion...and we have got to fight it with something better, not try to conceal the thinking of our own people."[78]

In the fall of 1953, McCarthy initiated an investigation into communist subversion in the US Army. McCarthy's investigations led nowhere, until he came upon a Dr. Irving Peress, a dentist who had been inducted under the doctor's draft law. Peress was commissioned and promoted to major (as required by law), despite his refusal to sign a loyalty oath because he didn't want to disclose that he was a member of the left-wing American Labor party.

Peress appeared before McCarthy's committee but refused to answer under his Fifth Amendment rights. Having discovered his affiliation, the next day Peress was given an honorable discharge from the Army. McCarthy was angry. He wanted to know who had promoted Peress. He called Peress's commanding officer General Ralph Zwicker to testify. When Zwicker refused to answer several of McCarthy's questions, the interrogation became abusive. McCarthy told Zwicker he did not have "the brains of a five-year-old child" and that he was "not fit to wear" his uniform.

The press, the military, veterans, and senators were outraged by McCarthy's abuse of Zwicker, a decorated World War II hero. But McCarthy's biggest mistake was he now had Eisenhower's attention. When Army Secretary Robert T. Stevens told Zwicker not to testify further, McCarthy simply ordered Stevens to testify. Trying to defuse the situation, McCarthy and Stevens had lunch, where McCarthy persuaded Stevens to permit further testimony by Zwicker and any others that were involved in the Peress case.

The reaction to the agreement was swift and negative. The *New York Times* headline read, "Stevens Bows to McCarthy at Administration Behest. Will Yield Data on Peress." Eisenhower had had enough. "This guy McCarthy is going to get into trouble over this," he told his press secretary, James Hagerty. "I'm not going to take this one lying down."[79] Given his military background and his role as commander in chief, Eisenhower was not about to sit idle while McCarthy abused and humiliated the armed services.

Eisenhower met with Senators Everett Dirkson and Karl Mundt and received agreement to seek a rule change requiring a majority vote when issuing subpoenas, which would eliminate McCarthy's ability to hold random one-on-one hearings. On February 25, 1954, the White House also issued a statement backing Stevens, adding that it would not tolerate abuse of Army personnel and that it had assurances from subcommittee members that such conditions would not occur in the future. That same day, the Republican Senate Policy Committee agreed to study investigating committee guidelines, which was seen by the press as the beginning of the end of McCarthy's ability to subpoena on his own.

More importantly, Eisenhower asked his attorney general to provide him with a memo on his legal grounds to deny access to executive personnel and records. As president, Eisenhower believed he could personally refuse to comply with a subpoena, but he wanted to protect his staff. Eisenhower was laying the foundation for "executive privilege."

Eisenhower continued to work behind the scenes with friendly senators to make sure any future hearings were fair. He also reinforced his beliefs to the cabinet in a formal memo: "Each superior, including me, must remember the obligation he has to his own subordinates. These obligations comprise, among other things, the protection of those subordinates, through all legal and proper means available, against attacks of a character under which they otherwise might be helpless. No hope of any kind of political advantage, no threat from *any* source, should lead anyone to forsake these principles of organizational leadership."[80]

On April 22, 1954, the McCarthy-Army hearings began and would continue for two months. Since they were televised, McCarthy had all the publicity he wanted. The problem for McCarthy was the more people saw, the less they liked. His overall approval ratings began to decline and actually went negative as the hearings rambled on for two months.

About a month later, McCarthy threatened to subpoena White House personnel to obtain the names of all Army personnel who had been involved in the Peress case. Eisenhower was set to refuse on the grounds of executive privilege. "Congress has absolutely no right to ask them to testify in any way, shape or form about the advice that they were giving me at any time on any subject," he told Hagerty.[81]

On May 17, Eisenhower met with Republican leaders. Eisenhower told them that he was about to issue orders to Secretary of Defense Charles Wilson "to keep confidential any advisory discussions in the administrative side of this government. Any man who testifies as to the advice he gave me won't be working for me that night...those people who are my confidential advisors are not going to be subpoenaed."[82]

Later that day, Eisenhower wrote to Wilson. "Because it is essential to efficient and effective administration that employees of the Executive Branch be in a position to be completely candid in advising with each other on official matters, and because it is not in the public interest that any of their conversations or communications, or any documents or reproductions, concerning such advice be disclosed, you will instruct employees of your Department that in all of their appearances before the Subcommittee of the Senate Committee on Operations...they are not to testify to any such conversations or communications or to produce any such documents or reproductions.... I direct this action so as to maintain the proper separation of powers between the Executive and Legislative Branches of the Government in accordance with my responsibilities and duties under the Constitution. This separation is vital to preclude the exercise of arbitrary power by any branch of the Government."[83]

This was a broad order, since it included all executive branch personnel rather than just the president's cabinet, and many in Congress were upset, especially McCarthy. If McCarthy couldn't get people to testify, he had no power. He appealed to federal workers to ignore the order, but that had no effect. When asked about rescinding or relaxing the executive order the next day at a press conference, Eisenhower said he had no intention of doing so. "It is a very moderate and proper statement of the division of powers between the Executive and the Legislative," he told the audience.

It would have been easy for Eisenhower to directly lash out at McCarthy, but he felt that would diminish the office of the presidency while giving the senator the publicity he wanted. Instead, Eisenhower continued to communicate about the need for fairness and tolerance. On May 31, 1954, Eisenhower gave an address at the two-hundredth anniversary of Columbia University.

"Without exhaustive debate—even heated debate—of ideas and programs, free government would weaken and wither. But if we allow ourselves to be persuaded that every individual, or party, that takes issue with our own convictions is necessarily wicked or treasonous — then indeed we are approaching the end of freedom's road. Effective support of principles, like success in battle, requires calm and clear judgment, courage, faith, fortitude. Our dedication to truth and freedom, at home and abroad, does not require — and cannot tolerate — fear, threat, hysteria, and intimidation. As we preach freedom to others, so we should practice it among ourselves."[84]

On June 18, 1954, the hearings ended. With Eisenhower's denial of access to people and information, McCarthy was left with little to investigate. He was reduced to exploring trivial bits of information, and he became increasingly irrational as the hearings progressed, which impacted his credibility. McCarthy's exposure on national television also accelerated his downfall, which eventually ended in a condemnation of him by the Senate in December 1954.

Some people argue that Eisenhower didn't react aggressively enough in response to McCarthy's attacks. But Eisenhower wanted to lift people up rather than tear them down. The last thing he wanted was to get into a gutter fight with a bully that would give him credibility he didn't deserve. Eisenhower's quiet "back room" actions to subvert McCarthy's powers were certainly effective. His initiation of executive privilege was the strategy that ultimately undermined McCarthy's ability to investigate. Not only did Eisenhower protect the people who worked for him, but it also set a precedent for future presidents to enforce the separation of governmental powers.

ASSESSING STRENGTHS AND WEAKNESSES

- -

"Pull the string, and it will follow wherever you wish. Push it, and it will go nowhere at all."

- -

One of the most important aspects of leadership is the ability to judge talent and determine the strengths and weaknesses of individuals. Behind his charm and easy smile, Eisenhower was highly judgmental of others, although most of the time he kept his views of others to himself. Early in his career, Eisenhower decided to write down his opinions of the people he met in his diary. He thought that "sometime in the future it will be fun to review these to determine whether my impression was a permanent one."

Of course, by looking back, Eisenhower would also be able to hone his skills on evaluating individuals and adjust his techniques accordingly. He thought this was one way to learn from those people who had achieved remarkable goals or those "who have attracted special attention in some field," by trying "to make an estimate of their character, their abilities and their weaknesses."

In his "Notes on Men," Eisenhower wrote paragraphs of his impressions of his seniors, peers, and friends, in both the military and government, and he would review and update them occasionally. The writings were unstructured, simply conveying his honest thoughts. He would sometimes note the person's physical appearance and mental capabilities, but he mostly focused on the person's strongest abilities.

General Mosely (to whom Eisenhower reported for a number of years) "works 'personally' as opposed to 'organizationally'" and was "mentally honest, and with great moral courage." Major General Fox Conner was "a wonderful officer and leader with a splendid analytical mind. He is loyal to subordinates as to superiors" and "quick to give credit to juniors." Major Gerow was his "best friend" and "intensely loyal, energetic, and possessed of a sound mind." Gerow's only fault, "if it is a fault, is that he is a little too respectful of rank." MacArthur was "essentially a romantic figure...very appreciative of good work, positive in his convictions—a genius at giving concise and clear instructions." He was also "impulsive-able, even brilliant-quick-tenacious in his views and extremely self-confident."[85]

This practice continued during World War II. In June 1943, after commanding the invasion of North Africa, Eisenhower noted the strengths and weaknesses of "several senior officers, for reference when I may need them at a later date." He had deep respect for Admiral Andrew Cunningham—"absolute selflessness, energy, devotion to duty and knowledge of his task, and in understanding to the requirements of allied operations." He felt that Air Chief Marshall Tedder ranked "close to Admiral Cunningham in qualifications, except in the one thing of broad vision...he is not quite as broad-gauged as he might be...certainly in all matters of energetic operation, fitting into an allied team, and knowledge of his job, he is tops. Moreover, he is a leader type."[86]

Eisenhower's entries tell as much about himself as those he wrote about. He was continually learning from others, both the good and the bad. He respected men of character and courage who were able to think and speak clearly and able to share the credit with those around them. Eisenhower certainly worked to maintain those qualities himself as his responsibilities increased dramatically in the 1940s.

One person operating at the extremes in terms of his strengths and weaknesses was George Patton, and he would test Eisenhower's leadership and resolve many times. Patton was an exceptional military commander and Eisenhower knew it, but he also knew Patton's limitations. Patton's indiscretions often led to embarrassing moments for everyone, but especially for Eisenhower.

Eisenhower and Patton had a conversation late into the night after the Casablanca conference in January 1943. Eisenhower knew Patton was an excellent leader of men and that he could play a critical role in future campaigns, if he could maintain some self-control. "As time goes on," he wrote to Patton the next day, "the United Nations are finding more and more that what we need is *fighting* Generals, and there will always be an increasing sphere of usefulness for people such as yourself. We must not forget, however, that superiors will frequently shy off from a man on account of impressions and I am anxious in your case that this does not occur. You are quick-witted and have a ready and facile tongue. As a result, you frequently give the impression that you act merely on impulse and not upon study and reflection...My advice is, therefore, (if you want it) merely the old saw to 'count to ten before you speak'. This applies not only to criticism of Allies, a subject on which I am adamant, but to many others.

"A man once gave to me an old proverb. It was this: 'Keep silent and appear stupid; open your mouth and remove all doubt.' I know that I have no more loyal and devoted friend and subordinate in this theater than yourself; there, I know you will take this letter...exactly as it is meant, and will take a little time to think over what I am trying to say."[87]

Despite Eisenhower's words of advice and subsequent orders to refrain from giving speeches unless he had permission, Patton made a major verbal blunder in late April 1944 that almost ended his career. This was particularly important given the politics and fragility of the Allied coalition at the time, and the memory of Patton slapping a soldier in Sicily in August 1943 was still fresh.

While speaking at what he thought was a private gathering, Patton indicated that the United States and Great Britain would rule the world in the future. This didn't exactly go over very well with the Soviets and other Allies, and soon the US Congress and the press were questioning Patton's fitness to command troops. To make matters worse, Marshall had submitted a list of permanent promotions to Congress, and this latest incident could jeopardize all the promotions, including Patton's.

Eisenhower didn't want to lose Patton. He knew Patton would be relentless in attacking the enemy in the upcoming invasion of Europe (Operation Overlord). But he also had to do everything to keep the Allies together and the War Department functioning, and if he had to lose his best general to do that, so be it. Eisenhower sent a letter to Marshall asking if Patton's behavior had compromised the confidence of the American public and the government in the War Department.

While he waited for a reply, Eisenhower sent Patton an intense letter demanding an explanation and warning him of the potential for dire consequences because of his speech. Eisenhower was leaning toward sending Patton home, since he didn't seem capable of "holding his tongue," which could lead to even more serious indiscretions.

Eisenhower sent a second letter to Marshall, indicating he was going to relieve Patton of his command, but it crossed in the mail with Marshall's response that what really mattered was the success of Overlord. The War Department could weather the criticism, and with a successful invasion, all of Patton's indiscretions would be forgotten.

"If you feel that the operation can be carried on with the same assurance of success with [Lt. Gen. Courtney H.] Hodges in command, for example, instead of Patton, all well and good," Marshall wrote to Eisenhower. Marshall gave Eisenhower complete authority to decide Patton's fate. He insisted that the position of the War Department was not to be considered in the decision, but "only Overlord and your own heavy responsibility for its success."

Eisenhower decided to retain Patton because his formidable military skills and "his demonstrated ability of getting the utmost out of soldiers in offensive operations" would be invaluable in Overlord. He told Patton he was keeping him "solely because of my faith in you as a battle leader and for no other motives." Secretary of War Henry Stimson praised Eisenhower's judgment "as well as the great courage which you have shown in making this decision."[88] Patton's achievements in leading the 3rd Army in World War II were outstanding. It's hard to imagine the same successes with any other battle commander; so, ultimately, Eisenhower probably made the right decision.

Immediately after the war, during the occupation of Germany, Eisenhower had to deal with yet another unpleasant confrontation with his friend. Allied directives included nonfraternization with the Germans and the denazification of Germany, which called for the removal of any Nazi party members from key positions in government. Patton disagreed with these policies, and, as usual, he was outspoken about his views. He respected the fighting abilities of the Germans, and he believed they were the most capable people available to run the country, regardless of their association with the Nazis.

On August 11, 1945, he wrote to Eisenhower, "It is no more possible for a man to be a civil servant in Germany and not have paid lip service to Nazism than it is possible for a man to be a postmaster in America and not have paid at least lip service to the Democratic Party, or the Republican Party when it is in power."[89] Eisenhower disagreed.

He wrote to Patton that "reduced to its fundamentals, the United States entered this war as a foe of Nazism; victory is not complete until we have eliminated from positions of responsibility and, in appropriate cases properly punished, every active adherent to the Nazi party." Eisenhower also made his expectations clear to Patton in terms of following this directive, writing, "I expect just as loyal service in the execution of this and other policies applying to the German occupation as I received during the war."[90]

Patton did his best to comply. He would tell Eisenhower, "You know, Ike, that I'm keeping my mouth shut. I'm a clam." But at a press conference on September 22, Patton said that the military government "would get better results if it employed more former members of the Nazi party in administrative jobs and as skilled workers." When one reporter asked, "After all, General, didn't most ordinary Nazis join their party in about the same way as Americans become Republicans or Democrats?" "Yes," Patton replied, "that's about it."[91]

Eisenhower was incredulous. "Press reports make it appear that you and I are of opposite conviction concerning methods to be pursued in de-Nazification of Germany, and that in spite of repeated orders, you have given public expression to your own views in the matter. I simply cannot believe these reports are accurate.... Smith tells me...that you are holding a press conference immediately to straighten out the matter. I hope you are completely successful because this question is a very serious one."[92] But Patton did little to resolve the uproar. Eisenhower wrote to Marshall that Patton's "own convictions are not entirely in sympathy with the 'hard peace' concept and, being Patton, he cannot keep his mouth shut."[93]

Eisenhower had to confront his friend on his indiscretions. He ordered Patton to his offices in Frankfurt. On the meeting day, Kay

Summersby, Eisenhower's chauffer and secretary, recalled the general "looking as though he hadn't slept a wink. I knew at once he had decided to take action against his old friend. He had aged ten years in reaching the decision, which was inevitable in light of Patton's past mistakes and the universal furor over this one. When General Patton came in...the door was closed. But I heard one of the stormiest sessions ever staged in our headquarters. It was the first time I ever heard General Eisenhower raise his voice."[94]

Once again Eisenhower expressed to Patton how critical the denazification program was to the future success of Germany. But Patton strongly believed that Russia was the real enemy and that Germany could help in battling them. Eisenhower was almost horrified by some of Patton's views on the Russians, and by his loose talk about driving the Red Army back to the Volga. He later told his son that he would have to remove Patton "not for what he's done — just for what he's going to do next."[95]

Eisenhower decided to reassign Patton. "The war's over and I don't want to hurt you but I can't let you be, making such ridiculous statements. I'm going to give you a new job." He put Patton in charge of documenting the lessons learned during the war, and while Patton did not want to leave his command, "he went to work on the new job, giving it the same enthusiasm he gave to command and battle. From then on he had no occasion to meet the press and I had no occasion to criticize George for indiscretions," Eisenhower wrote after the war.[96]

- -

"[The founding fathers] proclaimed to all the world the
revolutionary doctrine of the divine rights of the common man.
That doctrine has ever since been the heart of
the American faith."

- -

On September 8, 1953, President Eisenhower learned of the death of Chief Justice Frederick M. Vinson, "a close personal friend of many years, and a statesman and jurist" he greatly admired.[97] Eisenhower now had an opportunity to fill one of the most important positions in government. Eisenhower told his brother Milton and others he was looking for someone of national stature with a reputation of integrity, honesty, with experience in government and law, and a "middle-of-the-road philosophy."[98]

Previously, Eisenhower had a conversation with Earl Warren about the possibility of appointing the California governor to the Supreme Court. Their initial discussion focused on Warren joining the court as an associate justice, and not the chief justice role. Eisenhower was determined to find the best person for the job, and while Warren was certainly a leading candidate, he said he "owed Governor Warren nothing." Eisenhower's nominee would "not be charged to favoritism or to personal political indebtedness."[99]

As Eisenhower dispatched Attorney General Brownell to California to obtain more insight into Warren's record in his various legal roles, he also began considering other candidates, including his secretary of state John Foster Dulles, who was offered the position but declined. He also received hundreds of recommendations from various constituents, including his brothers. He told people his only decision so far was "to make no mistakes in a hurry."[100]

When the dean of the Columbia University School of Law wrote to Eisenhower with suggested candidates, Eisenhower explained his approach. "My principal concern is to do my part in helping restore the Court to the position of prestige that it used to hold, and which in my opinion was badly damaged during the New and Fair Deal days." In his view the court needed someone with "broad experience, professional competence, and with an unimpeachable record and reputation for integrity."[101]

Not everyone was happy about the potential appointment of Warren. Eisenhower's own brothers, Milton and Edgar, were against the appointment. Edgar wrote to Eisenhower that it would be a "tragedy" if Warren were appointed, and it "would result in the loss of a lot of support...the people of this country are looking for the appointment of a man who is a scholar and a lawyer...they hope you do not appoint either a politician or a professor to that job."

Eisenhower responded, "It appears that our respective ideas of government and of personnel to fill the key posts are characterized more by differences than by accord. What you consider to be a tragedy, I consider to be a very splendid and promising development." He added, "No one could seek comprehensive and exhaustive information and advice on these matters more than I do. However, I am unmoved by mere assertions of likes and dislikes, just as I pay little heed to opinion unsupported by some kind of factual statement." He told his brother that Warren "is a man of national stature, of unimpeachable integrity, of middle-of-the-road views, and with a splendid record during his years in active law work. In any event, I get a bit weary of having the word 'political' used with respect to such decisions. These appointments get my long and earnest study, and I am not trying to please anybody *politically*. So it is useless to talk to me in such terms."[102]

When Brownell returned from his trip with a report on Warren, Eisenhower decided to appoint Earl Warren as chief justice, which he announced on September 30, 1953. Eisenhower had outlined the criteria needed for the position, and Warren had all of them. He represented "the kind of political, economic, and social thinking" that Eisenhower believed was needed on the Supreme Court.[103]

But the most important reason Eisenhower chose Warren was because he sincerely believed he was the best person for the position, and some people believe this appointment was his most important domestic act. Eisenhower was a keen judge of character and talent, and whether people agreed with the decisions of his court or not, Warren and his associates crafted some of most noteworthy decisions of the court over the next fifteen years.

Eisenhower's Leadership Lessons: People

1. Build trust with your team to enable consensus and collaborative results.
2. Quickly replace people who don't work well together.
3. Create a unified team to compete effectively.
4. When you hear a lot of talk about morale, it's probably bad.
5. Explain the rationale for your decisions.
6. Discipline leads to dependability, teamwork, and results.
7. Morale is promoted by unity and destroyed by favoritism or injustice.
8. Workers like to see the executives directing operations.
9. Argue both sides of an issue to maintain flexibility and reach the optimal decision.
10. Develop a natural ability to mingle with people on an equal basis.
11. Provide realistic training.
12. Be precise and clear during disagreements with others.
13. Allow for respectful (even heated) debates for the free exchange of ideas.
14. Solve your own problems—only escalate issues as a last resort.
15. Stay true to your principles when arguing positions.
16. Take the high road in confrontations with others.
17. Protect your team from unnecessary and undeserved criticisms.
18. Keep a diary on your impressions of people for future reference.
19. Highly talented people are hard to find—develop a tolerance for their occasional indiscretions.
20. Hire the best and the brightest.

CHAPTER 4.

ON PLANNING AND ORGANIZING

"Rely on planning, but never trust plans."

VISION AND STRATEGY

"The success of...an alliance is to be judged...not by the amount of heat which may be engendered between the powers in their attempts to find a course of action which will most nearly preserve their individual aims while gaining a common goal, but rather by the degree to which the posers, which frankly working on a basis of self-interest, manage to achieve the one aim for which their forces were brought together. On that basis the Western Powers forged a unity seldom, if ever, achieved in the history of grand alliances. Their commanders, which striving to preserve national identity and gain individual honors for their forces, still waged a victorious war."

—Forrest C. Pogue

After serving briefly under General Leonard Gerow at the War Plans Division in 1942, Eisenhower became Marshall's chief planner of American strategy. He had an excellent relationship with Marshall, he had a staff of more than one hundred officers, and he worked tirelessly in developing various strategies in order to move the war effort forward.

In early 1942, Marshall asked Eisenhower to create a general strategy for the war, which would be presented to the president. Eisenhower knew only so much could be done given the current state of the US military, so he focused on the "high-value" areas and approached the problem by asking two questions. He considered them together, and then worked to find the proper response.

One question was, "What are the vital defensive tasks we must now perform in order that, pending the time when a major offensive effort can be staged, the strategic situation will not deteriorate so badly as to render all future effort practically futile?" Eisenhower's response was "that the immediate important tasks, aside from the protection of the American continent, are the security of England, the retention of Russia in the war as an active ally, and the defense of the Middle East." This was a major prioritization process, since there were many other activities that could contribute to winning the war, such as a major undertaking in the South Pacific.

However, Eisenhower was operating under the principle that the primary concern was to prevent "the arise of any situation that will automatically give the Axis an overwhelming tactical superiority; or one under which its productive potential becomes greater than our own."[1] Under these guidelines, other activities were important but not critical to the overall success of the war.

Eisenhower strongly believed "we must differentiate sharply and definitely between those things whose current accomplishment in the several theaters over the world is *necessary* to the ultimate defeat of the Axis Powers, as opposed to those which are merely *desirable* because of their effect in facilitating such defeat" and that the "distinction between what was necessary and what was desirable had to be rigidly observed, because of limitations on shipping equipment and trained troops."[2]

His other question was what was the "region or theater in which the first major offensive effort of the United Powers must take place" to inflict the most harm to the Axis powers. His response was clear and concise: "the principle target for our first major offensive should be Germany, to be attacked through Western Europe."[3] Eisenhower reasoned that despite the attack at Pearl Harbor, Japan had limited resources, and the major threat came from Germany, so any major efforts should be directed at that arena. He also believed that "time works in our favor. The hostile power is now at its maximum, ours will grow—provided none of the principle members of the United Powers is defeated and forced to capitulate."[4]

Marshall's thinking had been along these same lines for quite a while, so naturally he agreed with Eisenhower. It was a rather radical strategy given the poor state of the country's military status and the desire to retaliate against Japan, but it was the overarching strategy that the Allies would maintain throughout the next four years.

What Eisenhower did by asking questions was to separate the problem from the difficulty of the solution in order to create an unemotional, pragmatic response. In answering his own questions, he analyzed the various alternatives, determined the cost/benefit of each alternative and recommended both short- and long-term plans.

Reaching agreement among the Allies on the Europe-first strategy was an important next step, and Eisenhower was optimistic—"we are all definitely committed to one concept of fighting. If we can agree on major purposes and objectives, our efforts will begin to fall in line and we won't just be thrashing around in the dark."[5] Now Eisenhower and his team had to present alternative plans and the details on where and when to attack, and they had to get their British allies to agree. There were a number of factors to consider in planning the details:

- The people of Great Britain, America, and occupied Europe needed to see some kind of offensive action happen in 1942. Indeed, President Roosevelt "had specifically ordered the United States Chiefs of Staff to launch some kind of offensive ground action in the European zone in 1942."[6]
- Any action taken in 1942 would have to be on a smaller scale than the major cross-channel offensive, in order to prevent any distraction or redeployment of resources away from that major operation.
- A major cross-channel operation couldn't occur before late 1943 at the earliest because of a lack of men and equipment. Since the fall or winter was not the best time to proceed with an invasion of Europe, it meant that a 1944 operation was more likely.

There were a number of options of where to attack first in Europe, but Eisenhower preferred an operation called Sledgehammer, which would be a limited invasion of a relatively small force on the northwest corner of France. The plan called for capturing a small area and defending it against German attack, and, if successful, it could be used as a bridgehead for the larger cross-channel operation, called Roundup. Eisenhower knew that Sledgehammer had risks and was candid about them.

In his analysis on the "Probability of Success," he knew that the constraints included a "lack of suitable landing craft...aircraft operating from England can support the operation only at reduced efficiency," and "the danger of early defeat by enemy forces already in France, assuming a successful landing of the leading division, is always present." He placed the odds of a successful landing by the leading division at around 50 percent, and the overall odds of landing six divisions at about 20 percent. But this was a calculated risk, because he felt it was extremely important to open a second front against the Germans in order to keep the eight million Russians in the war.[7]

But there was strong disagreement from the British about undertaking any cross-channel operation. They were cautious after their experience at Dunkirk in 1940, and they would only approve of a mission to invade the continent if there was a very high level of confidence that the troops would stay there once they landed. Although no one really knew what the Russian situation was on the Eastern front, as Eisenhower wrote, the British thought that Sledgehammer "would have no beneficial effects on the Russian situation" and that "the chances of tactical disaster are very great." The political and morale consequences of another failed landing were unthinkable. Other risk factors were that both American commanders and troops were untested in battle, and amphibious landings were always dangerous.

The debates on the pros and cons of the Sledgehammer plan went on for days between the British and Americans, with Eisenhower and General Mark Clark providing Marshall with a number of memorandums outlining arguments for the plan. Eisenhower wrote to Harry Butcher, "We have sat up nights on the problem involved and have tried to open our eyes to see all the difficulties and not to be blinded by a mere passion for doing something."

But he felt strongly that forward progress was essential — "The British and American armies and the British and American people need to have the feeling that they are attempting something positive. We must not degenerate into a passive...attitude."[8] However, in the end, the British and the Americans were deadlocked in their debate, and President Roosevelt had to intervene. He again told Marshall of the requirement to engage in battle with the Germans sometime in 1942, and gave him the choices of an invasion of North Africa, fighting under the British in Egypt, an operation in Norway, or one through Iran. Once again, Marshall turned to Eisenhower and his team and asked that they create another position paper before deciding.

Eisenhower was disappointed by the decision to not move ahead with Sledgehammer. He felt that he was back to square one.

"Well," he told Clark the morning after the decision, "I hardly know where to start the day.... I'm right back to December fifteenth" of 1941, when Allied planning began.[9] But Eisenhower was never down for long, and, together with his team, he presented an eleven-page "Survey of Strategic Situation" paper that evening for Marshall.

The strategy paper presented an analysis of current conditions and assumptions, alternative solutions and their advantages and disadvantages, and ended with a general conclusion and recommendations. As with all of Eisenhower's papers, it was clear and precise. Eisenhower and his team recommended sending a division to the British Army in Egypt, primarily because it was the least disruptive to the buildup in resources for the eventual execution of Roundup.

Marshall conveyed the essence of Eisenhower's recommendation to Roosevelt. As he waited to hear the decision, Eisenhower told his dinner companions "that Napoleon had written that the most difficult thing for a commanding general is, after making a plan like ROUNDUP, to await the development of the plan and not allow himself to become impatient and diverted from the main plan by the starting of inconsequential side shows. Napoleon had learned that such distractions weaken the effect of the major plan, and, in fact, interfere seriously with its execution."[10] Eisenhower wondered if that's what was happening now. Word soon came from Roosevelt and Marshall of the decision to move forward with the invasion of North Africa, known as Operation Torch.[11]

If Eisenhower was upset that his latest recommendation was rejected on top of the decision to eliminate Sledgehammer, he never showed it. After the decision was made, Eisenhower got behind it, and he wanted his team to do the same. "General Eisenhower stated and restated that TORCH is an order from their Commander-in-Chief...and the Prime Minister; whether we like it or not, it has to be carried out, despite any obstacles."[12]

Indeed, after the war, Eisenhower believed that "those who held the SLEDGEHAMMER operation to be unwise at the moment were correct in their evaluation of the problem."[13] But Eisenhower's role in presenting plans, coordinating staff work, and overcoming disappointments was critical in developing an effective joint strategic plan.

- -

"In preparing for battle I have always found that plans are useless, but planning is indispensable."

- -

Max Hastings wrote that the planning of the invasion of France was "the greatest organizational achievement of the Second World War, a feat of staff work that has dazzled history, a monument to the imagination of British and American planners and logisticians which may never be surpassed in war."[14] Code-named Overlord, the plan required 130,000 Allied ground troops and 23,000 airborne troops to land in Normandy on the morning of June 6, 1944, supported by 195,700 Allied naval personnel. The coordination required between countries and military services, combined with ensuring the proper allocation of resources, was all but mind-numbing. As the supreme commander, Eisenhower was responsible for all aspects of the plan, including approval and oversight.

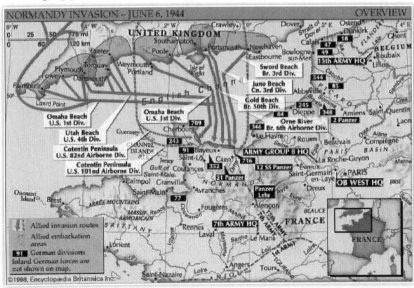

The Normandy invasion

When Eisenhower arrived in London in his new role, the first thing he did was organize his staff, clearly articulating to them what his expectations were. He told them Allied unity was critical and that problems would be solved through objective rather than nationalistic perspectives. He preferred to do business informally, and his door was always open. If he didn't understand something, he asked for their indulgence, and that they should make the subject understandable to him, since they were the experts. He wanted them to be honest and candid with him, as he would be with them. If he had an idea that had already been considered and rejected, he wanted to be told, not humored. Eisenhower told them no commander could possibly know everything, which is why he had a staff.[15]

As he proceeded with the planning, Eisenhower was guided by two principles. One was to completely defeat Nazi Germany. He understood that the quickest path to victory would be found by keeping the Allied coalition fighting together against the enemy — their combined knowledge and resources were much greater than their individual components. Even to the very end, Germany hoped that the Allies would fragment, offering cease-fire terms to the Allies fighting on the Western front only. Eisenhower and the Western leaders consistently refused these offers, telling Germany that it must surrender unconditionally to all of the Allies, including Russia.

The second guiding principle was to "avoid at any cost the freezing of battle lines that might bog down troops in a pattern similar to the trench warfare of World War I. At times in the conduct of any continental campaign, there develops a strain upon supply lines that largely prohibits the continuance of heavy, decisive attacks; during such periods, a certain degree of stabilization is unavoidable. But the Allied forces did not permit these periods of stabilization to develop," which led to "the long, dreary, and wasteful battles that bled Europe white in World War One."[16]

The most significant paragraph of Eisenhower's directive from the combined Joint Chiefs of Staff for liberating Europe was simple and straightforward: "You will enter the continent of Europe and, in conjunction with the other Allied Nations, undertake operations aimed at the heart of Germany and the destruction of her Armed Forces."[17] The entire mission to free Europe was written in a single, broad statement, leaving Eisenhower with the freedom to develop the most effective plans to achieve the required results. In developing the general plan, Eisenhower created his own objectives:

1. Land on the Normandy Coast.
2. Build up the resources needed for a decisive battle in the Normandy-Brittany region, and break out of the enemy's encircling position.
3. Pursue on a broad front with two army groups, emphasizing the left to gain necessary ports, and reach the boundaries of Germany and threaten the Ruhr. On our right, we would link up with the forces that were to invade France from the south.
4. Build up our new base along the western border of Germany, by securing ports in Belgium and in Brittany as well as in the Mediterranean.
5. While building up our forces for the final battles, keep up an unrelenting offensive to the extent of our means, both to wear down the enemy and to gain advantages for the final fighting.
6. Complete the destruction of enemy forces west of the Rhine, in the meantime constantly seeking bridgeheads across the river.
7. Launch the final attack as a double envelopment of the Ruhr, again emphasizing the left, and flow this up by an immediate thrust through Germany, with the specific direction to be determined at the time.
8. Clean out the remainder of Germany.

The specification of broad objectives rather than operational details allowed Eisenhower to maintain maximum flexibility to respond to changing events. Indeed, "this general plan...

was never abandoned, even momentarily, throughout the campaign."[18] In addition to the broad outlines, he was "charged with the location and timing of operations and with the allocation of forces and material made available to him by the Combined Chiefs of Staff, and his decisions would be subject to reversal by the Combined Chiefs."[19]

No one person could possibly develop the full set of Allied war plans of World War II because of its scope and complexity. Planning the strategy, implementing the organization, coordinating industry priorities for the building of ships and planes, training of hundreds of thousands of men, and determining supply and logistics were difficult enough. But when combined with coordinating decisions with political leaders, domestic military services, and the Allies, it's close to overwhelming.

As supreme commander, Eisenhower had the "power of his position," yet he preferred to exercise it judiciously, relying more on his considerable powers of persuasion to convince his superiors and subordinates to undertake the plans that would ultimately succeed. "In a war such as this, where high command invariably involves a President, a Prime Minister, 6 Chiefs of Staff and a horde of lesser 'planners' there has got to be a lot of patience — no one person can be a Napoleon or a Caesar!"[20]

However, in his prior role as head of the Operations Planning Division (OPD), Eisenhower came as close as anyone in developing and understanding almost all aspects of the initiative. He brought all his previous training and his considerable analytical skills to bear in assessing the proper strategic direction. He was thoughtful and pragmatic in solving large, complex problems, and he tended to solve them with the fastest and most direct option possible.[21]

In addition to invading France from the north, "The complimentary attack against southern France had long been considered…as an integral and necessary feature of the main invasion across the Channel." The Americans thought the attack, code-named Anvil, was vital to opening up additional ports to absorb the high volume of soldiers and supplies that were coming from the States.

Anvil would also draw in German resources to prevent their deployment to defend Normandy, ultimately helping to clear out any residual resistance in southern France, and support the broad front strategy as all the Allied forces headed east to Germany. However, in early 1944, there was not complete agreement among the Allies on the need to invade southern France.

The arguments centered on limited resources and the Mediterranean strategy. The resource limitation primarily involved LSTs (landing ship, tanks), which were needed to support a number of Allied efforts, including the pending D-day invasion, the continuing operation in Italy, and battles in the Pacific theater. The strategy issue was about how best to deploy Allied forces in the Mediterranean.

Eisenhower and the Americans wanted the forces to land in Marseilles and continue northward, eventually meeting up with Allied forces from the north for the advance eastward. This required suspension of Allied offenses in Italy after the capture of Rome, but that had been delayed. Eisenhower thought the entire discussion should focus on what was best for D-day, but everyone didn't share his opinion.

"The fighting in the Pacific is absorbing far too much of our limited resource in landing craft during the *critical* phase of the European war," Eisenhower wrote. "The forthcoming [D-day] operation should have every resource the two nations can produce until the moment when the invading force is firmly established on the continent.... But we are fighting two wars at once—which is wrong—so far as I can see from my own limited viewpoint."[22] Unanticipated heavy German resistance and the desire of Field Marshal Alan Brooke and the British Chiefs of Staff (BCOS) to continue on the offensive in Italy also absorbed LSTs.

Eisenhower's main concern was having enough resources and LSTs for D-day, even if it meant canceling Anvil. In writing to Marshall to seek his perspective and provide a unified front to the British, Eisenhower noted, "I honestly believe that a five division (100,000 soldiers) assault is the minimum that gives us a really favorable chance for success. I have earnestly hoped that this could be achieved by the 31st of May without sacrificing a strong ANVIL. One extra month of landing craft production in the United Kingdom and United States including LSTs should help a lot. I think late experience in Italy tends to confirm the necessity to have the OVERLORD landing force sufficiently strong so that it can achieve quick success, particularly securing ports. If we have to start small and wait for a buildup, we are running bigger risks than we should. Moreover, I believe that late developments in Italy create the possibility that the necessary forces there cannot be disentangled in time to put on a strong ANVIL...Some compensation would arise from the fact that as long as the enemy fights in Italy as earnestly and bitterly as he is now doing, the action there will in some degree, compensate for the absence of an ANVIL."

But Marshall was insistent on Anvil. He wanted to make sure that Eisenhower was not developing "localitis" and giving into the British under pressure. Marshall admitted that if the Allies didn't capture Rome by early April, it would be impossible to launch Overlord and Anvil simultaneously. However, he reminded Eisenhower that "canceling ANVIL would have the effect of losing eight to nine divisions that could not be employed either in Italy or northwestern France because of inadequate facilities."[23]

Eisenhower agreed with Marshall, emphasizing the criticality that the spring Mediterranean campaign "must strive in every way to promote a battle there that engages efficiently *all* the combat forces we can make available. The great advantage of a successful ANVIL is that it would open up a certain channel through which all our forces could be engaged, and would have an earlier effect upon the enemy situation in France than would be a continuation of the Italian campaign even on an intensive basis."

The issue was one of timing. Eventually the Allies would have to forecast the outcome of the Italian initiative and plan

116

Overlord and Anvil accordingly. The first sixty days of Overlord would "absorb everything [the Allies] can possibly pour into it," Eisenhower wrote. "At the same time we must have the strongest possible support from the Mediterranean, so planned as to utilize the great bulk of the forces we have there."

Eisenhower then reassured Marshall that his views were his own, and he continued to stress the need for Anvil. "In the various campaigns of this war I have occasionally had to modify slightly my own conceptions of campaign in order to achieve a unity of purpose and effort. I think this is inescapable in Allied operations but I assure you that I have never yet failed to give you my own clear personal convictions about every project and plan in prospect...no one here has tried to encourage me to present any particular view."[24]

Eisenhower convinced Marshall enough that the American Joint Chiefs of Staff (JCS) gave him "authority to decide the fate of ANVIL. From their point of view, he was in an ideal position to make the final determination since he was responsible for Overlord but had been involved in drawing up a plan for Anvil and had been a strong supporter of the operation. The British were amazed that the US Joint Chiefs would delegate this authority to a commander in the field."[25] While Eisenhower would try to persuade the British on the priority of Overlord and Anvil, Marshall would work to convince US Admiral Ernest King to move some of his LSTs from the Pacific to the European theater.

In representing the JCS in Anvil negotiations with the British, Eisenhower would now have the dual role of contributing to overall European strategy, while also acting as supreme commander for Overlord. As the JCS representative, Eisenhower attended the British Chief of Staffs (BCOS) meetings to discuss Overlord and Anvil.

At his first session, it quickly became clear to Eisenhower that the British were firm in their position that they would not suspend the offensive in Italy for any operation, including Overlord, and that he and Field Marshal Alan Brooke (the senior BCOS member) were at a standoff. However, Eisenhower did accept

Brooke's recommendation to solve the problem by first determining "what resources were required for OVERLORD and to allot them," and "then to consider how best to use the remaining forces so as to make the maximum contribution towards the success of ANVIL."[26]

The final review of Overlord occurred on May 15, 1944. The British king, Churchill, and over 150 senior officers attended the meeting. Eisenhower spoke first, prior to presentations by the air, sea, and land commanders. Although Eisenhower's speech lasted only about ten minutes, he was able to set the tone of the rest of the meeting and get the attention of his audience. "It has been said that his smile was worth twenty divisions," Leigh Mallory said. "That day it was worth more."

Eisenhower gave an overview of the plan, and he exuded enough confidence that the "mists of doubt dissolved. When he had finished the tension was gone. Not often has one man been called upon to accept so great a burden of responsibility. But here was one at peace with his soul." As Eisenhower concluded he said "Here we are on the eve of a great battle.... I would emphasize but one thing, that I consider it to be the duty of anyone who sees a flaw in the plan not to hesitate to say so. I have no sympathy with anyone, whatever his station, who will not brook criticism. We are here to get the best possible results and you must make a really co-operative effort."[27]

When the presentations were over, there was unanimous agreement to proceed as planned. Even Churchill, who previously wasn't fully convinced the effort would succeed and preferred alternative campaigns elsewhere, finally agreed that Overlord was the best way to achieve victory and end the fighting.

"Plans are nothing; planning is everything."

One of the reasons Eisenhower was such an effective leader was that he dedicated himself to learning how to lead, and, having mastered many of the principles of leadership, then fully immersed himself into every assignment he had. He thought deeply about how to move efforts forward and viewed problems from different perspectives. In weighing alternatives, Eisenhower had an ability to look beyond an initial first reaction to the longer-term effects of a decision, always keeping in mind the overall objectives and the well-being of his troops or constituents. Eisenhower's presidency spanned the Cold War, and one of the consistent issues confronting him was how to respond to the growing threat of communism.

Eisenhower's strategy against the spread of communism was containment, which was supported by three principles: He would deploy economic and military aid wherever and whenever needed, he would form defensive alliances, and he would threaten to exercise US military power if (and only if) all else failed. Eisenhower believed containment would be a winning strategy "only as long as the United States avoided three crucial errors: First, it should not allow anything to interfere decisively with free trade and should do everything possible to support its capitalist trading partners. Second, the United States could not let the Western Alliance be undermined, even as the old colonial empires collapsed and the nation's Communist opponents tried to break down the unity of the West. Third, America should not try to buy so much security that it weakened its economy over the long term."[28]

Throughout Eisenhower's presidency, the country was nervous about a surprise nuclear attack from the USSR, and the fears were valid considering the growing arsenal of nuclear weapons held by the two powers. These fears reached a new high when Soviet Premier Nikita Khrushchev said he would sign a treaty with East Germany that would effectively end any Allied rights in West Berlin. Khrushchev said that after the treaty was signed on May 27, 1959, the Allies would have to fight their way to West Berlin, since they did not have a similar treaty with East Germany.

Not only did Eisenhower have to deal with the threats from Khrushchev, he also was getting pressured by both political parties and the military to increase defense spending, and the public was getting restless about moving to the offensive in the Cold War, rather than reacting to events. People were becoming concerned that Eisenhower was underestimating the probably of going to war. The press was also becoming aggressive in questioning Eisenhower's stewardship through this difficult time.

At a press conference on March 9, 1959, Eisenhower was asked if he could imagine a scenario that would cause him to increase defense spending or delay the planned reductions in troop levels. Eisenhower responded that the goal was always to seek balance and achieve "a just peace from a position of strength," and the best approach was to follow the established plan and not get distracted with every world event.

"I have argued and urged for years," Eisenhower continued, "that we are living and we are going to live in a tense period because of the actions and the attitude of the Communist imperialism." Communists were always going to start something somewhere. "Whether it is Sputnik or it's Quemoy or it's Korea or whatever it is, what we have to do is to stand steady...to be alert, to watch what we are doing, and to make certain that we know how and where we would have to produce action, if action became necessary."

These spikes in tensions were not going to dictate defense levels. "We are certainly not going to fight a ground war in Europe," he told reporters. "What good would it do to send a few more thousands or indeed even a few divisions of troops to Europe? I do not see why we would think that we — with something of a half a million troops, Soviet and some German in East Germany, with 175 Soviet divisions [1.75 to 2.625 million troops] — why in the world would we dream of fighting a ground war?"

As far as troop levels, "I don't think that an army of 870,000 is a small army," he said. Eisenhower realized people were using the Berlin situation as a reason to have more ground forces. "What would you do with more ground forces in Europe?" Eisenhower asked. "Does anyone here have an idea? Would you start a ground war? You wouldn't start the kind of ground war that would win in that region" because you would still be outnumbered. "We just don't want to be fighting battles where we are always at a disadvantage, and I mean battles, whether they are political, economic, or military. I don't want to be at a disadvantage."

Eisenhower was then asked if the United States was prepared to use nuclear weapons if necessary to defend free Berlin. "Well, I don't know how you could free anything with nuclear weapons," Eisenhower said. However, "the United States and its allies have announced their firm intention of preserving their rights and responsibilities with respect to Berlin. If any threat, or any push in the direction of real hostilities is going to occur, it's going to occur from the side of the Soviets. Now, if that would become reality, and I don't believe that anyone would be senseless enough to push that to the point of reality, then there will be the time to decide exactly what the allies would, in turn, expect to do."

A reporter asked Eisenhower if he thought the American public was aware of the possibility of war over Berlin. Eisenhower thought Americans were more aware of the real situation than most of Washington DC, where events can take on a momentum of their own. Americans read enough newspapers and heard enough speeches to realize the situation was serious; otherwise, they would be protesting the amount of defense spending.

What Eisenhower counseled was patience. "Let's not make everything such an hysterical sort of a proposition that we go a little bit off half-cocked," he said. "We ought to keep our steadiness, is what I plead for, steadiness in meeting this whole business, whether it be in Quemoy or Berlin or anywhere else."

Eisenhower at one of his many press conferences

The discussion became even more lively with May Craig's question. "Sir, the Constitution gives to Congress the power to provide for the common defense and raise and support armies, maintain and provide a navy. Where do you get the right not to do what Congress says in providing for the common defense?" Eisenhower responded calmly, "First of all, I am Commander in Chief, and I use the forces that are given me. Now, I have pointed out a number of times that I am not going to try deliberately and continuously to, as you say, thwart the will of Congress." Congress sometimes makes mistakes, he said, but if they insisted that he add troops, he guessed he would just put them "some place where it's nice to keep them out of the way, because I don't know what else to do with them."

"Was his administration prioritizing a balanced budget ahead of national security?" Eisenhower was asked. "What if there was a budget surplus? Would he then spend more on armed forces?" Eisenhower said he would not increase military spending, but would rather "strengthen the United States in other ways," such as its educational system. He didn't understand the debate between a balanced budget and national security. "I say that a balanced budget in the long run is a vital part of national security. We have got the job of keeping the United States just as strong at home in everything we are trying to do as we have abroad."

In the last questions of the press conference, Eisenhower was asked if there was some other alternative in responding to the Soviets, since he seemed to rule out a ground war or the use of nuclear weapons. "I think we might as well understand this," Eisenhower responded. "I didn't say that nuclear war is a complete impossibility. I said it couldn't...free anything. Destruction is not a good police force. You don't throw hand grenades around streets to police the streets so that people won't be molested by thugs. This is exactly the way that you have to look at nuclear war, or any other. And, I must say, to use that kind of a nuclear war as a general thing looks to me a self-defeating thing for all of us. After all, with that kind of release of nuclear explosions around this world, of the numbers of hundreds, I don't know what it would do to the world and particularly the Northern Hemisphere; and I don't think anybody else does. But I know it would be quite serious."[29]

Eisenhower insisted that time and patience would eventually defeat the Communists, and he continued to focus on the larger picture and tried to calm everyone down. He repeatedly held meetings with the political parties and the military to stress the need to avoid overreacting because "in doing so we give the Soviets ammunition."

The president stressed the view that Khrushchev desired only to upset the United States. He expressed once again his view that "we must address this problem in terms, not of six months, but of forty years." The USSR wanted to disrupt America wherever it could, this time in Berlin, next time in Iraq or Iran. They would continue to do this, and "they would like us to go frantic every time they stir up difficulties in these areas."[30]

He patiently explained that if people wanted to understand Communist motives all they needed to do was to read their books and writings. The "Communist objective is to make us spend ourselves into bankruptcy." Eisenhower thought it was wrong to use Berlin as an excuse to respond dramatically. "This is a continuous crisis...that the United States has to live with certainly as long as we are going to be here." The long-term strategy was to contain the Soviets, until their citizens and others under Communist rule became educated, and this would eventually "sow the seeds of destruction of Communism as a virulent power. This will take a long time to settle."[31]

With the benefit of hindsight, Eisenhower was obviously right, and many of his insights are applicable to today's uncertainties surrounding the Middle East, terrorism, and economic security. However, in the late 1950s, Eisenhower was just about alone in this thinking. He continued his strategies of standing firm against the Soviets, while clearly stating the United States would not abandon West Berlin, but he would not overreact to this or other Soviet outbursts.

Khrushchev's May 27 deadline passed without incident, but Eisenhower wasn't satisfied. He thought it was "ridiculous that the world is divided into segments facing each other in unending hostility. He felt that decent men should be able to find some way to make progress toward a better state of things."[32] Eisenhower believed any problem could be solved if only people would sit down together and exchange ideas and solutions. This eventually led to Khrushchev visiting the United States, with Eisenhower playing host, to "take the crisis edge off the Berlin situation."[33]

In the end, Eisenhower's far-sighted, strategic thinking meant he never backed down from the Soviet threat, he didn't increase defense spending, and he avoided a war. It was a masterful performance. He took the time to understand the motivations of his adversary, he looked beyond the immediate crisis to the larger issues involved, he continued to listen and communicate his views to everyone, and he ultimately accomplished all of his goals.

124

ALLOCATING RESOURCES

"Every gun that is made, every warship launched, every rocket fired, signifies, in the final sense, a theft from those who hunger and are not fed, those who are cold and are not clothed. The world in arms is not spending money alone. It is spending the sweat of its laborers, the genius of its scientists, the hopes of its children."

One of the most important functions of a leader is to move resources from efforts with low returns to efforts with higher returns and be able to recognize the difference between the two. Eisenhower had the ability to visualize the resources required for massive initiatives, the wisdom to maintain the flexibility to redeploy resources as required to exploit advantages as they surfaced, the discipline and energy required to pay attention to even the smallest of operational efficiencies, and, most importantly, the ability to say no to unproductive activities that would potentially waste precious resources.

In his role as commander, Eisenhower was primarily responsible for what Churchill called the proper allocation of overwhelming force. As the capture of Sicily was coming to a close, Eisenhower and his team turned their attention to planning the invasion of mainland Italy, specifically at Salerno. This operation, code-named Avalanche, had many challenges "because of the distance from possible bases to provide fighter cover for the initial assault and...because of the increased effort required for neutralization of hostile air and disrupting lines of communication."

Eisenhower wanted to temporarily double the amount of heavy bombers for the campaign, so they could help to "paralyze the German air effort...and almost immobilize his ground units."[34] However, the bombers Eisenhower wanted were allocated to the bombing offensive against Germany, and Lt. General Jacob Devers, the commanding general of the European Theater of Operations, argued strongly against a redeployment of the aircraft, writing that in considering "the overall war effort, I must be guided by the greatest damage to the German enemy."[35]

Eisenhower countered that "in the possession a great numbers of long-range bombers, the United Nations possess a mobile strategic weapon that can be used for particular periods at any point," but Marshall decided against the transfer.[36] Eisenhower then tried an alternative approach to obtain the air resources. There were three B-24 bomber groups that were scheduled to return to England after participating in a bombing campaign of oil refineries in Romania. Eisenhower requested that these remain in the Mediterranean theater for use in the Avalanche campaign.

He made his case to Marshall, writing, "I am not submitting any detailed argument on this point because I am sure you understand that we are not asking for anything we do not believe to be absolutely necessary to carry out our mission.... The hostile bomber strength has been steadily building up in this theater for some days and we simply must get on top of this matter if AVALANCHE is to be a success."[37] But Marshall again declined the request, primarily because he wanted the strategic bombing of Europe to continue.

Even though he and his air commanders were "convinced that the immediate subtraction of these three groups would definitely add to the risks of the AVALANCHE operation," Eisenhower decided to move ahead with the invasion—"my plans for attack will not be altered as a result of this transfer." To Air Chief Marshal Arthur Tedder, who was assisting in planning Avalanche, "it was already plain enough...that Eisenhower accepted reasonable risks more willingly than did his British counterparts."[38]

While he accepted the decision, Eisenhower wanted to make it clear that there were major risks involved. There were already three divisions in the area with another reinforcement division expected soon, and German air support was increasing while Allied air support was decreasing. "As a consequence of these things our convoys will have to anticipate higher loses from air attack while at sea and lying offshore."[39] Eisenhower calculated that air support was vital to the success of the operation, and he fought hard to gain those resources. But with the decision against his proposal, he decided to do the best he could with the resources available to him.

However, within a month, Eisenhower's superiors would regret and reverse the decision to move the bomber groups away from the Mediterranean theater. Even after the redeployment of the bombers, the situation was risky. Eisenhower was betting that the Italians would be neutral during the conflict, or even turn against the Germans, but there was no guarantee that they wouldn't switch sides and fight against the Allies. Also, the Allies were not invading with an overwhelming force, as they would in the future in Normandy. They were going against almost twenty enemy divisions deployed throughout the mainland, and the Germans also had the ability to reinforce defenses at Salerno rather quickly.

As Geoffrey Perret explains, "Clark's amphibious assault consisted of only three divisions…with a follow-up force of two more divisions. His attack was going to hit Italy not so much with the impact of an avalanche as that of a snowball," and in his planning, he had "chosen to be strong nowhere and weak everywhere," because he was attacking across a broad front, with a river running through the beachfront.[40]

But it was a calculated risk by Eisenhower, and he was confident of eventual success. "My optimism, which never deserts me, is based upon the efficiency of our Air Force, the fact that the enemy cannot yet be sure that we will not attack still further north, and the fighting quality of our troops." He may not have had the amount of resources he wanted, but he knew the abilities of the resources he did have, and he would certainly need that optimism as the battle unfolded.

The invasion at Salerno started off well, but the situation quickly deteriorated. The Germans responded with strong resistance, and the conditions at the landing beaches caused the troops to become dispersed, which created confusion and caused difficulty in linking up the various forces. Eisenhower worked to find landing craft to get another division to Clark, and he pressed

Montgomery (who had entered with his forces at the toe of Italy) to move quickly in order to bring pressure to the Germans' left flank. With no landing craft available, Eisenhower ordered part of the 82nd Airborne Division to be dropped on the beaches to reinforce the positions.

After several pleas and refusals for additional landing craft, Eisenhower received eighteen landing craft, and he was able to get another division to Salerno. Even though the air force was performing well, Eisenhower could certainly use more—"I would give up next year's pay for two or three extra heavy groups right this minute."[41]

But he remained confident despite the turmoil around him. "I have great faith that even in spite of currently grim reports, we'll pull out all right," he wrote in his diary. "Our Air Force, the fighting value of our troops, and strenuous efforts by us all, should do the trick."[42] Ultimately he believed the Allies would "succeed because...our Air Force will finally disorganize the attacks against the Fifth Army and that very soon Montgomery's advance will have some effect on the enemy near Salerno. Moreover, we have adopted extraordinary measures to rush reinforcements to Clark and it is clear to me that if he can only hold on a week longer he will be in position to reorganize and resume the offensive."[43]

Almost as he wrote this, the situation began to stabilize, as the Allies held key positions and prevented a German breakthrough. When the Germans mounted a counteroffensive, he ordered Air Chief Tedder "to concentrate the full strength of his air force, to include every plane that could fly, in an attack upon sensitive spots in the German formations," and he supported the navy's decision to move closer to shore to hit German positions.[44]

Eisenhower also sent a note of encouragement to General Clark. "We know you are having a sticky time but you may be sure that everybody is working at full speed to provide the reinforcements you need," he wrote. "You and your people have done a magnificent job. We are all proud of you and since the whole operation depends upon you and your forces, you need have no fear that anything will be neglected in providing you all possible assistance."[45] As the Allies continued to resist the enemy's assault, Montgomery's army linked up with Clark's, causing the German army to withdraw.

While the crisis was over, the fighting was not. Now the Allies had to reorganize, move off the beaches, and secure "the two great initial objectives of the Italian invasion…the capture… of Naples as a satisfactory port from which to supply our troops, and, second of the airfields at Foggia from which to supplement the air bombardment of central Europe."[46]

In response to the stressful moments during the German counteroffensive, offers of support began to arrive at Allied headquarters. Churchill sent a telegram stating, "Ask for anything you want and I will make allocation of necessary supplies with highest priority irrespective of every other consideration." The British Chiefs of Staff (BCOS) were "most anxious to give all help possible at earliest moment" and requested that Eisenhower "state clearly…what further steps we can take to help."[47]

Eisenhower must have felt like asking everyone where they were two weeks ago; however, he resisted saying anything negative. He asked Churchill for long-range aircraft based in the UK to bomb northern Italy to disrupt communications and hopefully have a negative effect on the morale of the enemy all over the country. He also requested the return of the "three B-24 groups that had a considerable experience in this area." He wanted them deployed daily to disrupt "communications between the southern and northern enemy concentrations…even if these three groups could operate here for a period of two weeks only it should have a most marked effect on our present critical problem," which was additional air support.

He asked for a quick response, and he got it. The very next day, the BCOS told Eisenhower "that they approved of the movement of the B-24 groups and that the Bomber Command was waiting only for suitable weather to execute plans…for interrupting communications into northern Italy."[48] Within twenty-four hours, the long-range bombers were doing damage to enemy positions, and, within a week, the B-24 bombers were moved from England to the Mediterranean, and the Allies soon began their march across Italy, pushing the Germans back along the way.

Churchill sent a note of congratulations to Eisenhower, complementing him on the "landing and deployment in Italy" and on his willingness to take risks. "As the Duke of Wellington said of the battle of Waterloo, 'It was a damned close-run thing,'" Churchill wrote.[49] It was one of the most difficult and dangerous missions the Allies had undertaken throughout the war, and it was filled with risks from the beginning. Eisenhower knew the proper level of resources required to ensure rapid success, and he fought hard for them. When he didn't get them, he calculated that the potential benefits outweighed the risks, and he decided to move forward.

With the situation deteriorating, he didn't make excuses. Instead he took complete responsibility for the eventual outcome — good or bad. Rather than worry about his reputation or future, he got to work to support his team. He did everything possible to reinforce the efforts, from additional troops to working with his commanders to strengthen air and naval support, and by persistence and adapting rapidly to changing events, Eisenhower was able to lead his armies to a critical victory. Most importantly, Eisenhower learned an important lesson — he would insist upon the proper level and allocation of resources going forward. It wasn't long before the lesson had to be applied.

Soon after Naples fell into Allied control, Eisenhower received a cable from Churchill, who wanted "to exploit the Italian surrender in the eastern Mediterranean." In January 1943 Churchill had directed his Middle East staff to draft plans for the capture of Rhodes, "the largest and most strategically significant of the Dodecanese Islands." The plan was produced in March 1943, but it was delayed to give priority to the invasions of Sicily and mainland Italy.

Churchill reinitiated the plan using British soldiers under the Command of General Henry Wilson; however, "At the time of the Italian surrender, the Germans quickly overpowered the Italians on Rhodes and reinforced their garrison there. Unable to capture the main island, on September 14 the British landed small parties on Cos, Samos, Leros and other lesser islands."

Not able to overcome the German garrison on Rhodes, Churchill turned to Eisenhower, requesting reinforcement of the islands in preparation for an eventual takeover of the main island. Churchill sent two cables to Eisenhower stressing "that Rhodes was the key to both the eastern Mediterranean and the Aegean." Believing that the island should fall easily, Churchill requested that one-tenth of the Allied resources in the Mediterranean be redeployed to the effort, with another tenth deployed against the Adriatic, and the remaining forces used to strengthen the front in Italy. Churchill argued that "not only were the airfields of great value, but Allied possession of this strategic island might also bring Turkey into the war."[50]

Eisenhower knew of Churchill's desire for defeating Germany through its "soft underbelly" through the Mediterranean. He felt that Churchill "seemed always to see great and decisive possibilities in the Mediterranean, while the project of invasion across the English Channel left him cold," which was problematic to Eisenhower and the overall strategy.[51] But Eisenhower was never one to question people's motives, and as usual, he took Churchill's request seriously. Leaving his options open, he told Churchill that his office was "examining resources carefully," and he would get back to him shortly.[52]

Eisenhower discussed the resource request with his team—Alexander, Cunningham, and Tedder. They were "of one mind... that the operation against Rhodes...should be promptly abandoned." Given that existing resources in the Italian campaign were "barely sufficient," they "could not help fearing that in practice the requirements of" the Rhodes operation "would draw upon resources urgently needed for the main business at hand," which was the stabilization of the Italian mainland and the eventual redeployment of resources to OVERLORD."[53] Eisenhower was inclined to agree. He was against nonstrategic diversions and wanted to keep a concentration of resources in Italy to finish the job there. While the Italian and Rhodes operations were under separate commands, they were in effect inseparable because they were colocated in the Mediterranean.

He agreed with a number of the planning staff in London who "reported that the Middle East Commanders were overestimating the strategic importance of Rhodes. Possession of the island would of itself do nothing to drive the German Air Force out of Greece. Nor did the forces suggested for this operation against Rhodes seem to be sufficient. Further strength could only be provided at the expense of the effort in Italy. The Joint Planners thought it would be better to abandon Cos, Leros, and other islands we had taken, than to divert any proportion of the air effort from its main purpose, the destruction of targets in southern Germany, which was one of the principal reasons for entering upon the Italian campaign."[54]

Eisenhower "studied the problem with the greatest possible sympathy;" however, with intelligence reports indicating a massive build up of enemy forces north of Rome, it was becoming "clear that the battle there would not be won without a major struggle." Eisenhower concluded "that aside from temporary air support," they had little else to offer. Anything more "would be definitely detrimental—possibly fatal" to the Italian campaign.

As the German assault on the British occupied islands intensified, Churchill sent a cable to Eisenhower stating he was very "concerned about Cos and are sure you will do all in your power to prevent a vexatious injury to future plans occurring through loss of Cos."[55] Eisenhower had already authorized a number of air raids on enemy positions over four days, and he responded to Churchill, "We are already using all our available air power to assist in this project."[56]

Despite the response, Wilson submitted requests for additional support for the operation to Tedder, who was deeply concerned, not only about the potential dispersion of resources but in the lack of coordinated planning. He wrote to Eisenhower, "The participation of the air elements of this Theatre in this operation has never to my knowledge been properly considered and because of the shortness of the remaining time I feel this must be done at once."

It was clear that "the employment of any type of aircraft in support of Rhodes reduces by an equivalent amount the potential bombing effort which may be applied in Italy," which both Eisenhower and Tedder wanted to focus on. Tedder also made sure that the air commanding officer in the Middle East knew of his discontent with the current situation. He wrote that the "procedure by which Commanders-in-Chief, Middle East, launch operations without full consultation with me and Eisenhower is, I feel, most dangerous."

Eisenhower told Tedder not to be concerned. He wrote that our "first purpose must remain the defeat of the enemy in Italy," especially since he had not received any directive from the Combined Chiefs of Staff regarding Rhodes. While they were all certainly sympathetic to the situation, "At this time we cannot make any specific commitments other than those involving the blasting of enemy airfields in Greece," which they both committed to. "We cannot forget the mission given us in this theater by the Combined Chiefs of Staff and we cannot disperse strength where that strength is necessary to our own job."[57]

It wasn't long before Eisenhower's resolve was put to the test. The day after his note to Tedder, two additional messages arrived from Wilson reporting "that the island of Cos would probably fall to the Germans within twenty-four hours," and the other islands currently occupied by the British would also be lost unless reinforcements were sent. Wilson "requested immediate air and sea assistance to enable him to hold Leros until Rhodes was attacked and captured," noting that "the loss of Leros would reduce the air support available for the Rhodes operation."

Eisenhower escalated the matter to the US and British Combined Chiefs of Staff. He noted that while he appreciated the "importance which the British Chiefs of Staff attach to retention" of the islands, he had done all he could at this point without a major shift in strategic direction. The enemy was sending significant reinforcements to Italy, proving they were ready to "engage in major battle for the possession of Italy. Throughout the winter we shall be considerably inferior in ground forces, and it is essential to offset this by sustained and continued air attack upon German communications." He stressed that while the Rhodes operation may be "desirable in itself," it was "bound to place calls on us for a very considerable and continuing diversion of air effort from the main operations in Italy: I consider any material diversion highly prejudicial to the success of Italian operations," especially since "these operations will probably assume the aspect of a major bitter battle."[58]

After reading Eisenhower's note, Churchill responded, indicating that he was "disturbed over his reluctance to provide reinforcements" to the Rhodes effort. Stressing the importance of the Aegean, both in itself and in relation to Italy, he asked Eisenhower to approve the diversion of enough troops and supplies to insure the capture of Rhodes.

Churchill "contended that the diversion that would be forced upon the enemy would be greater than what Eisenhower would have to make, and an operation against Rhodes would give him an opportunity to engage and wear down the enemy's air power in a new region. 'Rhodes,' the Prime Minister declared, 'is the key to all this.' All that was needed was a first class diversion." Churchill was so concerned that he simultaneously sent a similar note to Roosevelt, again "urging the capture of Rhodes as the key to Greece and the Balkans."[59]

Churchill could be relentless in pursuing a course he believed to be right, and this was one of those occasions. But Eisenhower could be just as tenacious and firm. As Butcher noted in his diary, at the core of these arguments was a "fundamental difference between Britain and America as to the prosecution of the war. The Prime Minister wants to exploit our advantages throughout the Mediterranean as rapidly as possible. Ike and AFHQ [Allied Forces Headquarters] staff felt that every atom of our strength will be required to beat the Germans in Italy. The Germans have recently moved in another division...which will equal our ground strength. The balance in our favor comes in the air, where our superiority is appraised by Ike to be equivalent to ten ground divisions. Every subtraction from our strength makes more difficult our opportunity for the destruction of the Germans in the major battle to come in Italy."[60]

Eisenhower believed "that the greatest contribution we can make to the success of OVERLORD is, through a vigorous fall and winter campaign to attain a strong concentrated position in north Italy whence we can attack south France and threaten eastward as well. To do this immediate effort in establishing our air and ground forces in Italy is mandatory. Additionally it must be realized that unless we can keep all our efforts concentrated we may be forced onto the defensive and lose the initiative which we have struggled so hard to gain."

Despite these views, Eisenhower listened to Churchill's arguments, as he always did out of respect and admiration. Eisenhower decided to hold a conference with his commanders, Admiral Cunningham and the commanders in chief of the Middle East to reach a consensus on what—if anything—should be done.

Through Marshall, Eisenhower also requested a directive from the CCS on its position on the matter. Although Eisenhower never did receive the requested directive, he did receive timely support from President Roosevelt. Marshall forwarded a copy of Roosevelt's response to Churchill, stating that "he did not want to force any diversions that Eisenhower felt might jeopardize the present Italian situation nor any changes that might prejudice OVERLORD."[61]

That response didn't sit well with Churchill, so he sent another message to Roosevelt, repeating the same arguments and recommending "that he and the British Chiefs of Staff were willing to come to Eisenhower's headquarters to discuss plans with General Marshall or the President's personal representative." Marshall had grown weary of the debates and angrily told the prime minister "not one American soldier is going to die on that goddamned island."[62] But the president took a softer tone, telling Churchill "that this trip was unnecessary, advising him to wait for the outcome of the conference...scheduled the following day."[63]

Eisenhower called the session "the simplest, most unargumentative of any similar conference I attended during the war. I outlined the entire situation as we saw it and announced the decision I had reached, which was to be final unless overridden by the Combined Chiefs of Staff. Its purport was that detachments from the Italian command were not warranted and that we could and would do nothing about the islands. Those islands, in my judgment...did not compare in military value to success in the Italian battle. Every officer present agreed emphatically with my conclusions," and they all "knew that the decision would be a bitter one for the Prime Minister to accept. I reported these conclusions to the Combined Chiefs of Staff, who supported my decision."[64]

Churchill was extremely disappointed by the decision, and he was still not ready to give in. Churchill wanted to make sure all views were freely expressed at the conference, and that Roosevelt's previous message wasn't "taken as an order to close the subject." Eisenhower told Churchill that the "message was not even read at the conference," and he had instructed the group to "examine the problem on its own merits."[65] Churchill considered pushing his arguments further, but he finally relented when separate cables came in from Alexander, Wilson, and Cunningham, which all reinforced Eisenhower's decision.

"If you want total security, go to prison. There you're fed, clothed, given medical care and so on. The only thing lacking... is freedom."

"Ladies and gentlemen, there is no amount of military force that can possibly give you real security, because you wouldn't have that amount unless you felt that there was almost a similar amount that could threaten you somewhere in the world," Eisenhower told reporters early in his presidency, in March 1953. "Now, you finally have to make certain very tough decisions. I know of no better way to express it than George Washington did, many years ago. He said this country must always be careful to have a reasonable posture of defense."

With this, Eisenhower began the long pursuit of balancing between fiscal responsibility and the proper level of defense for the country during his presidency. Eisenhower hated waste, and having served in the military most of his career, he knew there were opportunities to save money without risking the safety of the country. He was "dedicated to one idea, which is to get less money spent for overhead and what I believe still to be certain duplications and unnecessary expenses, and to get out of that same money more combat strength."[66]

Eisenhower also believed a strong defense was only one aspect of national security. A strong economy with balanced federal budgets along with a strong foundation of intellectual capability and moral responsibility were also vital to the long-term success of democracy. America had the potential to lead the world to a better, less volatile place if the country was able to showcase how these values led to freedom and prosperity at home.

Achieving a balanced budget was a priority for Eisenhower, despite the Cold War and despite calls for tax cuts. And since the defense budget was the largest component of the federal budget, Eisenhower was determined to get it under control. Unlike many military men of the past, he understood the need to prepare to fight the next war, not the last one. The game had changed the moment the Soviets tested their first atomic bomb in 1949.

He wanted a fresh look at America's defenses, and he established five principles to guide him and his team: When attacked, America did not have to respond "in kind" (e.g., if Europe was invaded with troops, the United States did not have to use troops; it could use other weapons); since a nuclear war would be catastrophic, America needed enough strength to deter a conflict; "military and economic strength were intimate and indivisible;" modern armed forces were essential, since America could "no longer afford the folly...of beginning each war with the weapons of the last;" and lastly, the need for alliances, since America's resources were finite.[67]

It was also necessary to conduct a horizontal analysis — a strategic look across all military services to optimize the allocation and deployment of forces at home and around the world. The guidelines and analysis resulted in Eisenhower's "New Look" — a defense program that reallocated resources between the armed forces, with a greater reliance "on the deterrent and destructive power of improved nuclear weapons, better means of delivery, and effective air defense units." More resources would be moved from the other services to the air force, and an overall reduction in conventional services would occur, with the greater emphasis on nuclear deterrence.[68]

As he expected, Eisenhower received pushback from many quarters, from the army and the navy, from Congress, and even from within his own administration. When Dulles protested that the priority for a balanced budget would put the country at risk, Eisenhower disagreed, once again telling his cabinet that security required a sound economy, which required a balanced budget.

While past administrations had set targets for defense spending, with the goal of being ready for global war at any time, Eisenhower wanted to pay with available funds for a gradual buildup. He didn't believe in targets, because no one could predict what would be needed when. When asked at a news conference if he thought the buildup would "stretch out" over ten years, Eisenhower answered, "I would object to 10 years just as much as I object to" two years. "Anyone who bases his defense on his ability to predict the day and the hour of attack, is crazy. If you are going on the defensive, you have got to get a level of preparation you can sustain over the years. And I don't know — whether it's 1 year, 10 years, 20 years, or what; but if you try to build up all of a sudden to have an attack in '54, and it doesn't come, what do you do? Now, it just doesn't make sense."[69]

"The past speaks for itself. I am interested in the future."

The amount of defense spending was directly related to the perceived threats to America's national security. If Eisenhower could reduce tensions, he could reduce the amount of the funds allocated to military spending. He started giving considerable thought to a new approach to dealing with the Russians and other hostile governments in the world. He wanted to seize the initiative, and he was thinking of making a speech to outline a roadmap for peace. He knew it would be difficult. "You come up to face these terrible issues," he confided to his speechwriter Emmet Hughes one afternoon in March 1953, "and you know that what is in almost everyone's heart is a wish for peace, and you want so much to do something. And then you wonder...if there really is anything you can do by words and promises." But at least he was going to try.

As Hughes described the scene, he watched Eisenhower pace the Oval Office and listened as he began thinking out loud. "Look, I'm tired of just plain indictments of the Soviet regime. I think it would be wrong for me to get up before the world now to make another one of those indictments. Instead, one thing matters: what have *we* got to offer the world? What are *we* ready to do, to improve the chances of peace?" It had to be something of substance. "What are we *trying* to achieve?" he asked.

Eisenhower had stopped pacing and was quietly looking out the window as the room went silent. Eisenhower then turned quickly to face Hughes and told him "*Here* is what I would like to say. The jet plane that roars over your head costs three quarters of a million dollars. That is more money than a man earning ten thousand dollars every year is going to make in his lifetime. What world can afford this sort of thing for long? We are in an armaments race. Where will it lead us? At worst, to atomic warfare. At best, to robbing every people and nation on earth of the fruits of their own toil...Now, there could be another road before us — the road of disarmament. What does this mean? It means for everybody in the world: bread, butter, clothes, homes, hospitals, schools — all the good and necessary things for decent living.

"So let *this* be the choice we offer. If we take this second road, all of us can produce more of these good things for life — and we, the United States, will help them still more. We could do this by talking straight: *no* double talk, *no* sophisticated political formulas, *no* slick propaganda device." What would be said about the Soviet government? "I am not going to make an indictment of them. The past speaks for itself. I am interested in the future. The slate is clean. Now let us begin talking to each other. *And let us say what we've got to say so that every person on earth can understand it.* If the Soviet Union can improve on it, let's hear it.

"This is what I want to say. And if we don't really have anything to offer, I'm not going to make a speech about it." Eisenhower's enthusiasm was contagious, and his vision was compelling. When Hughes mentioned that this approach would be aggressively opposed by his hawkish secretary of state, John Foster Dulles, Eisenhower responded "All right then. If Mr. Dulles and all his sophisticated advisers really mean that they can *not* talk peace seriously, then I am in the wrong pew. For if it's *war* we should be talking about, I know the people to give me advice on that—and they're not in the State Department. Now either we cut out all this fooling around and make a serious bid for peace—or we forget the whole thing."[70]

Over the next two weeks, Eisenhower worked with his team to refine the speech, and on April 16, 1953, he gave his "Chance for Peace" address. Although he was to become ill, and he struggled to complete it, it was one of his finest oratories.

"In the Spring of 1953 the free world weighs one question above all others: the chance for a just peace for all peoples." After eight years of facing each other in hostility, "What can the world, or any nation in it, hope for if no turning is found on this dread road? The worst to be feared and the best to be expected can be simply stated. The worst is atomic war. The best would be this: a life of perpetual fear and tension; a burden of arms draining the wealth and the labor of all peoples; a wasting of strength that defies the American system or the Soviet system or any system to achieve true abundance and happiness for the peoples of this earth.

"Every gun that is made, every warship launched, every rocket fired signifies, in the final sense, a theft from those who hunger and are not fed, those who are cold and are not clothed. This world in arms is not spending money alone. It is spending the sweat of its laborers, the genius of its scientists, the hopes of its children. The cost of one modern heavy bomber is this: a modern brick school in more than 30 cities. It is two electric power plants, each serving a town of 60,000 population. It is two fine, fully equipped hospitals. It is some 50 miles of concrete highway. We pay for a single fighter plane with a half million bushels of wheat. We pay for a single destroyer with new homes that could have housed more than 8,000 people. This, I repeat, is the best way of life to be found on the road.

"This is not a way of life at all...Under the cloud of threatening war, it is humanity hanging from a cross of iron." With the recent death of Stalin, "the new Soviet leadership now has a precious opportunity to awaken, with the rest of the world, to the point of peril reached and to help turn the tide of history. Will it do this? We do not yet know. Recent statements and gestures of Soviet leaders give some evidence that they may recognize this critical moment. We welcome every honest act of peace. We care nothing for mere rhetoric. This we do know: a world that begins to witness the rebirth of trust among nations can find its way to a peace that is neither partial nor punitive. With all who will work in good faith toward such a peace, we are ready, with renewed resolve, to strive to redeem the near-lost hopes of our day."

Success in this endeavor would result in "the dedication of the energies, the resources, and the imaginations of all peaceful nations to a new kind of war. This would be a declared total war, not upon any human enemy but upon the brute forces of poverty and need.

"The peace we seek, rounded upon decent trust and cooperative effort among nations, can be fortified, not by weapons of war but by wheat and by cotton, by milk and by wool, by meat and by timber and by rice. These are words that translate into every language on earth. These are needs that challenge this world in arms.

"This Government is ready to ask its people to join with all nations in devoting a substantial percentage of the savings achieved by disarmament to a fund for world aid and reconstruction. The purposes of this great work would be to help other peoples to develop the undeveloped areas of the world, to stimulate profitable and fair world trade, to assist all peoples to know the blessings of productive freedom.

"The monuments to this new kind of war would be these: roads and schools, hospitals and homes, food and health. We are ready, in short, to dedicate our strength to serving the needs, rather than the fears, of the world. I know of nothing I can add to make plainer the sincere purpose of the United States. I know of no course, other than that marked by these and similar actions, that can be called the highway of peace.

"The purpose of the United States, in stating these proposals, is simple and clear. These proposals spring, without ulterior purpose or political passion, from our calm conviction that the hunger for peace is in the hearts of all peoples — those of Russia and of China no less than of our own country. They conform to our firm faith that God created men to enjoy, not destroy, the fruits of the earth and of their own toil. They aspire to this: the lifting, from the backs and from the hearts of men, of their burden of arms and of fears, so that they may find before them a golden age of freedom and of peace."[71]

The speech received enormous praise both at home and around the world. Newspapers called it "magnificent and moving," "the most effective speech of Eisenhower's career," and "an immense triumph." Newspapers from overseas were just as kind. Eisenhower knew he was asking a lot of Russia, especially since the country was currently focused internally on transitioning leadership after the death of Stalin.

But he had a long horizon, and he hoped this would set the tone for future discussions. Eisenhower had made a forceful argument about the realities of the Cold War tradeoffs, but unfortunately, it was ignored by the Soviets. The two sides soon reverted to the status quo, increasing the velocity of the arms race for the rest of Eisenhower's tenure. It would take decades for both countries to realize Eisenhower had been right — they couldn't afford to maintain their levels of defense spending without impacting the lives of their own citizens.

For the rest of his presidency, Eisenhower stood firm against pressure from the Pentagon, Congress, and others to increase defense spending in his goal to achieve the balanced budgets required for a sound economy. In his first federal budget for 1955, he was actually able to reduce overall defense spending from $48.7 billion in 1954 to $44.9 billion, which was in line with a decrease in the overall federal budget, and although the budget resulted in a deficit, it was smaller than the year before. In three of his eight years in office, Eisenhower managed to deliver a small budget surplus (1956, 1957, and 1960). The country did go through two recessions during his administration: one that he inherited in 1953 and another in 1957. But overall, the economy thrived under his leadership.

America had the strongest economy in the world in the 1950s. Business and manufacturing thrived, with exports at all-time highs, and US GDP grew from $284.6 billion in 1950 to about $500 billion by the end of the decade. The country prospered in large part because of Eisenhower's insistence on the proper allocation of resources and fiscal responsibility, especially his resistance to increase defense spending and reducing taxes.

CRITICAL THINKING

"The older I get the more wisdom I find in the ancient rule of taking first things first. A process which often reduces the most complex human problem to a manageable proportion."

Despite the enormous amount of information crossing his desk during World War II and his presidency, Eisenhower was able to separate the important from the trivial and achieve results through constancy of purpose. For example, at West Point, he spent more time enjoying the overall experience and his classmates and learning about leadership and military strategy than worrying about how many demerits he would get for being late or not cleaning his room adequately.

Early in his career, Eisenhower also realized that simplicity was better than complexity, and decisions and plans should be made completely unambiguous, or, as he would say, stated in a "positive" manner. In a 1926 essay targeted at military students, he wrote, "Two very important characteristics of every good solution are 'simplicity' and 'positiveness.' Not only should the dispositions and actions ordered by you be simple, but your order or plan should be of the same character. It is difficult to over emphasize this point...common sense solutions are always simple, and stated in clear straightforward terms." Even if the recommended solution is more complex than it should be, Eisenhower suggested to students "whatever you decide to do, state your decision in no unmistakable terms...your plan itself should always take into account the axiom that 'positive results are obtained only through positive action.'"[72]

Just after graduating from the Command and General Staff School at Leavenworth in June 1926, Eisenhower took it upon himself to write a paper on the attitude and work ethic that was required to succeed at the institution, which was subsequently published in the *Infantry Journal*. As mentioned earlier, Eisenhower finished first in his class, which he accomplished by working hard and smart. Eisenhower was refining his ability to perceive the core attitudes and activities that were required to be successful, and he wanted to convey these along with what to expect from the overall "Leavenworth experience" to incoming students.

Eisenhower began with a discussion on the need to be enthusiastic, optimistic, and self-confident in completing the work, and he said that students should trust the instructors, since they were there to help, not to "harass and obstruct." He continued with what was needed to prepare for the coursework at the school, including "correct habits of study; logical reasoning in the solutions of problems...and good health." He also discussed class schedules and resources available for studying.[73]

In a section titled "Mental Health," Eisenhower recommended that students keep the experience in perspective and not be concerned about "needless worry," since no one had failed to graduate from the school in the last four years. Eisenhower knew that there was always plenty to worry about, from standing in the class to absorbing the material, but he wrote that "it is obvious to anyone that there is no earthly use in worrying about something which is already an accomplished fact. So any thought and time expended in pondering or fretting over grades received, or to be received, on problems already solved is manifestly wasted. Worse, this tends to depress you to a certain extent and always takes away time that should be spent in regular study."[74]

In another section, Eisenhower talked about "Habits," and it revealed much about Eisenhower's own beliefs. He wrote, "As in everything else, your daily habits at Leavenworth should be normal and reasonable. If you carry any one of your daily activities to an extreme, something else must suffer. If you study too much you will lose some of your ability to carry a fresh active mind to the problem room. If you sleep and exercise too little you will gradually lose health, or at least become irritable and stale."

His balanced approach to attacking the assigned problems meant that Eisenhower had little use for cramming. "A man counts on getting a wonderful start by doing with less sleep and lengthening his study hours each night. He also cuts down his exercise and recreation to study some over the weekends. You should note the fact that knowledge alone will do you no good. You never get an examination at Leavenworth which consists of a list of questions to answer. Problems are so drawn that you are required to bring to bear your common sense and clear judgment in the application of the knowledge you have gained.

"If you are mentally fatigued or feel too stuffed up with facts and figures when you go to a problem, it is almost certain a poor mark will result.... Go to the problem room in good health, fresh in mind and body, and with a reasonable understanding of the principles the school has been teaching, and the results you obtain will be more than satisfactory."[75]

- -

"The test of truth is simple. There can be no persuasion but by deeds."

- -

In early November 1943, Eisenhower and his team went to Gibraltar to coordinate the Torch operation. This was Eisenhower's first combat and command experience, and the problems were many and extreme. The Allies were not sure how the Vichy French in

North Africa would react to the unprovoked invasion of neutral territory by British and American forces. Eisenhower also had to deal with the politics and egos of various French leaders such as de Gaulle, French General Henri Giraud, and Francois Darlan, the Vichy French admiral, who all wanted to play key roles in the future direction of their country.

There was also uncertainty about how Spain would react to Allied ships passing Gibraltar on the way to the landing sites, and he had to endure the "anticipation of action" — that anxious waiting period after all the long planning sessions are over and prior to the actual execution of the plans, when a leader can do no more than wait for feedback on progress and then respond accordingly.

The environment at Gibraltar didn't help with morale. Although it had the best communications facilities available in that area, the tunnels in the command center were deep, dark, and damp, adding to the gloom and anxiety. All involved in the operation were nervous about the outcome, and they looked to Eisenhower for comfort and reassurance. With time on his hands, Eisenhower did a lot of thinking and writing, and he realized a valuable lesson that would serve him well the rest of the war and his life.

"During those anxious hours" in Gibraltar was when Eisenhower "first realized how inexorably and inescapably strain and tension wear away at the leader's endurance, his judgment and his confidence. The pressure becomes more acute because of the duty of a staff to constantly present to the commander the worst side of an eventuality." Eisenhower realized that even during the most stressful and darkest hours, the leader must "preserve optimism in himself and in his command. Without confidence, enthusiasm and optimism in the command, victory is scarcely obtainable."

Eisenhower also recognized that "optimism and pessimism are infectious and they spread more rapidly from the head downward than in any other direction." He believed there are two major benefits in always asserting a positive attitude. One was that the "habit tends to minimize potentialities within the individual himself to become demoralized."

The other was that it "has a most extraordinary effect upon all with whom he comes in contact. With this clear realization, I firmly determined that my mannerisms and speech in public would always reflect the cheerful certainty of victory—that any pessimism and discouragement I might ever feel would be reserved for my pillow. I adopted a policy of circulating through the whole force the full limit imposed by physical considerations. I did my best to meet everyone from general to private with a smile, a pat on the back and a definite interest in his problems."[76]

Winston Churchill wrote that Eisenhower "was always very good at bearing stresses of this kind. The immensity of the stake that was being played, the uncertainty of the weather, ...the fragmentary news which arrived, the extraordinary complications of the French attitude, the danger from Spain—all, apart from the actual fighting, must have made this a very hard trial to a Commander, whose responsibilities were enormous and direct."[77]

When Eisenhower was assigned the role of supreme commander, he was guided in "all his actions by three paramount aims: (1) the prompt and complete defeat of Germany, (2) the earliest possible liberation of France, and (3) the fostering of democratic methods and conditions under which a French government may ultimately be established according to the free choice of the French people as the government under which they wish to live."[78] If an activity contributed to one of these aims, Eisenhower pursued it; if it didn't, he turned his attention elsewhere.

By August 1944, the Allies had obtained victory in Normandy, ending the campaign by closing the Falaise gap. Even though there was some disappointment in allowing more than forty thousand German troops to escape, the battle was a great victory. More than fifty thousand of the enemy were killed or captured, and those that did escape, left behind "masses of destroyed tanks, guns, transports and equipment of all kind."[79]

The losses sustained on its western front by Germany in the three months of fighting since D-day were more than 350,000, and when added to the more than 900,000 in losses on the Eastern Front, the situation looked very grim for the Germans and obviously very good for the Allies. There was a feeling of optimism throughout the Allied command and the Allied world. The stock market in New York fell dramatically with expectations of peace, and, at an August news conference, reporters asked Eisenhower how many weeks it would take to end the war. Eisenhower would hear this question again and again over the next few weeks.[80]

It seemed everyone was catching the so-called "victory disease," thinking that the winning trend would continue unabated.[81] Earlier in the war, the Germans and Japanese suffered from it, and it would surface time and again on the Allied side, usually after the adrenaline rush that comes from achieving victory and reaching objectives — after his initial battlefield successes, Montgomery wanted all available resources so he could march straight through to Berlin, and, after the war, Patton wanted to keep fighting as well, but this time against the Russians.

However, Eisenhower knew the German army would never give up so easily. They would fight back until they had nothing left to resist with. He "vehemently castigated those who think they can measure the end of the war in a matter of weeks."[82] He wrote to his wife that unfortunately, there was still a "lot of suffering to go through" and told her to not "be misled by the papers. Every victory...is sweet — but the end of the war will come only with the complete destruction of...forces."[83] Eisenhower strongly believed that "Hitler and his gang had nothing to lose" by continuing to fight, and everything to lose by surrendering. He suspected that Hitler "knows he will be hanged, if he doesn't hang himself...and, consequently, will fight to the bitter end."[84]

One clue that the Germans wouldn't give up was the way forty thousand Germans fought to escape rather than take the easy way out and surrender, and Eisenhower knew the fighting would intensify when the enemy began to defend its own soil. Not only did the Germans not give up, they also wouldn't settle into a defensive posture, and they would eventually launch one last desperate offensive campaign in December 1944 — the Battle of the Bulge.

Eisenhower worked hard to manage expectations and to discourage any discussions about an early end of the war. He didn't want any easing up in the activities required to prosecute the war, from the production and distribution of required supplies to the training of new troops. He didn't want any talk of the war being "almost finished" — he wanted it finished.

"A sense of humor is part of the art of leadership, of getting along with people, of getting things done."

In November 1945, George Marshall resigned from his position as chief of staff, and President Truman appointed Eisenhower to take his place. In this role Eisenhower reported to the president, and he was responsible for "the strategy, tactics and operations of the Army."[85] As he assumed his role, he held three basic principles based on his experiences before and after the war.

First, he was convinced that the most effective structure to conduct military action was under the unity of command, and that the military institutions and training needed to emphasize coordination and cooperation of activities among the various services, under the direction of a single command. Second, he believed that the country needed a strong peacetime army to quickly respond to any future emergency and avoid the problems of mobilizing an army in the midst of a crisis. This required strong leadership throughout the services, with an emphasis on running an efficient organization and a unified program of military training. "Third, if such a crisis was to be avoided, there had to be cooperation among the former wartime allies. Russia and the United States were the countries whose relations would necessarily be the prime determinants of world peace."[86]

However, Eisenhower soon found that he had to adjust his thinking to reflect the reality of the times. After four years of war, the country was anxious to reduce military spending and accelerate the demobilization process. There was constant in-fighting between the services for the allocation of scarce resources, and America's relationship with Russia quickly deteriorated. In contrast to his role as supreme commander, where he could focus primarily on military objectives, Eisenhower now had to engage in political debates in areas he felt were important to national policies. "He confronted situations that were far more complex and far less malleable than his administrative environment had been during the war and the occupation."[87]

Eisenhower dealt with the complexity and ambiguity by bringing structure and order to those things he could control, and by persistent follow-up and follow-through on areas beyond his control, as he tried to influence the outcomes. Shortly after assuming his new responsibilities, Eisenhower held a session to meet his staff and to give some overall guidance and express his expectations.

He began by empathizing with the difficulty of their roles: "No one knows better than I what tough jobs you have, how difficult your problems are to solve, and how you get irritated and resentful because of lack of progress due to circumstances over which you have no control whatsoever." But he urged his staff not to get down.

"There is one thing in any situation that I believe is always applicable, and that is optimism and a grin. Long faces are not going to be a bit of help. Just as in war, we have to keep our heads up. Keep grinning, and keep plugging." He expressed his desire to implement a military organization where each of the three services were equal and under a unified command. "We want to make certain that in establishing that kind of an organization we do not become guilty of duplications" of facilities or functions. He stressed that "we must have faith in each other. We have to depend each upon the other and believe that the other is going to perform the functions we expect of him and that each will deal with the other on a basis of fairness.... So in solving problems... let us proceed on the basis that...cooperation will be as great as possible."

Eisenhower also knew that one of the best ways to fight through complex issues was by encouraging teamwork, honesty, and communication. "I could never face a body of officers without emphasizing one word — teamwork...Our attitude one toward the other has to be that of a friend expecting assistance and knowing that he will get it. If we will always remember that the other fellow is trying to fulfill our common purpose just as much as each one of us is, I think no more need be said about teamwork."

Solving difficult problems while under extreme pressure required some finesse and "considerable tact. *Above all it demands integrity and fairness.* If we are honest in handling the whole problem we are certainly not going to get the War Department into a jam." He felt that everyone needed to "act according to our own good judgment after having examined every aspect involved" and that "tactfulness, trying to understand the other fellow's viewpoint, and using salesmanship instead of a club, seems to me to be called for...Patience is something we can't lose on the job. So we must be fair."[88] Overall, Eisenhower did well in achieving results in his brief tenure as chief of staff, even in areas that were beyond his sphere of control. He did especially well in the area with the most pressure—bringing the troops home after World War II

- -

"I hate war as only a soldier who has lived it can, and as one who has seen its brutality, its futility, its stupidity."

- -

What to do about French Indochina (Vietnam, Laos, and Cambodia) in the years of the Cold War was a continuous challenge to Eisenhower and a few future presidents. Even before becoming president, Eisenhower was convinced "the French...could *not* win the Indochina war and particularly could not get real American support in that region unless they would unequivocally pledge independence to the Associated States upon the achievement of military victory."[89] Having just brokered a peace in Korea the year before, it was a nonstarter for Eisenhower to consider committing other troops in Asia.

But as the situation unfolded in early 1954, Eisenhower's distaste for war was tempered by the strategic and political risks of losing Vietnam. He was inclined to provide aid to France, but he was adamantly against putting American troops on the ground. In a National Security Council (NSC) meeting in January 1954, Eisenhower said there "was just no sense in even talking about United States forces replacing the French in Indochina." He remained "bitterly opposed" to such a course, since American involvement would result in the Vietnamese transferring "their hatred of the French to us. This war in Indochina," he declared, "would absorb our troops by divisions!"

But Eisenhower felt something had to be done in the fight to help stop the potential spread of communism, so he reluctantly decided to provide "the French ten additional B-26 light bombers and to send 200 U.S. Air Force mechanics" to help train the French to maintain the existing fleet of C-26 and B-26 aircraft. "My God," Eisenhower emphasized, "we must not lose Asia — we've got to look the thing right in the face."[90]

Even with the aid, the French situation was grim. They were losing in their effort to defend the garrison at Dien Bien Phu, and Eisenhower believed they didn't seem to have anyone capable of "reversing the trend toward pessimism, defeatism and dejection. For those of us who have recognized and admired the basic virtues of the great mass of Frenchmen," Eisenhower wrote to Al Gruenther, "this spectacle has been saddening indeed. It seems incredible that a nation which had only the help of a tiny British Army when it turned back the German flood in 1914 and withstood the gigantic 1916 attacks at Verdun could now be reduced to the point that she cannot produce a few hundred technicians to keep planes flying properly in Indochina."[91]

As the situation at Dien Bien Phu deteriorated, Eisenhower realized his administration would come under pressure, so he established conditions for intervention into the conflict. First, there would need to be a coalition including the United States, Britain, and the free nations of Southeast Asia. Second, the French must guarantee independence to Vietnam, and lastly, the French needed to stay committed, even as new troops were added. Eisenhower deliberately made these conditions difficult to meet. He did not want to the United States going in at all, but, if it did, it would not be unilaterally.

On April 7, 1954, Eisenhower held a press conference and was asked about the strategic importance of Indochina to the free world. Eisenhower responded that there were both economic and humanitarian reasons to be engaged, but there were also "broader considerations that might follow what you would call the 'falling domino' principle. You have a row of dominoes set up, you knock over the first one, and what will happen to the last one is the certainty that it will go over very quickly. So you could have a beginning of a disintegration that would have the most profound influences."

In theory, he continued, events could spiral out of control, with "the loss of Indochina, of Burma, of Thailand, of the Peninsula, and Indonesia following, now you begin to talk about areas that not only multiply the disadvantages that you would suffer through loss of materials, sources of materials, but now you are talking really about millions and millions and millions of people."[92]

This was the historic Domino Theory speech—a simple metaphor which provided Americans and the free world with a rationale for at least attempting to stop the spread of communism. Eisenhower's Domino Theory would be referenced by future presidential administrations to justify increasing aid to South Vietnam, including the commitment of ground forces in Vietnam in 1965.

Privately, Eisenhower continued to believe any major involvement was a mistake. He believed that while the dominoes could fall, they probably wouldn't, because the communist system of government would eventually collapse on its own. He didn't think Vietnam was the place to make a major commitment and stand. "The jungles of Indochina...would have swallowed up division after division of United States troops, who, unaccustomed to this kind of warfare, would have sustained heavy causalities," he wrote in 1963. "Furthermore, the presence of ever more numbers of white men in uniform probably would have aggravated rather than assuaged Asiatic resentments."[93] Eisenhower excluded this passage from his memoirs, because he didn't want to criticize

Lyndon Johnson's escalation of US involvement in Vietnam, although tragically, his predication was correct.

Eisenhower's team continued to search for solutions. On May 1, Robert Cutler of the National Security Council presented Eisenhower with a draft paper exploring the feasibility of dropping atomic bombs on Vietnam. "I certainly do not think the atom bomb can be used by the United States unilaterally," he told Cutler. "You boys must be crazy. We can't use those awful things against Asians for the second time in less than ten years. My God."[94]

About a week later, Dien Bien Phu was lost to the communists. An agreement at the Geneva Conference divided the country in two, giving the communists control of the north. Vietnam was always a complex issue for America. No one wanted to see the country become communist, but committing troops to a distant country, largely made up of jungles, didn't make a lot of sense either.

In his Domino Theory press conference, Eisenhower insisted upon being guided by the principle that "no outside country can come in and be really helpful unless it is doing something that the local people want."[95] Eisenhower believed the most important reason for refusing to help the French was the US tradition against colonialism.

"Our deep conviction about colonialism has often brought us embarrassment in dealings with our friends in Western Europe... But the standing of the United States as the most powerful of the anti colonial powers is an asset of incalculable value to the Free World. It means our counsel is sometimes trusted where that of others may not be. It is essential to our position of leadership in a world wherein the majority of the nations have at some time or another felt the yoke of colonialism. Never, throughout the lone and sometimes frustrating search for an effective means of defeating the Communist struggle for power in Indochina, did we lose sight of the importance of America's moral position."[96]

Eisenhower's vision, principles, and communications skills led the nation through the chaos of Indochina. By mid-1954, Eisenhower's experience and leadership had stopped one war and kept the United States from entering another. He was a master at breaking down complex problems into their basic components so that guiding principles could be identified for the creation of both short- and long-term solutions. Anything that supported the guiding principles was worth pursuing; anything else was to be ignored.

"Of course, only time will tell how successful we have been," he confided to Al Gruenther. "Every day will bring its problems and many of these will cause much more talking and haggling — even some *thinking*! More and more I find myself, in this type of situation — tending to strip each problem down to its simplest possible form. Having gotten the issue well defined in my mind, I try in the next step to determine what answer would best serve the *long-term* advantage and welfare of the United States and the free world. I then consider the *immediate problem* and what solution can we get that will best conform to the long term interests of the country, and at the same time can command a sufficient approval in this country so as to secure the necessary Congressional action."[97]

ORGANIZING FOR SUCCESS

"Skillful and thorough organization of vast enterprises is essential to their operation."

Eisenhower spent a good part of his adult life in dealing with the problems and complexities of organization. He believed that the purpose of an organization was to "simplify, clarify, expedite and coordinate; it is a bulwark against chaos, confusion, delay and failure. Organization cannot of course make a successful leader out of a dunce, any more than it should make a decision for its chief. But it is effective in minimizing the chances of failure and in insuring that the right hand does, indeed, know what the left hand is doing."[98]

He understood that even the best strategy will fail without an effective organization to oversee and execute the plans, and he knew that the essence of organization was talented people. "The Chief Executive must first select his principle assistants from among the ablest, most dedicated and experienced men and women he can find." If these people "are strong, understanding, and devoted individuals of integrity, they can make even a jerry-built organization function."[99]

Eisenhower built several organizations throughout his military and political career. His personal writings and achievements during the World War II campaigns show that "Eisenhower concentrated his personal attention on two basic concerns. One was the creation of a command organization or structure. The other was the planning and carrying out of broad strategies to defeat the Axis force in Europe."[100] These were essential to each other, and they are fundamental to achieving results.

Allied war planning in early 1942 included a joint British and American operation called Bolero, the Europe-first strategy which authorized the accumulation of a massive amount of resources in England for an eventual cross-channel operation. Despite broad agreement on proceeding with the operation, Eisenhower had to be persistent in keeping the plan on course, including ensuring commitments to troop and other resource levels.

In the spring of 1942, Roosevelt had agreed to requests for additional troops and airplanes from MacArthur, the navy, and the Australian government, which, in effect, meant that the Bolero operation could not proceed. "BOLERO is *supposed* to have the approval of the President and Prime Minister," he wrote in his diary. "But the struggle to get everyone behind it, and to keep the highest authority from wrecking it by making additional commitments of air-ship-troops elsewhere is never ending."[101]

Eisenhower prepared a memorandum for Marshall that argued for an increase in troop commitments to Bolero, which could not occur if they were redeployed to Australia. When Marshall sent this to the president, Roosevelt restated his desire that Bolero move forward, and that his directive to send additional resources to go to Australia was a misunderstanding.

The same day that Roosevelt reiterated his commitment to Bolero, Eisenhower attended a discouraging committee meeting for the development of landing craft for the cross-channel assault. When he got back from the meeting he wrote some penetrating questions on his desk pad: "Who is responsible for bldg. landing craft? What types are they bldg? Are they suitable for cross-Channel work? Will the number of each type be sufficient? etc? How in hell can we win this war unless we can crack some heads?"[102]

It was a difficult time. The demand for resources from various quarters was intense. But Eisenhower had the tenacity and persistence required to overcome the barriers to progress and to keep the various parties focused on the organizational plans needed to succeed. His writings show that he became frustrated by the constant debates and the lack of progress in certain initiatives, but he persevered and continued to argue effectively for Bolero.

Marshall's deputy chief of staff, Major General Joseph T. McNarney, had drafted the proposed organizational structure for Bolero called the "U.S. Set up for Administrative Purposes." Marshall asked Eisenhower to review and comment on the proposal. In a written response, Eisenhower agreed with the overall command structure, which had one commanding general reporting to the Combined Chiefs of Staff of Britain and the United States, responsible for all US forces.

However, Eisenhower didn't like the use of the word "administrative" in the title. "The word implies definite limitations upon the authority of the commander, whereas the man occupying the position is the highest War Department representative in England and is the *Commander* of all Army forces preparing for the BOLERO Operation."

It also had to be made clear to the British that this commander was a "Theater Commander in every sense of the word." Unlike the British, it was standard US procedure to delegate as much authority as possible to the field commander, and Eisenhower wanted to make sure that the British relied on the Bolero commander rather than turning to Washington for answers.

Eisenhower also conveyed his views on the type of person that was needed to serve as the commanding general. His first requirement was that the person had to be of the same mind and work very well with the chief of staff (Marshall) in executing the Bolero plan. But he also stressed the person's responsibility and authority — "All planning in England for the U.S. Ground Forces, the Air Forces, and the Navy *must* be cleared through him; otherwise his position will be intolerable."

His second comment was that the person had to be adaptive and able to perform in a variety of roles. The war situation was fluid, and it was "impossible at this time to predict with certainty that BOLERO is going to develop along the lines now visualized," and the person needed to be flexible in assuming various roles "no matter the character the project may assume."

Eisenhower believed this person's role would change even if the plan did move forward as anticipated, with the forces building up to a critical mass. "It is easily possible that the *President may direct the Chief of Staff himself to proceed to London and take over command.* The officer previously serving as Commander should be one who could fit in (and would be acceptable to the new Commander) as a Deputy or as a Chief of Staff. This will insure continuity in planning and execution, and in understanding."

He also emphasized that the dynamic nature of the role had to be communicated to any potential candidates and that it needed to be filled as soon as possible. Regardless of whether the existing commander (General James E. Chaney) or someone else filled this role, "the whole task for preparation in the United Kingdom should be turned over to him as rapidly as possible, and he should be allowed to carry *out his task with minimum interference from this end.*"[103]

At the time Eisenhower wrote his analysis, it wasn't clear to Marshall whether General Chaney was the right person for the job. However, both Marshall and Eisenhower were anxious that the Bolero plan was falling behind schedule. Marshall told Eisenhower he "had become concerned because American officers on duty in London were not familiar with the broader problems and objectives of the War Department," and "they seemed to know nothing about the maturing plans that visualized the British Isles as the greatest operating military base at the time."[104] Eisenhower "had an uneasy feeling that either we don't understand our own C.G. [Commanding General Chaney] or they don't understand us. Our planning for BOLERO is *not* progressing!"[105]

Marshall sent Eisenhower to London to update Chaney and his staff on current Bolero plans and to "bring back recommendations involving future organizations and development of our European forces."[106] Eisenhower attended a number of meetings while in London. He met with Chaney and his team and found that they "had been given no opportunity to familiarize themselves with the revolutionary changes that had...taken place in the United States and were completely at a loss in their earnest attempts to further the war effort."[107] Eisenhower updated them on the plans, but he had additional concerns. He believed Chaney and his staff lacked discipline. They were working only eight hours a day and taking weekends off, and were not being proactive enough in understanding and implementing the new plans.

Eisenhower also met with the British, who presented two alternative organizational structures for the Roundup operation (the initial code name for the invasion of France). One structure was led by a supreme commander, and the other was led by a committee. Eisenhower told the British that "in principle the Americans believed that single command was essential and that committee command could not conduct a major battle." The British wanted a supreme commander named as soon as possible, but Eisenhower said there was no urgency to assign someone, since Roundup wouldn't occur for at least a year.

The British then wanted to know who their planners should cooperate with until a supreme commander was named. Surprised by the question, Eisenhower told them they should work with General Chaney and his staff. "This idea had apparently never occurred to the British Chiefs of Staff; they have looked on Chaney as something other than a Theater Commander."[108] Apparently the British were as concerned as Eisenhower was about Chaney's abilities, and they pressed Eisenhower to put a command structure in place as soon as possible.

As Eisenhower returned from his trip, it was clear that changes had to be made. "Our own people are able but do not understand what we want done," he wrote in his diary. "It is necessary to get a punch behind the job or we'll never be ready by spring, 1942, to attack. We must get going!"[109] He wrote a memorandum to Marshall recommending that two changes in leadership be made immediately.

He suggested that General Mark Clark command the troops accumulating in Britain for Roundup. He said that he had also given a "great deal of study" as to who should be placed in command of all US forces in England. He recommended Major General McNarney, because "he has the strength of character, the independence of thought, and the ability to fulfill satisfactorily the requirements for this difficult task."[110] But Marshall had just assigned McNarney as his deputy chief of staff, both because of his qualifications and because he wanted someone from the Air Corps to facilitate integration and cooperation. So he rejected that recommendation.

Eisenhower knew this was a critical position, so a few days later, he approached Marshall with some other thoughts on the role. He wrote that regardless of whether Marshall decided to make a change in command in London, he believed it was "highly desirable to promote the individual concerned." He knew that the "question of promotion might appear trivial," but he thought the British were more likely to respect a higher-level officer. He also provided more arguments for appointing McNarney to the position, including "his complete familiarity with the British organization and methods of planning, together with his characteristic of patience," which would be "highly necessary because of the complications in British procedure."[111]

To reinforce his arguments and to facilitate a decision, a few days later Eisenhower presented Marshall with a draft directive for the "Commanding General, European Theater of Operations."

In the draft, Eisenhower argued that because of the distance between the European theater and United States and the need for collaboration between all armed forces, it was essential "that absolute unity of command should be exercised by the Theater Commander to be designated."

The directive also gave specific instructions regarding the responsibilities, reporting structure, mission, and communication policies of the commanding general. The European theater leader would "command all U.S. Army forces and personnel" and would "exercise planning and operational control, under the principle of unity of command, over all U.S. Navy forces assigned to that theater for operation."

In carrying out his mission to "prepare for and carry on military operations in the European Theater against the Axis and their Allies," he was "charged with the strategical, tactical, territorial, and administrative duties of a theater commander" and "directed to cooperate with the forces of the British Empire and other Allied nations directed to the same mission." He was also instructed to "keep the Chief of Staff U.S. Army fully advised of all that concerns his command and will communicate his recommendations freely and directly to the War Department."[112]

When Eisenhower submitted his draft, he asked that Marshall give it his full consideration before sending it out, "because it was likely to be an important document in the further waging of the war." Marshall responded, "I certainly do want to read it. You may be the man who executes it. If that's the case, when can you leave?" Eisenhower was surprised, but he shouldn't have been. He was being asked to take the position because he achieved results, plus he had all the other leadership traits needed to fill the position. As Marshall said, "If he hadn't delivered, he wouldn't have moved up."[113]

As Eisenhower began to consider filling key roles in the European theater, he looked for people who were hardworking, energetic, loyal, efficient, reliable, honest, and team players. "War has become so comprehensive and so complicated that teamwork seems to me to be the essence of all success," Eisenhower once declared. "Each bureau, each section, each office…has to be part of a well-coordinated team."

Eisenhower strived to develop a feeling of family within his staff. He believed that "no successful team can have any personal enmities existing in it," and he insisted "on having a happy family…I want to see a big crowd of friends around me." He had little use for those who were self-serving or egotistical, but he could have a lot of patience with such people if the person was very good at what he or she did, such as Patton. He especially wanted people who were tested and had experience. Remembering what his mentor Fox Conner told him — that a commander must never have an enemy on his staff, since he will be motivated to undermine the leader — he made sure to get the most loyal people possible.

The day after his arrival as commander of the European Theater of Operations, Eisenhower began to restructure the organization. He believed "too many staff officers are merely pushing paper, and we can't win this war pushing paper. It takes imagination and initiative and a lot of it."[114] He immediately "instituted a seven-day work week…and groused a good deal about the lackadaisical attitude. 'After all,' he said, 'it is war and we're here to fight, and not to be wined and dined.'" He also held a series of meetings with his staff and emphasized "that each section must bear its share of responsibility and push incessantly toward the attainment of the objective, which is to have an army in the field, ready to attack, by early spring of 1944."

Eisenhower was most concerned with creating an environment of "determined enthusiasm and optimism in every member of his staff and every subordinate commander. He refused to tolerate pessimism or defeatism and urged everyone who could not rise above the recognized obstacles to ask for instant release from this theater. He "urged the greatest informality in the staff work" and told them "they are free to solve their own problems and not get into the habit of passing the buck to him."

He stressed "we are not operating or writing for the record, but to win the war," and "emphasized that no set scheme of organization, training, or concept of command was to prevail over common sense and in adjusting to meet our needs. Absolute freedom in planning to meet our requirements has been granted in this headquarters. This imposes a corresponding responsibility to act decisively and promptly and with no alibis."

Eisenhower "announced his intention of moving General Headquarters outside London, where all hands could live together like a football team and think, plan, and execute war in all our waking hours."[115] Eisenhower had little use for subordinates "who feel they have fulfilled their responsibility when they simply report a problem to a superior and do not bring the proposed solution with them."[116]

Because of Eisenhower's leadership and organizational skill, progress was soon being made with the Bolero operation. About 375,000 US troops would make their way to England, but the buildup of troops in Europe was soon put on hold, because by late July 1942, the decision was made to move forward with Operation Torch — the invasion of North Africa — with Eisenhower as commander.

- -

"Good organization provides for the allocation of authority and fixing of responsibility in each echelon of the entire establishment."

- -

Even before winning the presidency in 1952, Eisenhower was thinking about his potential cabinet team and how to organize the massive and often chaotic work of the executive branch. With his now deep experience in leadership, he was well aware of the importance of putting the right person in the right job. He also learned during the campaign that "in politics fitness for a job is only *one* of the factors to be considered in making assignments."[117]

Teamwork, collaboration across political lines, and critical thinking skills (with a slant toward political nuances) were also needed. Eisenhower was looking for highly competent leaders with proven track records — honest brokers he could go to for advice, who would share in the successes and challenges ahead.

Eisenhower moved quickly to staff his cabinet. The day after the election, he asked Herbert Brownell and Lucius Clay to provide him with candidates "of the highest possible standing in character, integrity, and ability, to assist me in carrying on the proper functions of government."[118]

A little more than two weeks after the election, Eisenhower put the nominees forward. For secretary of state, he selected John Foster Dulles, who had spent the better part of his life preparing for the role. Eisenhower appreciated his bipartisanship and considered him "a man of strong opinions and unimpeachable character."[119]

Eisenhower wanted a corporate executive — Charles E. Wilson, CEO of General Motors — for secretary of defense. He believed the "huge procurement, storage, transportation, distribution, and other logistical functions of the Defense Department" needed an expert. He also wanted to eliminate the duplication of effort between the army, navy, and air force. "We have tried two investment bankers, a lawyer and a soldier and we are not yet unified. I believe it takes a man who is used to knocking heads together and who is not easily fooled."[120]

For secretary of interior, Eisenhower nominated Douglas McKay, a successful businessman with an excellent reputation who had just ended a term as governor of Oregon. Eisenhower's advisors recommended George Humphrey for Treasury secretary, as a man who was "impeccable in integrity and character, able as an administrator, and dedicated to sound fiscal and financial policies." Although Humphrey was reluctant to take the post, Eisenhower appealed to his patriotism and convinced him to take the job. They quickly developed a mutual respect that developed into a warm friendship.

Eisenhower asked another close friend, Herbert Brownell, to fill the attorney general role. Eisenhower never really considered anyone else — he admired Brownell's "alert mind" and "respected him as a man and a lawyer."[121]

Having worked closely with White House personnel and processes for more than ten years, Eisenhower believed there were a number of opportunities to improve the efficiency of the executive branch, especially by optimizing the organization and the White House staff. Eisenhower's experience in running large, complex organizations convinced him of the need to create a chief of staff role in the White House — someone who could coordinate activities across departmental lines, liaise with Congress and the press, ensure that decisions being made at lower levels were adhering to established policies, and most importantly, make sure the president's time wasn't wasted.

Eisenhower wanted a competent administrator and someone he could trust. He had several extremely capable military officers to choose from, including Bedell Smith and Lucius Clay. But he thought they may have given the perception of too much military influence in the White House. He offered the position to Sherman Adams, who was direct, honest, and extremely efficient. After some initial reluctance, Adams accepted the position, and Eisenhower made sure the position was at the cabinet level, to empower Adams to work at the same level of authority as the others reporting to the president.

He also created a small personal staff to maximize his time efficiency by taking care of routine matters, such as paying personal bills and taking care of his mail. In essence, he had taken a page from his military experience and created two staff functions — one for the White House and one personal — which have been adopted by every subsequent presidential administration.

By December 1, 1952, less than a month after the election, Eisenhower had completed the selection of his cabinet. Some cabinet members went with Eisenhower on a trip to Korea; others spent the time informing themselves (at their own expense) on their new roles by traveling the country. The early selection also let them all have informal conversations about the challenges ahead and attend a pre-inauguration cabinet meeting on January 12, 1953.

Eisenhower had several objectives for the meeting: to discuss the roles of the cabinet and the National Security Council, to convey the operating principles of the White House, to get feedback on his inaugural address, and to build rapport and camaraderie within the team. Eisenhower made sure there was mutual understanding on the work to be done by each department, and stressed that each cabinet member was "free to be concerned not only with the affairs of his own department but with virtually any question that concerned the government. No one was relieved of his responsibility or the opportunity to think broadly and to make suggestions."

Eisenhower told his team that while prior administrations had informal cabinet and NSC meetings, he wanted to operate differently. Together they would make policy decisions, provide ideas, and debate solutions to both immediate and long-term problems. He told them he believed a more disciplined approach, combined with a strong White House staff, would help coordinate activities across the administration, which was needed, since policy activities tended to involve more than one department.

The discussion then turned to the inaugural address. Eisenhower wanted the speech to include simple but effective words, so it could be understood by everyone, both at home and abroad. When he received applause after he started reading the draft, Eisenhower stopped and told them he "had not read it for praise but for analysis and criticism."[122] Suggestions were made for both form and content. When Eisenhower agreed, he would pass them on for the next version. When he didn't agree, he would say so and explain why, which gave him an informal opportunity to express his thoughts and rationale on various topics to the team.

Eisenhower also took time during the session to urge his cabinet to practice what he thought was fundamental to an effective and efficient organization—"spontaneous mutual coordination." He told them he hoped that before too long they would all consider each other as best friends, "so that you can call up and do your own coordinating. That is the perfect way" to get things done. The friendship Eisenhower was referring to was somewhat social, but it was more about cultivating mutual trust, which enables people to get beyond personalities to develop strong working relationships. He also suggested they go to dinner on a regular basis to get to know each other outside of work.[123]

The two-day meeting was a great success. Eisenhower was able to present the formal operating procedures the team would follow for efficiency, but also show flexibility and camaraderie in working with his team. In essence, he showed his team the kind of leadership they could expect from him. He was proactive, communicative, efficient, adaptable, and formal yet informal at the same time. A few weeks into his presidency, Eisenhower wrote in his diary, "All of my early Cabinet meetings have revealed the existence of a spirit of teamwork and of friendship that augers well for the future. Everybody is working hard and doing it with a will."[124]

While Eisenhower worked to prepare his team for the work of the administration, he was as ready as anyone for the demands and intensity of the office. His experience in international affairs, dealing with complex problems, and leading large organizations was extensive, and more importantly, he did it very well. He was also smart enough and humble enough to know he didn't have all the answers. "I don't believe this government was set up to be operated by anyone acting alone," he said. "No one has a monopoly on the truth and on the facts that affect this country."[125]

As Eisenhower started his first term, he made a note to himself. "My first day at President's Desk. Plenty of worries and difficult problems. But such has been my portion for a long time—the result is that this just seems (today) like a continuation of all I've been doing since July '41—even before that!"[126] Eisenhower was used to being responsible for making difficult decisions under extreme stress. Even at age sixty-two, he needed only a few hours of sleep to feel rested, and he had an extraordinary ability to focus on a problem until resolution.

At times his mind was at work before he got out of bed in the morning. "Ever since the hectic days of the North African campaign," he wrote to his boyhood friend Everett "Swede" Hazlett, "I find that when I have weighty matters on my mind I wake up extremely early, apparently because a rested mind is anxious to begin grappling with knotty questions. Incidentally, I never worry about what I did the day before. Likewise, I spend no time fretting about what enemies or critics have said about me. I have never indulged in useless regrets. Always I find, when I have come awake sufficiently to figure out what may be then engaging my attention, that I am pondering the same question that is still unanswered. So I think it is fair to say that it is not worry about the past, but a desire to attack the future, that gets me into this annoying habit."[127]

Eisenhower would typically begin his day at 6:00 a.m. and would read several morning papers over a light breakfast. In his office by 8:00 a.m., Eisenhower would work through the morning until breaking for lunch at 1:00 p.m. He would then continue work until 6:00 p.m. or later. Many evenings would include dinner with a list of guests including politicians, celebrities, clergy, and academics. After drinks and dinner, guests would be invited to the White House residential quarters for further conversations. Although the conversations were informal, Eisenhower would usually guide the discussions to reinforce strategies and policies or obtain the advice and insights of his guests on various problems.

One of his top priorities was to bring structure and process to running the White House. His primary vehicle for operating his administration would be his cabinet meetings. He would attend the meetings regularly, where an agenda would drive the discussion topics and keep digressions to a minimum and minutes documenting key decisions or follow-up would be published.

Eisenhower didn't believe the right organizational structure could help an "incompetent" leader or by itself "make the decisions which are required to trigger necessary action." But "on the other hand, disorganization can scarcely fail to result in inefficiency and can easily lead to disaster. Organization makes more efficient the fathering and analysis of facts, and the arranging of the findings of experts in logical fashion. Therefore, organization helps the responsible individual make the necessary decision, and helps assure that it is satisfactorily carried out."[128]

Eisenhower was used to making decisions quickly, and he was relentless in using time efficiently to do so. Although it wasn't unusual for Eisenhower to read volumes of detailed reports, he told his staff he preferred one-page memos, and Sherman Adams edited pages to three hundred words whenever possible. Larger reports would include an executive summary, which Eisenhower would read, and then drill into the larger report for more details if he needed to.

Eisenhower had an active mind and was intellectually curious, and he wanted the people around him to confront and challenge him. He continually told his team that he wasn't the only one to come up with ideas. As in the service, he encouraged his staff and cabinet to bring various solutions to problems and to be prepared to debate them from different perspectives.

When one person would finish discussing a point, Eisenhower would ask another member of his team for his thoughts. On non-crucial matters, he would ask for a vote, and a decision was made. The process for key, critical matters was the same, except after the discussion, Eisenhower would thank everyone and then let them know of his decision, either at that time or later after he had time to think through the problem.

Eisenhower also relied heavily on the smaller, non-cabinet teams to help shape policy and solve problems. For the US Council of Economic Advisors, he worked closely with Arthur Burns, who was a professor at Columbia University. Eisenhower thought Burns was "one of the most brilliant economists in the United States." Burns, who had known and worked with some of the most powerful men in the United States, thought "Eisenhower was the best administrator I have ever known."[129]

Another non-cabinet team, the Planning Board, served the National Security Council (NSC) and was led by Robert Cutler, a Boston trust company executive. Eisenhower established a number of new policies at the NSC to rationalize and reinvigorate their work. Eisenhower had seen an NSC report from the prior administration, which recommended programs that would result in an additional $44 billion in deficit spending over the next five years. To broaden the understanding of the relationship between economic and military strength, Eisenhower had Secretary of Treasury George Humphrey attend NSC meetings going forward.

The degree of animated discussion at cabinet meetings depended on the topics the various participants would raise and on Eisenhower's desire and ability to promote discussion from various perspectives. The NSC meetings were more formal and designed to encourage disagreement and debate on critical issues to help identify the best solution.

The Planning Board essentially conducted scenario-based policy discussions and was responsible for setting the NSC agenda. The board was given guidelines to "facilitate the formulation of policies" by engaging with resources across various departments to determine possible alternatives and to work to avoid "undesirable compromises which conceal or gloss over real differences." Any differences had to be "clearly defined" and reduced to as "narrow an area as possible prior to reference to the Council."[130]

The Planning Board would meet for three hours twice a week to draft a major agenda paper for a policy discussion at an NSC meeting, such as "U.S. Policy in the Event of Renewal of Aggression in Vietnam, September 16, 1953." The draft would include a summary of general considerations (facts), proposed general objectives (broad policy aims), recommendations for policy guidance (detailed operational suggestions), and cost estimates for the recommended policy.

During the NSC meeting, the paper would be read with specific attention brought to the areas of disagreement. Each agency would then articulate its position on the topic of disagreement during a free-flowing discussion. Eisenhower was "an active participant in the Council discussions." Sometimes issues that were in conflict were decided in the course of the discussion.[131]

However, Eisenhower was very careful not to speak too early in the discussion, since his views could influence the debate too heavily and potentially short-circuit the discussion. While everyone was heard from, a majority didn't always rule when deciding policy. If a decision was required, Eisenhower would always exercise his right to make the final call. After debating in these sessions or with smaller teams in the Oval Office, Cutler would document the policy in a "Statement of Record."

This scenario-based planning approach provided an opportunity for Eisenhower to interact with his team and leverage their talents. The proactive, iterative process of discussing alternative situations and possible responses allowed the administration to think through the best approach in a formal, non-crisis atmosphere, rather than reacting to a situation as it occurred, when the dynamics were different. If a crisis did occur somewhere in the world, the documented policy would act as a guideline in how to respon.

Eisenhower's Leadership Lessons: On Planning and Organizing

1. Ask questions to help frame problems and discover solutions.
2. Prioritize initiatives and allocate resources to "high value" areas.
3. Differentiate between the necessary and the desirable.
4. Separate the problem from the difficulties of the solution.
5. Measure the "probability of success."
6. Don't allow diversions or "sideshows" to distract the focus from the main objectives.
7. Don't present a problem without alternative solutions and a recommended approach.
8. Once a decision is made by senior management, get behind it, even if you don't agree.
9. Stay on the offensive, provide solutions, and execute.
10. Specify broad strategic objectives to enable maximum flexibility when developing plans.
11. When confronted with a problem, solve it by the most direct and quickest method possible.
12. View problems from different perspectives.
13. Proactively seek out those who disagree with your own points of view.
14. Be confident and open to criticism when presenting plans and progress reports.

---

15. Balance fiscal soundness and investment opportunities.
16. Don't fight the battles where you are disadvantaged.
17. Stay calm under pressure.
18. Insist upon the required level of resources for critical initiatives.
19. Conduct a "horizontal analysis" to identify opportunities to improve efficiencies.
20. Provide a collaborative, non-threatening environment.
21. Optimism and pessimism are infectious and can spread rapidly, especially downward.
22. Develop your ability to persuade and influence through effective communications.
23. Avoid the "victory disease" — don't celebrate success too early.
24. An effective organization will minimize chaos, confusion, delay, and failure.
25. Establish clear lines of authority and responsibility, including "unity of command."
26. Move quickly to fill key positions.
27. Encourage informal "spontaneous mutual coordination."
28. Everything is possible with teamwork, nothing is easy without it.
29. Use scenario-based planning to anticipate competitive pressures and events.
30. Two characteristics of every good solution are simplicity and positivity.

CHAPTER 5.

ACHIEVING RESULTS

"The United States never lost a soldier or a foot of ground in my administration. We kept the peace. People asked how it happened — by God, it didn't just happen, I'll tell you that."

DECISIVENESS

"Suaviter in modo, fortiter in re (Gently in manner, strong in deed)."
- Eisenhower's Presidential Desk Ornament

During the campaigns in North Africa and Italy, Eisenhower struggled with inferior air support, and both campaigns suffered as a consequence. In planning for Overlord, he was determined to marshal all the air resources he could before and during the operation. As Eisenhower had learned from prior experience, a coordinated effort of air, naval, and troop resources offered the clearest path to success. As a result, one of Eisenhower's top priorities was to make certain that he had an effective air strategy and the proper organization in place to execute the plan.

"My insistence upon commanding these air forces at that time was further influenced by the lesson so conclusively demonstrated at Salerno; when a battle needs the last ounce of available force, the commander must not be in the position of depending upon request and negotiation to get it," he wrote after the war. "It was vital that the entire sum of our assault power...be available for use during the critical stages of the attack. I stated unequivocally that so long as I was in command I would accept no other solution."[1]

When Eisenhower assumed responsibility for Overlord, the air plans called for little more than a cursory bombing of the Normandy coastal defenses and outlying regions a few weeks prior to the campaign in order to clear the way for the invasion forces. Eisenhower thought these plans were flawed. If the bombers focused only on Normandy, the Allies would lose the element of surprise, since it would become obvious to the enemy where the invasion was to occur once the bombing started.

Another problem was the possibility that the enemy could rush reinforcements to Normandy and build up their defenses quicker than the Allies could get their people ashore and cut off any advances — the campaign could be stalled or even fail soon after it started. Eisenhower wanted an integrated approach. He wanted to use air power before and during the invasion, along with the navy, artillery, and ground troops to ensure a successful landing.

Eisenhower saw three factors contributing to the lack of urgency in air support for Overlord. First, the air command structure was somewhat fragmented, with each Allied commander acting independently and with their own agendas. The major players included Sir Charles Portal as chief of air staff; Sir Arthur Harris, responsible for the Royal Air Force (RAF) bomber command; Sir Trafford Leigh-Mallory, the most senior commander at SHAEF; Army Air Force Commander in Chief General Henry

"Hap" Arnold; U.S. Strategic Air Force Commander General Carl Spaatz; and Air Chief Marshal Sir Arthur Tedder. Tedder had broad experience in air command, but, as Eisenhower's deputy supreme commander, he was without portfolio.

Secondly, there was an almost complacent attitude by many, especially within the air command, that the Allied forces would be able get ashore in Normandy. Eisenhower's experience in Italy told him it wasn't that easy. The Germans would certainly try to push them back into the English Channel with everything they had, and Eisenhower wanted to eliminate that threat through the proper use of all the air power at his disposal.

A third factor was the allocation of air resources to support the strategic bombing effort against Germany, also known as operation Pointblank. Based on a directive from the Combined Chiefs of Staff (CCS) in June 1943, the Allied commanders were focusing their energy and resources on destroying Germany's air production facilities to sharply reduce their ability to conduct any air battles. Spaatz and Harris were deeply committed to Pointblank.

The good news was that the Allies were close to having air superiority over Europe. Now the question was how to use the superiority in conjunction with Overlord. Eisenhower wanted to deploy an overwhelming force in the invasion of France, and he wanted responsibility for all available resources, but he was under no illusion that it would be easy to get direct control of strategic and tactical air forces. "I anticipate that there will be some trouble in securing necessary approval for integration of all air forces that will be essential to success of OVERLORD," he told Smith. "I suspect that use of these air forces for the necessary preparatory phase will be particularly resisted."

Eisenhower wanted to present a case for the alignment of air and other resources in executing Overlord, and he wanted Tedder to lead the planning effort. "To support our position it is essential that a complete outline plan for use of all available air craft during this phase be ready as quickly as possible," he said. "I therefore believe that Tedder should proceed to the new station at once and consult with Spaatz and others in order to have the plan ready at the earliest possible date."[2]

Eisenhower's first challenge was to reorganize the fragmented air force commands. He already had control of the British and American tactical air forces at SHAEF under Air Chief Marshal Sir Trafford Leigh-Mallory. But he also wanted responsibility for the large bombers under Spaatz and Harris—at least for several weeks—in order to provide a concentration of air force against the enemy prior to and during the operation. He wanted to simplify the organization by bringing Harris and Spaatz under Leigh-Mallory, who would report to Eisenhower.

Tedder got to work on developing the plan, and, with significant help from Professor Solly Zuckerman (a British scientist), a strategy was developed, which became known as the Transportation Plan. At Tedder's request, Zuckerman had analyzed the effects of Allied bombing in Rome. Zuckerman concluded that any bombing effort had to be strategic with specific attacks extended over a period of time, well before D-day. Tactical bombing a few days before the invasion wouldn't be sufficient.

Zuckerman went to London to work with Leigh-Mallory. He explained that the best way to support D-day was to execute air attacks against France's railroad network and bridges and roads in the Low Countries prior to the invasion. Even a limited number of attacks at key points could paralyze the entire rail system. Leigh-Mallory was convinced.[3]

As the team worked to finalize the details, Eisenhower wrote to Marshall. "Within a day or so I will have a complete draft of our Air Preparation plan," which would "not only lay out exactly what we have to do, with priorities, but will also fix our recommended dates for the passage of command over Strategical Air Forces to this Headquarters." Eisenhower wanted buy-in from all the parties before submitting it to the Combined Chiefs of Staff, so he decided "to have a full Commanders-in-Chief meeting on it so that thereafter it becomes doctrine so far as this Headquarters is concerned."[4]

Attempting to obtain pre-approval from all stakeholders is almost always a good idea. But it can also trigger long and heated debates, and the adoption of this plan generated discussions between the Allies that would last another three months.

In January 1944, Leigh-Mallory presented the Transportation Plan to the US and British bomber commanders. They opposed it immediately, believing it was a distraction from the Pointblank initiative and that attacking targets in France would have limited return. There were some agreements about the plan, such as the need to destroy the German air force in France prior to D-day, providing air cover just prior to and during the invasion, and attacking communication targets and airfields after the troops were on shore, but there were serious conflicts over both strategy and structure.

Harris and Spaatz architected Pointblank and were strongly in favor of the status quo. They argued that "the continuing success of the operations against aircraft production and oil refineries would assure greater support for both OVERLORD and POINTBLANK, whereas turning from these targets to railways would allow German production to return to high output." Spaatz even went so far as to say that the US Air Strategic Forces alone could finish the war "with twenty or thirty clear operational days" over the next few months.[5]

Churchill and Portal also had deep reservations about the Transportation Plan. Portal reminded everyone that one of the mandates of the British War Cabinet was to forbid any attacks against occupied countries that could cause a high number of civilian casualties. With the Ministry of Home Security estimating 80,000 to 160,000 civilian deaths and injuries, the plan was a political nonstarter, Portal argued.[6] Churchill was appalled by the thought of large civilian casualties both on moral and political grounds. He was also strongly opposed to giving Leigh-Mallory command of British and American strategic air forces, because his experience to date had been exclusively with fighters.

Even if it were possible for the air forces to win the war on their own, there was a timing issue. The Western Allies had committed to Russia that they would establish another front in Western Europe as soon as possible, and if the invasion was to take place in 1944, it had to happen in May or June, when the tides were right and there were months of fair weather ahead. No one could guarantee that the air force could bring the enemy down by June.

In essence, "long-range strategic bombing inside Germany could have no favorable effect on the OVERLORD battlefield."[7]

The other reality was that Pointblank was not a complete success. While the relentless air attacks since June 1943 did keep Nazi fighters inside German boarders, by early 1944, enemy fighter production had actually increased, and "the cost in lives and aircraft were astronomical, with 96 of 795 RAF bombers lost in a single night raid on Nuremburg on March 30, 1944."[8]

Precision bombing was essentially a notion, Eisenhower argued. Allied raids were more likely to kill cows and land in open fields than hit a German factory.[9] Eisenhower, Leigh-Mallory, Tedder, and Zuckerman argued that the Transportation Plan "would not only be invaluable to OVERLORD by making the movement of German reserves and reinforcements exceedingly difficult but would also reinforce the objectives of POINTBLANK" by reducing the enemy's ability to move oil and other resources from its dispersed sites throughout France.

Eisenhower weighed the various arguments carefully. While he conceded it was never a good idea to constrain "these great bomb units, with their ability to strike at any point in Western Europe, to assist in a single ground operation," Eisenhower also stressed that this was no ordinary ground operation: Britain and the United States "were placing all their hopes, expectations, and assets in one great effort to establish a theater of operations in Western Europe. Failure would carry with it consequences that would be almost fatal."

Eisenhower added, "Such a catastrophe might mean the complete redeployment to other theaters of all United States forces accumulated in the United Kingdom, while the setback to Allied morale and determination would be so profound that it was beyond calculation." He concluded that "such a failure would certainly react violently upon the Russian situation and it was not unreasonable to assume that, if that country should consider her Allies completely futile and helpless in doing anything of a major character in Europe, she might consider a separate peace."[10]

----

*"Every war is going to astonish you in the way it occurred,
and in the way it is carried out."*

Eisenhower met with Churchill to press his case for the Transportation Plan. Churchill told Eisenhower he was strongly opposed to appointing Leigh-Mallory as the overall air commander in chief. Instead, Churchill suggested that Eisenhower put Tedder in charge of the operation, where he "would be responsible for making an air plan; Leigh Mallory would execute orders received from Tedder in Eisenhower's name. Tedder would also issue orders to Spaatz, Harris and Sholto Douglas (British coastal command) with respect to any employment of their forces for OVERLORD that the Combined Chiefs sanction." Through the CCS, Tedder would agree to "assign forces from those commands to Eisenhower as the need arose."

In essence, Churchill didn't want to give Eisenhower control of British air resources. Certainly an understandable view—it would be hard to imagine the United States ever giving another country commander control of American air forces—but given the urgency of the invasion, Eisenhower resisted. He agreed that he shouldn't have control of the coastal command, but he was strongly opposed "to submitting his plans to the CCS," and he was adamant about having "complete operational control of the whole Bomber Command and the American Strategic Force."

He was certainly willing to have Tedder responsible for all the resources (except coastal command), but it had to be an authoritative command, without the need to negotiate for resources at any time. "Eisenhower felt so strongly that he must have final say as to air during OVERLORD that he told the Prime Minister that unless he received full cooperation from the British, he would 'simply have to go home.'"[11]

Eisenhower had never pressed his case so strongly, and he had never issued an ultimatum before. He was quite willing to give up the most important command in the history of warfare on the principle of unity of command. It was not an arbitrary threat, and his passion made an impression on Churchill. The prime minster backed off and suggested that Eisenhower work with Portal to devise a solution he could approve.

As Tedder and Portal worked on a directive for the command structure, Eisenhower provided Marshall with an update: "As we always anticipated, the Air features of our plans have been difficult to get completely in line. It is now my impression that Tedder will become at least the defacto Commander-in-Chief of Air with Spaatz', Harris' and Leigh-Mallory's forces each coordinate bodies under Tedder... I must say that the way it is now shaping up I am far happier than I was a week ago."

The draft solution was published a few days later. Tedder was to "supervise all air operations for OVERLORD," and Eisenhower and Portal "were to approve the air program developed for OVERLORD." Once the plan was approved, Eisenhower would assume "responsibility for supervision of air operations out of England of all the forces engaged in the [Overlord] programme including U.S. Strategic and British Bomber Command together with any other air forces that might be available," at least until the Allies were "established on the continent." After that, "the employment of strategic bombing forces was to be reviewed."[12]

The draft was exactly what Eisenhower wanted, but not everyone was satisfied. When the US Chiefs argued for changing the directive to use the word "command" rather than "supervise," the British hedged and "answered that Eisenhower had not only approved their draft but had even written part of it." This seemed rather petty to Eisenhower, and he began to suspect that the British would not give him command of the strategic bombers after all.

Eisenhower admitted using the word "supervise," but he had done so in good faith. "The question of exact terms and phraseology did not arise at that time but it was clearly understood that authority for operational control of forces definitely allocated to OVERLORD, whether they were engaged on close in targets or in deep penetrations for the destruction of the German Air Force should reside with me." Eisenhower thought they had settled the command structure and the use of air forces, excluding the coastal command. They had also agreed that he would respond to any air "emergency tasks" that were assigned by the CCS.

"I am somewhat astonished that in view of all these agreements there should have been any reluctance on the part of the British Chiefs of Staff to accept the word *command*," Eisenhower wrote in his diary. "In all our conversations this point seemed so well and clearly understood that it never occurred to me to question the complete intent to make me clearly and definitely responsible for operational control of these forces," at least until "OVERLORD was established." At this point, all Eisenhower wanted was "some word that leaves no doubt as to the right of the Supreme Commander to control these air forces under the conditions stated."[13]

Eisenhower was becoming frustrated. The air command structure was still unsettled, with debates at the highest level over semantics. Despite his efforts to remain unbiased, he felt the British hesitancy to use the word *command* showed a lack of good faith. Meanwhile, the air strategy was still undecided. He was still in favor of the Transportation Plan, but he had to reach agreement with all parties once the organizational issues were resolved.

When Tedder reported that Spaatz, Harris, and Leigh-Mallory were not cooperating, Eisenhower turned and said, "Now listen Arthur. I am tired of dealing with a lot of prima donnas. By God you tell that bunch if they can't get together and stop quarrelling like children, I will tell the Prime Minister to get someone else to run this damned war. I'll quit."[14]

Again Eisenhower retreated to his diary to reflect. "The air problem has been one requiring a great deal of patience and negotiation." He was surprised to find "that the British had a great fear that the American idea was to seize all the air in Great Britain and apply it very locally in the preparation of OVERLORD." That was hardly the case, and "it took long and patient explaining to show" that the Americans had "no interest in Coastal Command." They also did not want a total shutdown of Pointblank, because it was the "only means of forcing the German Air Force to fight," which would allow the Allies to gain eventual superiority. He was surprised that the British "did not trust Leigh-Mallory to be the directing head of my Air Forces, since he had been especially selected by the British themselves for this post." Since having Leigh-Mallory in charge wasn't an option, Eisenhower selected Tedder to be his commander of air forces.

Now he wanted to work with Portal to approve "a general air preparation plan which would take into account all of the objectives of POINTBLANK so far as they were consistent with our great need for preparing OVERLORD." Meanwhile, "in the messages coming back and forth from Washington a sudden argument developed between [sic] the use of the word 'command.' This whole matter I had considered settled a week ago, after many weeks of argument." Eisenhower had enough to do without revisiting old arguments—he wanted to move forward.

"The actual air preparatory plan is to be the subject of a formal meeting on this coming Saturday, March 25, between Portal, Spaatz, Harris, Leigh-Mallory, Tedder, and myself," Eisenhower wrote to Marshall. "If a satisfactory answer is not reached I am going to take drastic action and inform the Combined Chiefs of Staff that unless the matter is settled at once I will request relief from this Command." Eisenhower soon got word that the Chiefs of Staff settled on the word "direction" in place of "command," to which he responded, "Amen."[15] Now they could work on the actual air plans.

Eisenhower was determined to walk away from the March 25 meeting with a strategy, and he hoped to reach a consensus. Tedder wanted to reach closure as well, and on the day before the meeting, he sent Portal a note with his reasoning. Tedder felt "what was now required was an adjustment of POINTBLANK." The Allies "could only derive full value from our immense airpower, our strongest single asset, if this target system were based...on one common object towards which all the available air forces can be directed. We would waste much of our power if the U.S. Strategic Air Forces were to operate against one system of objectives, Bomber Command against another, and the A.E.A.F. [Allied Expeditionary Air Force] against yet another.

Concentration against one common system, by both day and night, is essential."[16]

The day of the meeting, each side presented its case. Leigh-Mallory argued for the Transportation Plan, with a consistent attack against rail facilities (yards, roundhouses, turntables, etc.) which "would destroy the Germans' capacity to move reinforcements to the beachhead; interdiction would only prove to be a temporary irritant." Spaatz disagreed. He "thought interdiction was sufficient to isolate the battlefield and maintained that it would be a grave error to divert heavy bombers from POINTBLANK to railroad capacity" and "shattering France's railway system would make Allied movement difficult once OVERLORD was completed."

Spaatz wanted to extend the bombings in Germany to include oil and rubber plants, and, as a concession, send bombers to hit railroad targets when the weather prevented any operation inside Germany. Spaatz believed "the effects of such bombings [on oil and rubber plants] on German industry and troop mobility on all fronts would be so drastic that the enemy high command might consider whether or not to oppose OVERLORD, or even continue the war." Spaatz suggested a continuation of Pointblank's effort to destroy the German air force, move aggressively against Germany's oil and rubber facilities, and provide tactical support just prior to D-day.

Tedder argued strongly for the Transportation Plan. "He held that the worth of any plan at the moment lay in the aid it would bring to OVERLORD before D-Day."[17] While he agreed that Spaatz's Oil Plan would ultimately do serious damage to the German war effort, the problems were that Germany had many oil reserves scattered throughout France that they could fall back on, and there was the matter of timing — it would take four or five months for the Germans to feel the impact of the oil bombings. There was simply "not enough time before D-day for Spaatz's oil and rubber campaign to have much effect." Both Portal and Harris were persuaded and threw their support behind the Transportation Plan.

Eisenhower listened quietly to the arguments. The decision came down to choosing between Spaatz's Oil Plan and the Transportation Plan. He believed the Germans would fight to the end, and bombing German industry and oil would not get the job done by itself. The Allied armies would have to liberate Europe by entering the continent with an overwhelming force, so Overlord was the critical campaign of the war.

He entered the discussion by cutting to the chase and restating his belief that the priority was to make sure the troops landed and stayed there. "The greatest contribution that he could imagine the air forces making to this aim was that they would hinder enemy movement." Everything Eisenhower had heard and "read had convinced him that apart from the attack on the German Air Force, the Transportation Plan offered the air forces a reasonable chance of making an important contribution to the land battle in the first vital weeks after the landing." He believed that even a small reduction in enemy movement justified the plan.[18]

Eisenhower chose the Transportation Plan, and he reached his decision in a collaborative, cooperative manner. None of the air officers could complain they didn't have a chance to present their specific ideas for moving forward. Not everyone was happy with the decision, and some warned of continued political debates (especially from Churchill) in the near future, but they all respected the decision. The Allies now had the organization and framework for an air strategy in support of D-day. Eisenhower asked Tedder to formalize the plan, and he suggested integrating Pointblank and Overlord objectives, since they couldn't overlook "the tremendous advantages accruing to OVERLORD through current POINTBLANK operations."[19]

Tedder's plan called for a continuation of raids against the German air force and industry while applying maximum resources to affect the Transportation Plan. "This meant, in effect, that Spaatz and Harris should be allowed to continue bombing in Germany, although on a reduced scale. It was a necessary concession; without it the airmen might have grown sullen and done everything by half measures."[20]

The strategy offered a balanced approach to achieving long-term objectives while supporting the most critical campaign of the war—the invasion of France. The military issues were resolved, but the political debates continued. While Churchill had said he would approve the air plan submitted by Eisenhower and Portal, he and the British Cabinet still had serious reservations. They had trouble reconciling the benefits of the Transportation Plan with "the possible deaths of thousands of French civilians," which some estimated as high as one hundred thousand.

After consulting with Tedder, Eisenhower responded to Churchill on April 5 by stressing "we must never forget that one of the fundamental factors leading to the decision for undertaking OVERLORD was the conviction that our overpowering air force would make feasible an operation which might otherwise be considered extremely hazardous if not foolhardy." Eisenhower agreed that "the weight of the argument that has been brought against the bombing of transportation centers in occupied territories is heavy indeed. Serious considerations are involved. I admit that warnings will probable do very little in evacuating people from the points we intend to hit. On the other hand I personally believe that estimates of probable causalities have been grossly exaggerated.

"The French people are now slaves," Eisenhower argued. "Only a successful OVERLORD can free them. No one has a greater stake in the success of that operation than the French. As a consequence of all these considerations I am convinced that while we must do everything possible to avoid loss of life among our friends I think it would be sheer folly to abstain from doing anything that can increase in any measure our chances for success in OVERLORD."[21]

But Churchill still wasn't convinced, and no one could be more tenacious for a cause. He was still deeply concerned about French reaction to accidental casualties as a result of the Transportation Plan. But Eisenhower had managed to persuade a number of decision makers in the necessity of the plan. The British Chiefs supported the plan, and Portal, who was once against the plan, now supported it. Tedder continued to advocate for the plan, adding "the estimates of casualties were much too high." Churchill was unmoved, and he decided to withhold final approval until early May. The debate continued.

On April 29, Churchill met with his war cabinet to discuss the issue and came to the conclusion that "the cost of the plan outweighed its gains." Churchill made his case to Eisenhower once again, going over the same arguments and pressing "that attacks on railway centers be limited to those where estimated casualties did not exceed 100-150." Eisenhower was careful to maintain that his decision was based on military priorities. These priorities could always be overruled at any time by Churchill or Roosevelt due to political concerns, but until that happened, "Eisenhower continued to insist that, as far as he was concerned, military strategy necessitated the bombing of the transportation system."[22]

During these discussions Eisenhower received some support from Major General Pierre Joseph Koenig, head of the French forces in the United Kingdom. When informed of the plan by Smith, he responded, "This is War, and it must be expected that people will be killed. We would take twice the anticipated loss to be rid of the Germans."[23]

Eisenhower and Tedder refused to give into the considerable pressure applied by the prime minister and his staff. "The British Government has been trying to induce me to change my bombing program against the transportation systems, so as to avoid the killing of any Frenchman. I have stuck to my guns because there is no other way in which this tremendous air force can help us, during the preparatory period, to get ashore and stay there."[24]

In a formal response to Churchill's protests, Eisenhower reiterated his familiar arguments but also agreed to hold off on bombing targets with the greatest risk of civilian casualties until just prior to D-day, so that the French people may take the warnings seriously and avoid transportation centers. "Although this postponement does inevitably affect the full efficacy of the Plan, since some of the targets involving heavy casualties are...some of the most important, I feel this handicap can be accepted in view of the weighty political considerations put forward by the British Cabinet."

However, Eisenhower could not agree to limit bombing to those targets that would limit casualties to 100 to 150, since "such a modification would emasculate the whole plan. The OVERLORD concept was based on the assumption that our over-whelming Air power would be able to prepare the way for the assault. If its hands are to be tied, the perils of an already hazard-ous undertaking will be greatly enhanced."

On May 2, Churchill reviewed the document with his cabinet. "Churchill spoke of Eisenhower's onerous responsibilities and said care should be taken not to add to his burdens unnecessar-ily." Churchill hated to "interfere with essential military opera-tions on political grounds, but had not fully realized that our use of air power before OVERLORD would assume such a cruel and remorseless a form."

Churchill and many in his cabinet continued to worry about the long-term effects of the killing of such a large amount of civil-ians in post-war Europe. When Brooke, Tedder, and others tried again to persuade Churchill, he responded: "You will smear the good name of the Royal Air Force across the world."

Churchill had one last appeal. He took his case to the presi-dent to settle the issue. The prime minister argued, "The War Cabinet have been much concerned during the last three weeks about the number of Frenchmen killed in the raids on the rail-way centres in France" and questioned "as to whether almost as good military results could not be produced by other methods." But Roosevelt refused to intervene, saying decisively that mili-tary considerations must dominate. The debate was over—the Transportation Plan would be implemented.[25]

The bombing offensive was a strategic and tactical success. Bridges were destroyed all along the Seine from Rouen to Mantes-Gassicourt. By the end of May, all rail traffic along the Seine north of Paris was shut down for more than a month. Civilian casu-alties were kept under ten thousand, and, while even one was too many, the amount was significantly less than the worst esti-mates, and it's impossible to estimate how many lives the cam-paign actually saved by preventing the enemy from reinforcing their troops during the invasion and in the days following. And despite the bombing, there wasn't any evidence of pro-German sentiment by the French.

At this stage of the war, the German army relied on horse-drawn carriages to move equipment and railroads to move supplies and reserves. With the destruction of these supply lines, the Germans couldn't reinforce their defenses in Normandy, and the infantry was without adequate supplies or artillery.

On D-day, German defenses began to fade as they ran out of ammunition. The destruction of the rail network and rail supplies across France and around Paris was so relentless and total that many Germans considered it pointless to try and repair any of the damage. As a result of the Transportation Plan, the Allies were assured of a successful landing even before June 6, 1944.[26]

Throughout the war Eisenhower had numerous arguments with Churchill and the Combined Chiefs of Staff, some major, some minor. But the only time he ever threatened to resign was over the issue of having complete command over the Allied strategic forces.

By insisting upon having unity of command, Eisenhower positioned himself to take full responsibility for all major military decisions. He knew that to succeed, one commander had to have unquestioned control over all military resources and plans, and he never doubted his belief. In one of Eisenhower's last interviews in 1968, he told Stephen Ambrose "that he felt the greatest single contribution he personally made to the success of OVERLORD was the insistence on the Transportation Plan."[27]

- -

"When you appeal to force, there's one thing you must never do — lose."

- -

In making decisions, Eisenhower paid a lot of attention to detail, and he had a great ability to know exactly which details to pay attention to. In the weeks leading to D-day, Eisenhower would take time from his schedule for a daily meeting with his chief weatherman, Group Captain James Stagg. Eisenhower would listen to Stagg's weather forecast for the next few days, and then observe and question him about the actual weather and his prediction. Eisenhower was testing Stagg. He wanted to know how good he was for the moment the time came for Eisenhower to make the decision of a lifetime.[28]

Having pushed back the invasion of Normandy from May to June 1944 to allow more time for training and obtaining additional equipment, Eisenhower decided the attack would occur on June 4, when the tides would be most favorable for a beach landing. The month of May was spent finalizing logistics and making sure the landing zones were kept secret.

On May 30, Leigh-Mallory told Eisenhower he was concerned about reports that the Germans were reinforcing the areas where the 82nd and 101st Airborne Troops would be landing. Leigh-Mallory estimated that only 30 percent of the troops would land safely and be able to fight. The airborne plan was a critical part of the invasion strategy, and it was required to ensure that the Allies kept pressure on the Germans from the rear as the landings occurred. Bradley believed the landings would fail without the help of the 82nd and 101st, never mind the loss of up to 70 percent of two of the finest units in the American military.

"It would be difficult to perceive of a more soul-racking problem," Eisenhower would later write. Eisenhower went off by himself to think through the problem and alternatives. He decided that the airborne operation would go ahead as planned, and he told Leigh-Mallory that all the commanders could do was to "work out to the last detail every single thing that may" be done to eliminate the risks. "Like all the rest of the soldiers, they must understand that they have a tough job to do but be fired with determination to get it done."[29]

On Saturday, June 3, Eisenhower believed everything would go as on schedule. However, during the day, he began receiving forecasts of stormy weather for June 5. At 4:30 a.m. on June 4, he met with his commanders to discuss the launch. With the weather conditions continuing to deteriorate, Eisenhower decided to delay the invasion for twenty-four hours.

On the evening of June 4, as Eisenhower sat in the dining room with his commanders, Stagg came in to report a break in the weather. The rain would stop within two or three hours, followed by thirty-six hours of relatively calm weather and mild winds. Eisenhower sat quietly. Smith told him it was a "helluva gamble." Eisenhower looked at Montgomery. "Do you see any reason for not going on Tuesday?" he asked.

"I would say — go!" Montgomery replied.

"The question," Eisenhower said, was "how long can you hang this operation on the end of a limb and let it hang there?"[30]

At this moment, Eisenhower was completely alone. It would either be now, or delay the landings until July, when the tides would be aligned again. But a July landing would allow for only a few months of fighting before the unpredictable autumn and winter weather months. The burden of making a monumental decision was his alone. At 9:45 p.m., as he stared out the window at the rain, Eisenhower calmly and thoughtfully weighed the alternatives. "I am quite positive that the order must be given," he said.[31]

With this, the command was given to start moving five thousand ships toward France. With the weather getting worse, there was one more opportunity to stop the airborne operation and the invasion, and delay to July. At 3:30 a.m. on June 5, Eisenhower met with Stagg and his commanders again. The weather prediction was the same — a small window of opportunity for the invasion. As the meeting continued, the rain stopped and the clouds began to disappear.

Eisenhower asked his team for their opinions. Everyone wanted to go, although Leigh-Mallory thought the conditions were below acceptable. Once again, it was Eisenhower's decision to make. If the ships sailing into the Channel were to be called back, now was the time. With an order to proceed, there would be no turning back. Eisenhower thought for a moment, and then said, "OK, let's go." The commanders rushed out with their orders, and within a minute, the dining room was empty, except for Eisenhower.[32]

It was one of the most courageous and important decisions ever made by a leader. And as history shows, it was the right one. Later that day, Eisenhower went to visit the 101st Airborne for informal conversations and to wish them well. The men told him not to worry—one even offered him a job after the war. Eisenhower stayed until the last plane left. He went back to his headquarters to wait and listen for the results of the invasion.

Eisenhower visiting troops prior to D-day invasion

At noon on June 6, Leigh-Mallory sent Eisenhower a note, stating although it was sometimes hard to admit one was wrong, he was very happy to report that he was on this occasion. The airborne causalities were dramatically less than he had estimated. He apologized to Eisenhower for adding to his worries and congratulated him on his decision to proceed with the airborne operation.

- -

"The hard way is to have the courage to be patient."

- -

On the evening of September 3, 1954, Eisenhower was told that Chinese Communists had started a heavy artillery assault on

Quemoy Island, about two miles off the coast of mainland China. Two Americans soldiers had been killed and fourteen were being evacuated. This event ignited a crisis that would continue for several months, once again putting the United States on the brink of war.

Since the beginning of the Korean War in 1950, the United States had been committed to protecting Formosa (Taiwan), a small island about one hundred miles off the southeastern coast of China, the home of the Chinese Nationalists led by Chiang Kai-shek. Several naval ships from the Pacific fleet were stationed in the Formosa Strait in a blockade to prevent either side from attacking each other. However, given Asia's animosity toward China's aggression in the Korean War, Eisenhower's view was the fleet was actually protecting the Chinese Communists, so he ended the naval blockade. The United States made it very clear to Communist China and the world that it would still defend Formosa against any aggression. At a press conference in August, when Eisenhower was asked what the response would be if the Communists attacked Formosa, he answered that the 7th Fleet had had standing orders to defend Formosa since early 1953, so "any invasion of Formosa would have to run over the 7th Fleet."[33]

What wasn't clear was what the United States would do to defend two small groups of islands much closer to the mainland, which were also inhabited by soldiers and civilians loyal to the Chinese Nationalists—Quemoy and Matsu. Since Chiang and his people had fled to Taiwan in 1949, they considered Quemoy and Matsu to be part of their country and were determined to defend them, believing if they were to lose control of the islands, then Formosa and possibly other South Pacific territories would be the next to fall. Chiang also believed the islands would be instrumental as beachheads for a reinvasion of the mainland.

With the lifting of the blockade, both sides began building up troop strength—Communist China on the mainland, and Chinese Nationalists on Quemoy and Matsu. Observing this buildup of troops, and remembering Chiang's promise to attack the mainland in the near future, Chinese Communist Prime Minister

Zhou Enlai said it was time to "liberate" Taiwan, and against US warnings, began the bombardment of Quemoy on September 3.

As tensions deepened about what either side would do next, Eisenhower began to consider his options. The Joint Chiefs of Staff disagreed with defending the islands, since they weren't vital to protecting Taiwan. However, other civilian and military advisors believed the islands were of strategic importance and that the United States should go on the offensive and begin bombing mainland China.

Eisenhower disagreed. "We're not talking now about a limited brush-fire war. We're talking about going to the threshold of World War III. If we attack China, we're not going to impose limits on our military actions, as in Korea. Moreover," Eisenhower reminded them, "if we get into a general war, the logical enemy will be Russia, not China, and we'll have to strike there."[34]

Eisenhower was asked at a news conference if he would consider a preventive war with the Communists, as suggested by some in high places. All of us have heard this term "preventive war" since the earliest days of Hitler, Eisenhower responded. "A preventive war, to my mind, is an impossibility today," given the destructive force of atomic weapons.

"How could you have one if one of its features would be several cities lying in ruins, several cities where many, many thousands of people would be dead and injured and mangled, the transportation systems destroyed, sanitation and systems all gone? That isn't preventive war; that is war. I don't believe there is such a thing; and, frankly, I wouldn't even listen to anyone seriously that came in and talked about such a thing."[35]

Meanwhile, Eisenhower was getting conflicting advice from overseas, ranging from former British Prime Minister Clement Attlee's suggestion to get rid of Chiang, to British Foreign Minister Anthony Eden's counsel to avoid war over the islands, to South Korean President Syngman Rhee's suggestion to join him and Chiang in a holy war of liberation.

In November, anxieties escalated as the Chinese Communists bombed the Tachen Islands, about two hundred miles away from Taiwan, and the Red Chinese announced that thirteen American airmen were found guilty of espionage in a Communist court (they were captured on Eisenhower's first day in office). This sparked a number of his advisors and senators to urge Eisenhower to act—to place a naval blockade around Communist China or consider using atomic weapons. But again he said no. At a news conference in early December, he spoke without notes about the realities of war and the need for diplomacy backed by military strength.

"This struggle we now are in, we call the cold war," Eisenhower said. "The great hope of mankind is that we can find methods and means of progressing a little bit, even if by little steps, toward a true or real peace, and that we do not go progressively toward war. Now, on our side we must make certain that our efforts to promote peace are not interpreted as appeasement...but we must, on the other hand, be steady and refuse to be goaded into actions that would be unwise."

He reminded the audience that the American prisoners had been held for two years, and that the timing of the guilty announcement was intentional—"everything they do is deliberate and well thought out," and it was intended to provoke the United States into "some impulsive action in the hope of dividing us from our allies." The goals of communism have always been "to divide the free world, to divide us among ourselves as the strongest nation of the free world, and by dividing to confuse and eventually to conquer, to attain through those means their announced aim of world domination."

Now Eisenhower wanted to get personal. It would be easy for him to respond aggressively. "A President experiences exactly the same resentments, the same anger, the same kind of sense of frustration almost, when things like this occur to other Americans, and his impulse is to lash out," he said. "That would be the easy way for this reason: those actions lead toward war. Now, let us think of war for a second. When this Nation goes to war, there occurs automatically a unification of our people. Traditionally, if we get into trouble that involves war, the Nation closes ranks behind the leader. The job to do becomes simply understood—it is to win the war. There is a real fervor developed throughout the

Nation that you can feel everywhere you go. There is practically an exhilaration about the affair."

Eisenhower said there was a reason Robert E. Lee said "It is well that war is so horrible; if it were not so, we would grow too fond of it." That's "because in the intellectual and spiritual contest of matching wits and getting along to see if you can win, there comes about something, an atmosphere is created, and an attitude is created to which I am not totally unfamiliar."

But there are sad consequences to war. Eisenhower personally had the "very sobering experience" of writing "letters of condolence by the hundreds, by the thousands, to bereaved mothers and to bereaved wives and others who have lost dear ones on the battlefield." We should not go to war "in response to our human emotions of anger and resentment." We should do it "prayerfully," and as a last resort. "Let us recognize that we owe it to ourselves and to the world to explore every possible peaceable means of settling differences before we even think of such a thing as war," Eisenhower said.

"The hard way is to have the courage to be patient, tirelessly to seek out every single avenue open to us in the hope even finally of leading the other side to a little better understanding of the honesty of our intentions. There is no question; they honestly, in certain instances, do question our intentions. They do not believe always, or at least universally, that we are peaceably inclined. We have got a job yet of our own to do—as well as to demand action from others—the courage and the patience to keep after this kind of thing."

Regarding the blockading of Communist China, Eisenhower considered that type of action to be a wartime tactic "to bring your adversary to your way of thinking or to his knees." There were well-defined rules of engagement for blockades, which were all essentially acts of war. "So far as I am concerned, if ever we come to a place that I feel that a step of war is necessary," Eisenhower concluded, "it is going to be brought about not by any impulsive individualistic act of my own, but I am going before the Congress in the constitutional method set up in this country, and lay the problem before them with my recommendation as to whatever it may be."[36]

Eisenhower wasn't going to show any lack of will, which could be misinterpreted as weakness by the Communists, but he wasn't going to be rushed into war either, by anyone. He had been here before. Throughout 1954, most of his advisors, both military and civilian, had pressed him to go on the offensive in Asia.

Whenever a major event occurred during the Vietnam conflict, and now during the Formosa crisis, there were calls all around him to unleash the US military and use atomic weapons. He seemed almost alone in his desire to find a peaceful resolution to the crises, but he believed his primary purpose was "keeping this world at peace." He was determined to keep his options open as long as possible to get the most optimal solution, one that would end the crisis, without embarrassing either side.

"Unless we progress, we regress."

With the New Year came new tensions. Chiang Kai-shek announced in January that war was imminent. The Chinese Communists were building airfields on the mainland opposite Taiwan, and they continued their assault on the Tachen Islands and began attacking other islands north of Taiwan as well. Eisenhower believed the time had come to make a stand and to make sure the Communists took the US defense of Taiwan seriously.

Having signed a mutual defense treaty with the Chinese Nationalists in early December, Eisenhower requested and received approval for a Congressional resolution authorizing the use American armed forces to protect Taiwan. The resolution's language about defending the surrounding islands was intentionally vague, to allow Eisenhower maximum flexibility and to confuse the Chinese Communists about US intentions.

With the resolution in place, Eisenhower was free to use whatever he wanted in his arsenal. Having just returned from a trip to Southeast Asia, Dulles was pessimistic and thought that atomic weapons would be needed to defend Quemoy and Matsu. Eisenhower was more interested in understanding the will and the capacity of the Chinese Nationalists to defend Taiwan without atomic weapons or US troops, so he sent Colonel Andrew Goodpaster to the Pacific to get more information.

On March 15, 1955, Goodpaster reported that the Chinese Communists would need a major assault to overtake the islands, but they probably wouldn't be ready for about another four to six weeks. The Chinese Nationalists were building up their defenses on the islands, but the next ten days were critical — if the Chinese Communists launched a surprise attack, they could take over the islands.

Eisenhower decided to ratchet up the rhetoric. At a March 16 news conference, he was asked if tactical atomic weapons would be used in a general war in Asia. Eisenhower responded, "Yes, of course they would be used...I see no reason why they shouldn't be used just exactly as you would use a bullet or anything else."[37] Eisenhower knew that statement would get the Chinese Communists' attention. At the next news conference, when asked about when he would use an atomic weapon, Eisenhower's response was intentionally confusing. He talked about a police action versus a war, large versus small explosions, and then turned philosophical.

"Suppose you won a war by the indiscriminate use of atomic weapons; what would you have left? Now, what would you do for your police action, for your occupation and restoration of order, and all of the things needed to be done in a great area of the earth? I repeat, the concept of atomic war is too horrible for man to endure and to practice, and he must find some way out of it."

But would the United States use an atomic weapon or not, a reporter asked in frustration. "I must confess I cannot answer that question in advance," Eisenhower said. "The only thing I know about war are [sic] two things: the most changeable factor in war is human nature, and the only unchanging factor in war is human nature. And the next thing is that every war is going to astonish you in the way it occurred, and in the way it is carried out. So that for a man to predict, particularly if he has the responsibility for making the decision, to predict what he is going to use, how he is going to do it, would I think exhibit his ignorance of war; that is what I believe. So I think you just have to wait, and that is the kind of prayerful decision that may someday face a President."[38] This commentary would certainly send the Communist intelligence analysts spinning.

While many members in Eisenhower's cabinet were predicting war, Eisenhower continued to be optimistic that it wouldn't come to that. "I have so often been through these periods of strain that I have become accustomed to the fact that most of the calamities that we anticipate really never occur," he wrote in his diary. On April 23, Eisenhower got the break he had been waiting for. At an Asian-African conference, Zhou Enlai said that Red China had no desire to go to war with the United States, and that they were ready to negotiate about Formosa. By mid-May an informal cease-fire was in place.[39]

Eisenhower succeeded once again. He had guided the country and his administration through treacherous times and averted a nuclear catastrophe. Eisenhower had secured peace by leveraging his experience, perseverance, and communication and diplomatic skills. There was no gloating over who had backed down or any victory celebrations. The crisis was ended with dignity, humility, and honor for all. When faced with a choice between war and peace, the supreme commander of World War II chose peace, both for his country and the Chinese Communists and Nationalists.

ADAPTIVE LEADERSHIP

- -

"The problem in defense is how far you can go without destroying from within what you are trying to defend from without."

- -

Eisenhower's leadership style avoided dramatics or unnecessary confrontations. He was also pragmatic, adapting tactics to circumstances without comprising the strategic goals. He was extremely confident in his abilities and didn't feel threatened by having highly talented people around him. In the chaos "of a military campaign — or a political effort — loyal, effective subordinates are mandatory. To tie them to the leader with unbreakable bonds one rule must always be observed — take full responsibility, promptly, for everything that remotely resembles failure. Give extravagant and public praise to all subordinates for every success."[40]

On August 6, 1942, Roosevelt sent Churchill a formal note on the appointment of Eisenhower as Allied commander for Operation Torch (the British-American invasion of North Africa). Although he played a major role in developing the Torch plan, Eisenhower was originally against the idea. He thought all efforts and resources should be applied to the Allied invasion of France.

However, once the decision was reached to move forward, Eisenhower was determined to succeed. "From the instant that I was authorized to assume executive charge of the propositions," he wrote to Marshall, "I laid down a specific charge to all subordinates that the time for analyzing the wisdom of the original decision had passed, and that we were going to accept, without question, whatever the two governments could make available, and that our problem was first to make the best possible plan within the framework of visible assets. Then by leadership, organizing ability and intensive preparation to do all that lay within our power to insure success."

He insisted that his team focus on the possible, rather than the obstacles preventing progress. He also understood that his attitude was fundamental to the morale of those under his leadership. He added, "It seems to me that the rougher the prospects, the more necessary it is that superior commanders allow no indication of doubt or criticism to discourage efforts and dampen the morale of subordinates and of troop movements."[41]

"War brings about strange, sometime ridiculous situations."[42] Little did Eisenhower know how true that would be when he wrote it just as the North African campaign was starting in November 1942. Eisenhower had to deal with military issues as well as the strange and twisted politics of Vichy North Africa. "It isn't this operation that's wearing me down," he wrote. "It's the petty intrigue and the necessity of dealing with little, selfish, conceited worms that call themselves men."[43]

Almost as soon as the Torch campaign began, Eisenhower had a major problem. After many hours of debate, he had finally come to terms with having General Henri Giraud lead the armies of North Africa (the local French) once the Allies were on shore, only to find that no one would follow him. As the Allies were landing on the beaches, they were fighting against the French as well as the natural elements. Eisenhower and his team soon realized that the French soldiers in North Africa would take orders only from their existing chain of command, and that meant dealing with Francois Darlan, the Vichy French admiral.

"Without exception every French commander with whom General [Mark] Clark held exhaustive conversations declined to make any move toward bringing his forces to the side of the Allies unless he could get a legal order to do so...or could give any order to cease firing unless the necessary instructions were given by Darlan."[44]

Eisenhower decided to approve an agreement, which exchanged Allied military rights in North Africa for allowing Darlan and the French to maintain administrative control of the region. However, while the agreement with Darlan had eventually stopped the fighting in Casablanca and Oran, the confusion and delay in getting the deal done allowed the Germans to take Tunisia, a key objective in the campaign.

A few days into the invasion, Eisenhower's view of the results in North Africa was mixed. Although they were ashore and were working to completely secure the ports at Casablanca and Oran, the Allies had no force in the Tunisia area to counter the German buildup of their defensive positions. He then received a surprise cable from the Combined Chiefs of Staff (CCS), who were apparently very satisfied with the progress of the campaign.

"In their enthusiasm over Eisenhower's quick victories and the agreement that had been reached with the French," the CCS wanted Eisenhower to consider expanding the campaign in the Mediterranean with an attack on Sardinia. They also "questioned the necessity of building up TORCH to the strength originally contemplated and felt Eisenhower should return to London for a general strategy conference."

Eisenhower couldn't believe it. Now he had pressure from the front and the rear. Somehow, the CCS were under the impression that the state of affairs was more under control than it actually was. Eisenhower knew they needed a reality check, so he set out to define the current state and manage expectations accordingly.

"I am unalterably opposed to any suggestion at this time for reducing contemplated TORCH strength," he wrote. The situation was extremely fluid, especially in Tunisia, where it was "touch and go," the two ports in Casablanca and Oren were "seriously blocked" with sunken ships, the "country is not pacified completely, and communications are a problem of first magnitude. Moreover, every effort to secure organized and effective French cooperation runs into a maze of political and personal intrigue." Yet without local organized cooperation, "we have a tremendous job on our hands in this sprawling country." Eisenhower was certainly in favor of looking forward, "but for God's sake let's get one job done at a time." The operation was less than five days old, and "this is the time to push rather than slacken our efforts," in order "not to lose momentum" in gaining the offensive.

To Eisenhower, any suggestion of expanding the campaign at this time was a nonstarter, but what really concerned him was that the CCS in London didn't have a strong appreciation of the events and environment in North Africa. "I am disturbed by the apparently bland assumption that this job is finished. It would take only five minutes actually on the ground to convince anyone that nothing could be further from the truth."[45] Later that day he told Smith not to let "anybody get any screwy ideas that we've got the job done."[46]

No sooner had that fire been put out when serious concerns began to surface in England and America about the Darlan deal. Many in the United States and Britain were questioning the rationale of doing business with someone like Darlan, who was deeply involved in Vichy and pro-Fascist politics. The British were especially stunned. Darlan had abandoned them in the fight against the Nazis in 1940 and had joined the Vichy French, who collaborated with the enemy.[47] In describing the deal, "Some of the London papers speak of the act, by Eisenhower, as 'revolting' and 'disgusting.'"[48]

Churchill was sensitive to the political storms the deal had caused, but he was also pragmatic about the needs of the situation—just before leaving England for his command post in Gibraltar, Churchill told Eisenhower, "Kiss Darlan's stern if you have to, but get the French Navy"[49] and "If I could meet Darlan, much as I hate him, I would cheerfully crawl on my hands and knees for a mile if by doing so I could get him to bring that fleet of his into the circle of Allied forces."[50]

But now that the deal was done, there was a curious lack of support from either Churchill or Roosevelt, and it wasn't long before American politicians and reporters joined in denouncing the deal, deploring the idea of working with traitors. Eisenhower was taking a lot of heat, and as he worked to defend the deal, he was once again distracted from the battlefield activities.

"Can well understand some bewilderment in London and Washington with the turn that negotiations with French North Africans have taken," he wrote to the CCS. But he had considered a number of objectives and facts in securing the deal with Darlan. First, the Allies needed someone who could work with the local politicians in maintaining stability in the region, so time and resources could be focused on the enemy rather than the civil population. "Without a strong French Government of some kind here we would be forced to undertake complete military occupation. The cost in time and resources would be tremendous."

Second, the Allies also needed someone who the French soldiers would take orders from—to not only stop fighting the Allies but to also start fighting the Germans. Third, there were the military factors to consider. Two of the major objectives of the campaign were the capture of Tunisia and securing the French fleet for the Allied cause. Neither of these would happen "unless there is accepted a general agreement along the lines which we have just concluded with Darlan." Eisenhower knew they needed someone to work with, and "that man is Darlan... All concerned profess themselves to be ready to go along with us provided Darlan tells them to do so, but they are absolutely not... willing to follow anyone else."

Eisenhower closed by writing that together with his staff, "I have made what we consider to be the only possible workable arrangement for securing advantages and avoiding disadvantage. I am certain that anyone who is not on the ground can have no clear appreciation of the complex currents of feeling and of prejudice that influence the situation." He suggested that those who were "still dissatisfied with the nature of agreement made" should visit "headquarters, where, in ten minutes the can be convinced of the soundness of the moves we have made."[51]

The bottom line for Eisenhower was that Darlan could deliver. His primary objective was to push the Germans out of North Africa, and he was willing to let Darlan help him. He saw no other choice given the circumstances. Eisenhower must have been somewhat reassured when he received congratulatory notes from both Churchill and Roosevelt on the success of the operation.

But Eisenhower's explanatory note did little to appease many British. Churchill wired Roosevelt that "deep currents of feeling are stirred by the arrangement with Darlan," and the British Foreign Office sent a note to the British Embassy in Washington, noting "It may well be that Darlan's collaboration is indispensable for military reasons as an interim measure," but they had to consider "our moral position. We are fighting for international decency and Darlan is the antithesis of this."[52]

There were heated arguments between Churchill and his staff, with Churchill refusing to renounce Darlan. Roosevelt was impressed and satisfied with Eisenhower's explanation, but he still didn't publicly support him until a number of people such as

Marshall and Secretary of War Harry Stimson urged him to do so. At his regular press conference, Roosevelt explained that he supported the political arrangements in North Africa, but he considered them "a temporary expedient, justified solely by the stress of battle"[53] and to save Allied lives. He added that ultimately, the French people would decide what form their government would take once they were liberated.

As for Eisenhower, he would rather be focusing on battlefield objectives than deeply involved in the political quagmire. "Since this operation started," he wrote Smith, "three quarters of my time...has been necessarily occupied in difficult political maneuver in attempting to explain to people, far from the scene of action, the basic elements of the local situation." The need to continually communicate the rationale of the Darlan deal was distracting from the main priorities of the campaign.

"If we don't get to Tunisia quickly, we surrender initiative, give the Axis time to do as it pleases in that region, and encourage all our enemies in the area" to increase resistance. "The potential consequences of delay are enormous because this battle is not yet won, and we have not concentrated here all the forces we need to insure stability." He added, "I do not...expect any encouragement and hurrahs from the rear, but I regret that I must use so much of my own time to keep explaining these matters."[54]

Despite the detailed explanations and the efforts of Marshall to reduce the level of rhetoric and questions, Eisenhower continued to receive requests for information, including one from the State Department regarding the exact nature of Darlan's position. He realized he needed to put an end to these constant inquires and force the issue of whether or not the campaign would continue under the Darlan agreement. Plus, the agreement with Darlan had already started to pay off. He had already witnessed "evidence on every hand of the effective way in which the French are cooperating," and he realized that "this must not stop!"

He approved of a protocol outlining the agreements reached with Darlan. His original thought was to send it down throughout the chain of command, but his staff wanted him to send it up the chain of command. He hesitated. He didn't want to be viewed as avoiding responsibility for the deal. But, as he explained to Clark, "when [Admiral Andrew] Cunningham, whom I consider about as bold a man as I know of, joined the chorus," he gave in and sent the protocol onto his seniors. He was forcing them to commit themselves in approving the political decisions he had made in order to achieve his primary objectives. And it worked. Roosevelt ratified the deal, and the questions and distractions began to dissipate.

Despite all the anxiety, the deal turned out to be beneficial to the Allies. Darlan kept to his word. He stabilized the region, he assisted the Allies in attaining the required ports, and he was determined to restore property and individual rights to the local people.

It was a difficult time for Eisenhower, who was not totally immune to the criticism coming his way. He knew his performance wasn't exceptional, but the Allies were ashore and preparing to move forward now that the political and administrative environments were established. Eisenhower tried to keep it all in perspective.

To his son he wrote, "From what I hear of what has been appearing in the newspapers, you are learning that it is easy enough to be a newspaper hero one day and a bum the next. The answer is that just as one must not let his head get swelled too much by a bit of acclaim, he must not be too upset and irritated when the pack turns on him. Apparently, the people who have been creating the storm do not like Darlan. The answer to that one is 'Who does?' The only thing that a soldier can use for a guide is to try to do what appears right and just at the moment of the crisis. If it turns out wrong — or if it even appears to turn out wrong — the reaction may be serious, but there is no other course to follow." He believed his role "in a moment of emergency" was to "get down to the essentials of the situations and not be too much disturbed about popularity or newspaper acclaims."[55]

"Neither a wise man nor a brave man lies down on the tracks of history to wait for the train of the future to run over him."

As Eisenhower turned his attention to the battlefield, he realized they were not making the progress he had hoped for. With both Eisenhower and Clark distracted by political problems, there was a sense of drift in the campaign. The weather and lack of suitable transportation were also factors. The heavy rains affected the ability to create the required airfields, road transport was inadequate, and there was only one frail railroad running along five hundred miles of the Mediterranean coast available to move equipment to the front. The Allies had also lost many aircraft because the lack of air facilities caused them to group planes close together, which made them vulnerable to air raids.

Eisenhower had expected some problems in moving quickly to Tunisia. "When I made the decision to rush our forces into Tunisia as rapidly as possible, I did so in full realization that we were assuming the inescapable risk of having bases damaged, of sabotage on lines of communication, and of having some of our small columns get into bad tactical situations. However, I felt that the Axis was startled and upset by our initial landing and that I was perfectly justified in assuming any risks that did not actually jeopardize...what we had already gained." Indeed, the emphasis on speed had enabled Lieutenant General Sir Kenneth Anderson (one of the ground commanders) to advance quickly to the front.

But now Eisenhower's challenge was to get Anderson the supplies, reinforcements, and air support he needed. "My immediate aim is to keep pushing hard," he wrote to Marshall. He first needed to fine-tune his leadership style, organization, and directives to meet current realities. "In a confused, fluid situation, such as this, rumors flow thick and fast and are so conflicting that it is a real job to separate the true from the false. By the same token, a commander quickly learns which of his subordinates are to be trusted under all circumstances to do a fine workmanlike job and which ones he has to watch closely and handle by special means in order to get the best out of them."[56]

He jump-started his organization by providing clear direction to his widely dispersed staff to act in a coordinated manner. He then worked to get each of his forces in shape. He asked for more planes and replacement parts, explaining that "in rushing forward into Tunisia with every bit of available tactical strength that could be moved, we have been forced to do so without the methodical preparation and prior defense of bases and lines of communication that are normally the first concern of a commander."[57]

Eisenhower received the requested equipment, and he turned his attention to the ground forces, where Anderson's forward movement was stalled due to continual strafing from Nazi planes and the lack of equipment to rapidly move material and men. Eisenhower worked with his staff to eliminate the logistical bottlenecks and get personnel transports and other equipment to Anderson as soon as possible, but it was a struggle. The distance between Algiers—where the supplies arrived—and Tunisia was relatively far at 386 miles, and the lack of transport and poor weather conditions were all working against the Allies.

Eisenhower decided to travel to the front. During the trip he experienced the difficulties of his troops firsthand—while on the road, he was exposed to constant air raids, and, at one point while riding at night, his jeep ended up in a ditch. When he got to the front, he found that despite "physical conditions" that were "almost unendurable," morale was high.

"Troops and commanders were not experienced, but their boldness, courage and stamina...could not have been exceeded by the most battle-wise veterans." In addition to the enemy, they were fighting the elements, including the oncoming winter cold and mud, which "deepened daily, confining all operations to the roads, long stretches of which practically disintegrated." Even though they outnumbered the enemy, Anderson's troops were spread thin across a broad front, and the lack of supplies, artillery, and air support prevented a sustained drive into Tunis. "Day by day, following the first contact, fighting grew more bitter, more stubborn, more difficult and the enemy was more rapidly reinforced than were our own troops."[58]

Eisenhower had some concerns about his commander, telling Marshall he felt that "Anderson is apparently imbued with the will to win, but blows hot and cold," yet he was determined to give Anderson all the forces and equipment he could for a final push onto Tunis.[59] He decided to gamble and "bring up to General Anderson every available fighting man in the theater," which was risky considering the enemy could attack from the rear, but Eisenhower was "quite willing to take all later criticism if only the Allied forces could turn over Tunis to our people as a New Year's present!"[60]

However, while the Allies were building up their reinforcements, the Germans began a series of offensives, including a very effective use of their superior air support in the region. Anderson reported "if he did not take Tunis or Bizerte within the next few days, he would have to withdraw" because of "ineffective administration (systematic command structures had been deliberately disregarded during the dash for Tunis), the enemy's air superiority and his rate of reinforcement."

Eisenhower met with his team and decided to delay the offensive for a few days. He wrote to the CCS that "in the pell mell race for Tunisia, we have gone beyond sustainable limit of air capabilities in support of ground forces...the scale of possible air support is not sufficient to keep down the hostile strafing and dive bombing that is largely responsible for breaking up all attempted advances by ground forces."[61] Eisenhower wanted to pause the offensive to allow the air force to recover and strengthen for an assault and to take advantage of the pending arrival of additional British troops and armor.

To help prevent the Axis from reinforcing its positions, Eisenhower ordered heavy bombers to attack enemy ports and communications facilities. He was now targeting December 9 as the date for an advance on Tunisia, but cautioned that the plan could be affected by weather, since it would make airfields unusable, and it could limit the amount of heavy bombing operations.

The CCS sent Eisenhower a note confirming that the revised date seemed reasonable. But they also stressed that "losses in the initial assault may be heavy, but should be less than those that are bound to occur if you become involved in a long drawn out attrition battle,"[62] which essentially meant that they were concerned that Eisenhower was becoming too cautious.

But that was hardly the case. "Courage, resourcefulness, and endurance though daily displayed in overwhelming measure," he wrote, "could not completely overcome the combination of enemy, weather and terrain." Eisenhower was pressing as hard as he could, but he also knew when to regroup in order to prevent a massacre.

Conventional means of warfare had been discarded in taking the calculated risk of moving rapidly to Tunisia. Eisenhower sent a note to General Thomas T. Handy, his successor at the Operations Planning Division (OPD) in Washington DC about the current situation. "I think the best way to describe our operations to date is that they have violated every recognized principle of war, are in conflict with all operational and logistic methods laid down in text-books, and will be condemned, in their entirety, by all Leavenworth and War College classes for the next twenty-five years."[63]

The Allied buildup continued. But as December 9 approached, it was becoming clear the Allies still weren't strong enough to launch an attack. The weather also continued to hamper progress, so Eisenhower delayed the offensive for a week to ten days. These offensive postponements were extremely frustrating to Eisenhower, and the return of political problems didn't help his mood.

Darlan had started to make statements and behave as if he was the head of the French state, and he had done little to reform the administration of North Africa. After meeting with Eisenhower, Darlan agreed he would issue a press statement renouncing any personal political ambitions and expressing opposition to the Axis. Eisenhower hoped this would bring an end to the controversy surrounding Darlan, and just when he needed it, he received a word of encouragement from Marshall.

"With completion of negotiations regarding Darlan, I want you to feel that you have not only my confidence but my deep sympathy in conducting a battle, organizing a fair sixth slice of a continent, and at the same time being involved in probably the most complicated and highly supervised negotiations of history, considering the time element and all the other circumstances,"

Marshall wrote. "Your judgment throughout has been sound and your action in each instance completely justified."

Eisenhower was grateful for the positive reinforcement. "No other person's complete understanding of this complicated situation and commendation for its handling to date could possibly mean so much to me as yours," he responded to Marshall.[64]

As the poor weather continued and the Allies strived to launch the major offensive before the end of the year, Eisenhower tried hard to maintain his customary optimism. "All in all, I would rate our prospects for the present as good. We are having our troubles; so is the enemy. If we can make up our minds to endure more and go further and work harder than he does and provide only that the comparative logistics of the situation does [sic] not favor him *too* much, we can certainly win!"[65]

December 24 was the new target date for an ambitious offensive attack. Efforts "continued twenty-four hours a day to build up the strength that we believed would, with some temporary improvement in the weather give us a good fighting chance to capture Northeastern Tunisia before all operations were hopelessly bogged down" in the rain and mud of the Northern African winter. The Allies had built up enough artillery to have a superior advantage, which they hoped would lead the way in securing a victory. But as winter approached, the news from the front wasn't promising—the weather continued to deteriorate. Eisenhower was "determined to not give up unless" he was "personally convinced that the attack was an impossibility."

Eisenhower took a car to the front to survey the situation. Because of the poor weather conditions, it took him almost two days to get there. The rain continued nonstop, and the entire landscape was saturated. When he arrived, some small elements of the battle had already begun, with the major attack scheduled for the next night.

Eisenhower and his team went out to look over the terrain where the Allies were to advance, and he "observed an incident which, as much as anything else...convinced me of the hopelessness of an attack. About thirty feet off the road, in a field that appeared to be covered with winter wheat, a motorcycle had become stuck in the mud. Four soldiers were struggling to extricate it but in spite of their most strenuous efforts succeeded only in getting themselves mired into the sticky clay. They finally had to give up the attempt and left the motorcycle more deeply bogged down than when they started."[66]

Eisenhower decided to postpone the attack until the weather improved, but "probably in not less than two months." It was a difficult but courageous decision. "The abandonment for the time being of our plan for a full-out effort has been the severest disappointment I have suffered to date," Eisenhower wrote to the CCS. "However, the evidence is complete, in my opinion, that any attempt to make a major attack under current conditions in northern Tunisia would be merely to court disaster."[67]

By nature Eisenhower had a strong bias toward offensive action. He certainly did not want to get bogged down in holding defensive positions and conducting a war of attrition. The Allies finally had enough resources assembled for the offensive, and Eisenhower could have easily given the order to attack. But to mount an offensive this late in the year under the extreme weather conditions could result in complete failure and catastrophic losses, which were unacceptable.

Still, "it was a bitter decision," Eisenhower wrote. Even though the capture of Tunisia was something of a stretch goal, and the Allies had accomplished many of their objectives, the Torch operation could not be considered a complete success because it continued to be held by the enemy. There was a natural letdown for all of those involved, and Eisenhower knew that "in such circumstances it is always necessary for the commander to avoid an attitude of defeatism; discouragement on the part of the high commander inevitably spreads rapidly throughout the command and always with unfortunate results." But even Eisenhower found "that on this occasion it was exceedingly difficult to display any particular optimism."[68]

Clearly, everyone involved in the operation had underestimated the impact of the logistical and weather-related problems involved in North Africa. However, with the decision made, there was some sense of relief. The Allies could now focus on holding their positions and building up their strength for an attack when the weather improved. The day Eisenhower decided to cancel the offensive, Darlan was assassinated, which had the rather morbid effect of improving the political situation in the area.

"I never worry about what I did the day before. Likewise, I spend no time fretting about what enemies or critics have said about me. I have never indulged in useless regrets."

Rather than dwell on the things he couldn't control (like the weather), Eisenhower turned his attention to things he could control. He certainly had no intention of giving up any positions that had been gained or allowing his team and the troops to become complacent. "Idleness by our ground forces during this period would constitute a failure to take advantage of the enemy before he can solidify himself." He also believed "a period of almost complete stagnation...would be bad psychologically for this army."[69] He wanted an aggressive defense.

He gave orders for his forward troops to conduct small, tactical attacks to keep the enemy off-balance. He also wanted the airfields protected so he could launch air raids on enemy positions and supplies. Churchill had sent Eisenhower a note that he was "concerned about the decision to call off the drive for Tunis." The two-month delay made him "particularly anxious about the condition of the First British Army."

But Eisenhower assured him that "my plan is not to have the First Army stay idle during the several weeks that it will be building up for a final punch. It will conduct a very aggressive type of defense so as to facilitate an operation that I now have mind for regaining the initiative and for upsetting and weakening the enemy." He added "we are adopting the one course of action that promises definite and positive results."[70]

He also saw the delay as an opportunity to improve the performance of his organization and operations. He stressed that he would be addressing command weaknesses "so that future operations will be characterized by complete coordination of effort. Signal communications and every other feature of our command arrangement will be thoroughly studied and, where necessary, suitable recommendations will be made to higher authority." In addition, British and American units were fighting together but there were "considerable logistic and other type of difficulty," which was to be expected since there were "inherent differences in organization, equipment, training and doctrine," but Eisenhower wanted these "corrected at once."[71]

He immediately established a forward Allied command post to take "personal charge of the Tunisian front" in order to improve coordination between the British, American, and French forces. Where there were equipment shortages, with motor transport for example, he pressed for efficiencies in the logistical supply chain. He also moved to solve the problem of air support. "From the beginning of TORCH coordination in operations involving air units have not been completely satisfactory." After studying the problem and getting advice from a number of subordinates, Eisenhower decided he needed a single air commander.[72]

His recommendation of General Spaatz as commander of Allied air forces was approved within a few days. While he knew this appointment wouldn't ensure success, he believed it would unify the command structure in the expanding Tunisia theater and facilitate cooperation with long-range bomber commanders in Europe.

Improving the operation, getting the right people in place, and placing continued pressure on the enemy was somewhat cathartic for Eisenhower. While he was still disappointed that they hadn't taken Tunisia, he was getting things done that would set the stage for the offensive to come. In communicating his plans to the chiefs of staff, Eisenhower told them that everyone was "devoting the maximum in unceasing effort and determination." He added that despite the setbacks, "Personally, I do not consider the picture to be excessively dark, providing always of course that no great catastrophe overtakes us."[73]

Eisenhower knew he had to maintain his optimism since everyone took their cues from him, and, for the most part, he did.

He wrote to a friend in the Operations Planning Division: "On the whole, I think I keep up my optimism very well, although we have suffered some sad disappointments. In fact, I can scarcely call them disappointments, because they were only things to be anticipated in the event that the enemy reacted aggressively and strongly. None of this business is child's play and only the sissy indulges in crying and whimpering because everything does not go as he would like. We have constantly got to get tougher and tougher — all of us — take our losses in stride with full preparation made for replacing them promptly, and keep on everlastingly pounding until the other fellow gives way."[74]

He then turned his attention to a major concern. In his many trips to the front, Eisenhower had recently seen some major shortfalls in the attitudes and skills of some of his new American junior commanders and troops. He sensed a lack of urgency, poor discipline, and inadequate knowledge of routine military tactics. Eisenhower and his team could make all the changes they wanted to improve logistics, communications, and supplies, but at the end of the day, if the commanders and troops wouldn't — or couldn't — fight effectively, the campaign and maybe even the war was a lost cause.

Eisenhower wanted his commanders to make the most effective use of the offensive delay by conducting continuous training exercises and instilling discipline in the troops. In a letter to his senior commanders in January 1943, he noted, "Nothing has impressed me more in connection with our operations in this theater than our deficiencies in training." The shortfall had become clear because they stood out "in operations against a skillful and practiced enemy."

Eisenhower believed that while the training doctrine and methods were sound, "it is in the application of them that we fail. If only we can, even now that we are at grips with the enemy, impress upon our junior officers, the deadly seriousness of the job, the absolute necessity for thoroughness in every detail — then we will begin to get results. But seemingly we have been unable to do this. We must try again, harder." He then went on to list several of the most critical areas where he wanted changes made:

Discipline. Despite the efforts which have been made in the past to improve the discipline of troops in the European Theater of Operations, it is still unsatisfactory. It is now reflecting itself in battle loses by failure of officers to carry out orders, by men failing to construct fox holes or slit trenches, by disregard of orders requiring use of vehicle blackout lights, by running vehicle columns closed up. Innumerable instances of these and other derelictions could be cited which can be attributed directly to poor discipline. The only kind of discipline that is acceptable is the kind which will be carried onto the battlefield, and survive a period of combat operations. This applies alike to officers and enlisted men. The officer, however, has the additional duty of exacting discipline from his subordinates. Too often minor offenses against discipline are condoned. Every infraction, from a mere failure to salute, a coat unbuttoned, to more serious offenses, must be promptly dealt with; or disciplinary action taken against the officer who condones the offense. It is only in this way that the kind of discipline can be developed that service in this theater demands.

Basic individual and small unit training has left much to be desired. This must be corrected by requiring frequent combat exercises involving the squad, platoon and company, followed by critiques in which errors are unmistakably pointed out in such a way that they will not be repeated. An exercise should be repeated until proficiency is attained. Principle mistakes have been frontal attack instead of envelopment, being diverted from the objective by minor incidents, loss of control by failure to maintain communications, lack of adequate reconnaissance. Aggressiveness both in attack and defense must be stressed.

Troops must be hard; capable of marching distances up to twenty-five miles without a long halt, going days without sleep, subsisting on short rations. Frequent rapid short marches or runs across country will be of great value.

Training in air support of ground troops must be conducted — and must be applicatory. We have published a doctrine that has not been proved faulty. The air and ground forces must get together in training, or they will not be able to do so in combat.

Perhaps the above may appear elementary. It is so intended. The defects in training in elementary subjects are the most outstanding of the lessons learned in this campaign. The mistakes made in maneuvers nearly two years ago are now being repeated on the battlefield almost without variation – but this time at the cost of human life instead of umpire penalties. I cannot urge too strongly that emphasis be placed on individual and small unit training. Thoroughness – thoroughness achieved by leadership and constant attention to detail – will pay maximum dividends.[75]

Hard training, easy battle. Easy training, hard battle. Eisenhower wanted his team to succeed, which meant providing them with the training and the skills to do so.

- -

"It is far more important to be able to hit the target than it is to haggle over who makes a weapon or who pulls a trigger."

- -

While Eisenhower and his troops prepared for the coming offensive, the Allies held a military strategy session in Casablanca in January 1943. All the senior Allied leaders attended the meetings, including Roosevelt, Churchill, Brooke, and Marshall. Many of the events leading up to the conference had been the most difficult of Eisenhower's career, and many were disappointed in the results of the Allied campaign in North Africa so far.

As the date for the Casablanca conference approached, Eisenhower's performance included both successes and failures, and he was objective about both. On the positive side, the Allies had landed and stayed there, and they had liberated much of Northern Africa. He had navigated through the bizarre politics in the region, and his approach had been vindicated by the stability of the region and the cooperation of the French armies.

In his first command of troops, he had held the Allied coalition together and had developed an efficient Allied headquarters with little friction between nationalities. Most importantly, he was learning—how to command, how to cope with uncertainty, how to deal with the politics—and he was gaining confidence.

On the negative side, Eisenhower had failed to capture Tunis. He had been unable to leverage the Allie's advantages of initiative and surprise, and everyone, including Eisenhower, had underestimated the obstacles to supplying and deploying an effective fighting force against the enemy. With the Germans rapidly reinforcing their defensive positions, it was now a logistical battle to see who could build up the most resources prior to engaging in a "slugfest" when the weather cleared later in the year.

Although the meeting was primarily about strategy, Eisenhower was more interested in discussing tactics, such as how the British and American armies were going to come together for the advance on Tunisia. Eisenhower was at the conference for only a day, and in the one session he did attend, "the military situation in North Africa was thoroughly discussed."[76] With all the senior political and military advisors present, Eisenhower "gave, from memory and without the aide of notes, a detailed account of operations in North Africa."[77]

Eisenhower discussed the current situation and immediate plans to advance toward the eastern coast of Tunisia, which was still rather risky because the buildup was not complete, and it was contingent on the enemy remaining quiet. But Alexander, who was commanding the British armies east of Tunisia, "interrupted to say that we could drop considerations of the offensive move because British forces would" soon be in Tripoli, and, in about six weeks, they would be "at the southern border of Tunisia." "This was great news," Eisenhower wrote, because now he could continue the buildup of resources in preparation for a concentrated joint attack with Alexander's forces against the enemy.

Later that day, Roosevelt asked to see Eisenhower privately. Eisenhower didn't know what the topic would be, and he thought there was a good possibility that he would be relieved of his command, given the political turmoil that had occurred and the failure to reach all the objectives of the mission. Regardless of what was to be discussed, "Eisenhower had decided that he owed the

President absolute candor rather than the bull too often spoon-fed to political leaders, and if Roosevelt fired him, so be it."[78]

However, Roosevelt wanted to discuss the future of France in Europe, and "the military and political developments of the preceding ten weeks." Eisenhower found Roosevelt to be upbeat and energetic, "obviously and outspokenly delighted with the progress" that had been made and optimistic about the future. Eisenhower tried to manage Roosevelt's expectations by explaining the "possibilities for reverses that the winter held for us." Roosevelt then pressed Eisenhower for a date that the enemy would be forced out of Tunisia. Eisenhower "blurted out...May 15." (This had to be his "most miraculous guess of the war," since the last enemy surrendered to Allied forces on May 13[79]).

Eisenhower set high standards for himself, which is why he may have been overly anxious about his performance to date. It certainly could have been better, but given the circumstances, he had done everything he could. Despite his concerns he had the full support of most of his superiors, including Marshall, who wasn't the type of leader to offer praise on a regular basis — McNarney told Eisenhower that based on "his daily conversations with Marshall...you have his complete confidence."[80]

After ten days, many major agreements were reached, and a final report, "The Conduct of the War in 1943," was generated. It called for offensive action against Sicily, a maximum air offensive against the German war effort, and the rapid accumulation of a massive amount of resources in Britain for a potential invasion of France in late summer 1943.

Many from the American contingent were disappointed in the resulting strategy, including Marshall and his staff from the Operations Planning Division (OPD). They favored Roundup (the Allied invasion of France) in 1943 and a suspension of alternative campaigns after removing the enemy from North Africa, while the British wanted to continue fighting in the Mediterranean. As one American participant wrote, "We came, we listened, and we were conquered."

From Eisenhower's perspective, Roundup couldn't happen until 1944 anyway, and "inaction in 1943 could not be tolerated.

One may question…the specific objective chosen…but in all such cases the pros and cons are usually rather evenly balanced and I am happy that a firm decision was reached." Eisenhower emphasized the importance of continuing to commit to Allied unity despite the differences in strategy.

"I am not so incredibly naïve that I do not realize that Britishers instinctively approach every military problem from the viewpoint of the Empire, just as we approach from the viewpoint of American interests. But one of the constant sources of danger to us in this war is the temptation to regard as our first enemy the partner that must work with us in defending the real enemy. Every man, of course, has to use his own methods in developing the idea of complete unity and coordination. The method that I have used is brutal frankness."

Eisenhower would openly challenge any nationalistic attitudes and viewpoints—stressing that the United Nations' view was the only one that mattered, and he "would ruthlessly eliminate any man who violates" his convictions on an Allied approach to solving problems. He emphasized that "I am not British and I am not ambidextrous in attitude. But I have got a very wholesome regard for the terrific tasks facing the United Nations in this war, and I am not going to let national prejudice or any of its related evils prevent me from getting the best out of the means that you fellows struggle so hard to make available to us."[81]

Besides strategy and politics, the conference also provided Allied leaders an opportunity to restructure the command system in light of the current situation and future plans. The CCS decided to make Eisenhower commander in chief of the Allied Forces Headquarters (AFHQ), with three principal subordinates: Tedder would control a single Mediterranean air force, Cunningham commanded the naval forces, and Alexander was to command all land forces, including British, American, and French troops.

Eisenhower was extremely pleased with the decision—not so much because it placed him in a key leadership position, but because it offered "complete unity of action in the central Mediterranean and it provided needed machinery for effective tactical and strategic coordination."[82] However, as Eisenhower would soon realize, some people had other incentives for creating the structure than what appeared on the surface. Not everyone was pleased with the progress of the North African campaign, especially General Sir Alan Brooke, the chief of the Imperial General Staff (CIGS).

Although Brooke was impressed with how well the Allied Forces Headquarters functioned, where "there was remarkably little friction at [AFHQ] between the staff officers of the two nations," he had little confidence in Eisenhower's ability to command the Allied force. Brooke felt that Eisenhower had "neither the tactical nor strategical experience required for such a task." With Alexander and the other British commanders now under Eisenhower, Brooke felt they were moving Eisenhower into more of a political and administrative role, which would allow Alexander to conduct the day-to-day operations of the campaign in coordination with the other British commanders.

"We were carrying out a move which could not help flattering and pleasing the Americans in so far as we were placing our senior and experienced commander...under their commander who had no war experience...We were pushing Eisenhower up into the stratosphere and rarefied atmosphere of a Supreme Commander, where he would be free to devote his time to the political and inter-allied problems, whilst we inserted under him one of our own commanders to deal with the military situations and to restore the necessary drive and coordination which had been so seriously lacking."[83]

But Brooke underestimated Eisenhower. He didn't understand the depths of Eisenhower's passion and resolve to succeed as the supreme commander, not just in title but in reality. Eisenhower's belief in the unity of command—one person responsible for all activities—was total. He was convinced it was the only way the Allies would succeed in deploying their combined resources effectively. It didn't matter to him if he was the supreme commander or if Alexander was placed in the role, just so long as there was only one leader. Now that he had received the appointment, he intended to behave and act as that one leader.

Brooke also didn't realize just how well Eisenhower had succeeded in leading the alliance so far. There was "tremendous admiration and affection for him of the British officers who had served with him, most importantly, Admiral Cunningham, a fighting sailor who was held in very high esteem."[84]

Eisenhower's resolve was tested soon after the conference. Two directives arrived from the CCS, which essentially dictated what his subordinates were to do and how they should do it. One directive discussed the organizational structure of the air command and the execution of the battle plans in Tunisia.

It stated that "the detailed organization of the command must, however, be left to the decision of the Air Commander-in-Chief," and it gave Alexander the authority to "coordinate the operations of all three armies in the Tunisia theater." The other directive involved the invasion of Sicily (known as Operation Husky), which gave Alexander the responsibility for the "detailed planning and preparation and with the execution of the actual operation when launched" and ordered him to "cooperate with Cunningham and Tedder" on the project.

When Eisenhower first read these directives, he pushed back hard, "challenging such intrusions into the organization set-up of an Allied commander. Each intrusion dulls the principle of unity of command," he wrote. But at his staff's urging, he never sent the message. Eisenhower believed that the organizational structure, communications, and planning were his responsibility as supreme commander. He didn't want Alexander to "coordinate;" he wanted him focused on engaging with the enemy at the front.

After the Casablanca conference, Marshall had warned Eisenhower that this might happen, and he had urged Eisenhower to be firm in his role as supreme commander and not let the committee system imposed at the conference undermine his authority. Eisenhower wrote to Marshall about the events and how he would approach his new position going forward. He wrote, "In each case the influence of the British tendency toward reaching down into a theater and attempting to compel an organization along the lines to which they are accustomed, is readily apparent."

In terms of the directive regarding the air command organization, Eisenhower said, "As far as I'm concerned, no attention will
be paid" to it: "It is my responsibility to organize to win battles."
He also disagreed with giving complete authority to Alexander in
the planning of Husky because "responsibility again falls directly
on me...I would consider it a definite invasion of my own proper
field if they attempted to prevent me, for example, from setting
up Alexander as a Task Force Commander for the tactical phases
of the operation."

Eisenhower didn't think "there was anything vicious or even
deliberate in the British actions; they simply reflect their own
doctrine and training just as we do ours. But when the two governments accept the principle of unified command in a particular
theater, I not only believe that they must leave him a considerable freedom in organizing his own forces as he sees fit, but that
when it becomes necessary to organize subordinate task forces,
he should be free to do it under the principle of unified command, if he so chooses."

In addition to venting his frustration, Eisenhower was letting
Marshall know that he understood what he had told him earlier
and that he would handle the situation himself. "By no means am
I proposing or suggesting that anything be done with respect to
the examples I have just quoted," he wrote. "I am merely trying
to say that I believe I have grasped your idea and that I will be
constantly on my guard to prevent any important military venture depending for its control and direction upon the 'committee'
system."[85]

This was Eisenhower's first confrontation with those who
questioned his leadership capabilities, and it certainly wouldn't
be his last. Eisenhower believed that conducting affairs by committee was unproductive and the directives telling his team what
and how to perform were misguided, but what really concerned
him was *how* it was done. If the British wanted to change the
organizational structure and process, they should have been
upfront about it rather than doing end runs.

But until told otherwise, he would see to it that he would *be*
the supreme commander, in both title and function—he had the

responsibility, and he would make sure he carried the authority. Not because he was power-hungry or egotistical, but because he believed it was the most effective way to run the organization and achieve the desired results. He knew it would be unproductive and time-consuming to directly confront the British on these disagreements. He wanted to fight the enemy, not his friends, so he tempered his anger and got to work to turn the situation around to favor his view of an effective and efficient operation.

In the coming months, he would quietly assert his leadership, and, through the power of his persuasion, personality, and hard work, he developed the mutual trust required with his subordinates to establish a functional organization that achieved results. He and his team would suffer occasional setbacks in the campaign, such as in Kasserine Pass and allowing the enemy to escape from Tunisia, but, overall, Eisenhower was successful in forming an effective command structure that led the Allies to victory in North Africa, and he established a model for organizing future campaigns in Italy and Europe.

"Pessimism never won any battle."

On December 7, 1944, as he traveled to a meeting with his commanders in Maastricht, "Eisenhower had noticed how spread out the troops in the Ardennes were, and he questioned Bradley about the vulnerability of this sector of the 12th Army Group's front, where four divisions held seventy-five miles. Bradley said he could not strengthen the Ardennes area without weakening Patton's and Hodges' offensives and that if the Germans counterattacked in the Ardennes they could be hit on either flank and stopped long before they reached the Meuse. Although he did not expect a counterattack, he had taken the precaution of not placing any supply installations of major importance in the Ardennes."[86]

Eisenhower agreed with Bradley's analysis and approach. The Allies had the entire 30th Corps and the XVIII Airborne Corps available for deployment, which included the highly competent 82nd and 101st Airborne divisions. "With the resources available to us, we were confident that any attack the Germans might launch could eventually be effectively countered. But we were under no illusions concerning the weakness of the VIII Corps line or the ability of any strong attack to make deep penetrations through it. We agreed, therefore that in the event the German advance should prove to be an all-out assault we would avoid piecemeal commitment of reserves. The temptation in such circumstances is always to hurl each individual reinforcement into the battle as rapidly as it can be brought up to the line. This was a weakness of Rommel's. In the face of a great attack, it merely assures that each reinforcing unit is overwhelmed by the strength of the advance."[87]

On December 16, 1944, the German army launched its last counteroffensive in the Ardennes, which became known as the Battle of the Bulge. The attack included three German armies, with up to twenty-four divisions engaged at any one time. Although they knew the Ardennes was vulnerable, the timing, speed, and strength of the attack had caught the Allies by surprise.

The Allies had been hammering the Nazis for the last four months, reducing their fighting capacity significantly. No one had anticipated that the enemy would be able to assemble the required resources for a major counteroffensive as soon as they did, and some still couldn't believe it, despite the penetration against the Allied forces.

Bradley thought he was facing a "spoiling attack" meant to disrupt his pending offenses. But Eisenhower immediately recognized it as a major assault and told Bradley, "I think you'd better send Middleton [whose troops were in the Ardennes] some help." Eisenhower wanted to quickly send the Ninth Army's 7th and the Third Army's 10th Armored Divisions to reinforce Middleton. Bradley knew the volatile Patton would be upset about losing his division and slowing his own offensive, and when he relayed his apprehension, Eisenhower showed he had no patience for such nonsense at this critical moment. Eisenhower told Bradley to tell Patton, "Ike is running this damn war."[88]

While they were surprised in many ways, Eisenhower and his team believed an offensive attack would eventually occur, and they had anticipated that it might occur in the Ardennes. They had a general idea of how to respond, and Eisenhower especially wanted to turn this problem into an opportunity. How he personally responded to this crisis was critical.

Eisenhower felt that "in battles of this kind it is more than ever necessary that responsible commanders exhibit the firmness, the calmness, the optimism that can pierce through the web of conflicting reports, doubts, and uncertainty and by taking advantage of every enemy weakness win through to victory. The American commanders reacted in just this fashion."[89] Even in the early hours of the German attack, Eisenhower wrote, "If things go well we should not only stop the thrust but should be able to profit from it."[90]

By the evening of December 18, Eisenhower had enough information regarding the enemy's counteroffensive and Allied capabilities that he called for a meeting with his commanders the next day in Verdun to review the situation and reach agreement on their plans going forward. Bradley still had reservations that this was an all-out counteroffensive, so prior to the meeting, Eisenhower sent a note to his team outlining his probable directives after the next day's meeting.

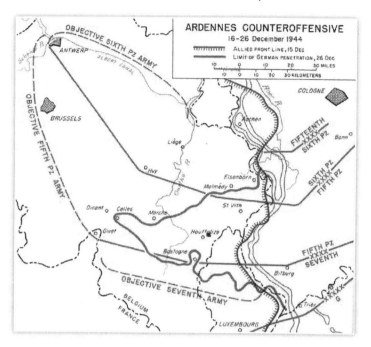

Battle of the Bulge

"The enemy is making a major thrust through the Ardennes. He still has reserves uncommitted. He may therefore use these reserves to increase the strength of this attack, or use them to launch a second attack north of Aachen." Eisenhower thought the enemy would continue to attack south of the Moselle, using all of his armored reserves, and he intended to "take immediate action to check the enemy advance" and then "launch a counter-offensive without delay."[91]

The Allies quickly realized that the defense of Bastogne was critical to stopping the enemy. Through countless and amazing heroics, the soldiers in Bastogne and elsewhere frustrated and slowed down the Germany army. However, with overcast skies, the Allies could not use their air power to counter the German offensive or provide supplies to Bastogne. The enemy continued to penetrate further into Allied territory, and there was still a small chance that they could overrun the Allies.

Despite an underlying confidence, there were many under-standably anxious people in the cold, damp room. As the meeting started, Eisenhower told his team: "The present situation is to be regarded as one of opportunity for us and not disaster. There will be only cheerful faces at this conference table." Patton broke the ice a bit by responding, "Hell, let's have the guts to let the sons of bitches go all the way to Paris. Then we'll really cut 'em up and chew 'em up." Eisenhower smiled, replying "the enemy would never be allowed to cross the Meuse."

Eisenhower and his team decided the primary principle was to take the offensive as soon as possible. "In the strategic sense," Eisenhower wrote, "we were on the offensive, but because I firmly believed that by coming out of the Siegfried [Line], the enemy had given us a great opportunity which we should seize as soon as possible."[92]

Senior American military officials of World War II.
Seated are (from left to right) Gens. William H. Simpson, George S. Patton, Carl A. Spaatz, Dwight D. Eisenhower, Omar Bradley, Courtney H. Hodges, and Leonard T. Gerow; standing are (from left to right) Gens. Ralph F. Stearley, Hoyt Vandenberg, Walter Bedell Smith, Otto P. Weyland, and Richard E. Nugent

Eisenhower wanted the Allies to close any gaps and begin attacking from both the north and south, but it didn't have to be done simultaneously. In the north, where the enemy's assault was strongest, Eisenhower told Montgomery he was willing to give up some ground, "in order to shorten our line and collect a strong reserve for the purpose of destroying the enemy in Belgium," as soon as the situation stabilized.[93]

In the south, Eisenhower wanted to initiate an attack as soon as possible. Based on previous intelligence from his staff, Patton had already developed plans to turn north if needed. Patton's troops had already suspended their offensive and had two corps headed north, where they would travel about seventy-five miles and attack within three days — an extraordinary accomplishment.

As the battle continued, it became clear that a command change was required. The Germans would soon divide the 12th Army Group, making it impossible for Bradley to communicate from his headquarters south of the bulge in Luxembourg with the US First and Ninth Armies to the north. Eisenhower's aides suggested a temporary reorganization, giving Montgomery operational control over all Allied forces north of the Ardennes. Bradley would continue to command Patton's Third Army in the south.

"Because of my faith in the soundness of teamwork that we had built up," Eisenhower wrote, "I had no hesitancy in adopting this solution."[94] However, Bradley wasn't pleased with the decision, and when Eisenhower called to communicate the change, he responded angrily. "By God, Ike, I cannot be responsible to the American people if you do this. I resign." Eisenhower, shocked and angry, took a deep breath and said "Brad, I — not you — am responsible to the American people. Your resignation therefore means absolutely nothing." Bradley continued to protest vigorously, until Eisenhower ended the debate by telling him, "Well, Brad, those are my orders."[95]

Despite the national political uproar that would inevitably emerge about moving two-thirds of Bradley's command to Montgomery (and later back again), Eisenhower knew it had to be done. He was intentionally blind to national concerns when it came to allocating resources for the greater good of the battle and the war.

While Eisenhower wouldn't let egos drive battlefield decisions, he was sensitive to the potential perception that Bradley had failed. To offset this, he asked Marshall to promote Bradley to the rank of a four-star general. "While there was undoubtedly a failure, in the current operation, to evaluate the power that the enemy could thrust through the Ardennes...all of us, without exception, were astonished at the ability of the *Volkssturm* division [Hitler's recruits of sixteen to sixty years old] to act offensively. Nevertheless Bradley has kept his head magnificently and has proceeded methodically and energetically to meet the situation. In no quarter is there a tendency to blame Bradley."[96]

Eisenhower also sent a note of encouragement to Hodges and Simpson, who would both be reporting to Montgomery with the command shift. "In the recent battling you and your army have performed in your usual magnificent style and your good work is helping create a situation from which we may profit materially." He told them it was important that "all of us look and plan ahead with calm determination, and with optimism, to taking advantage of all opportunities."[97]

While the battle continued to rage, the German offensive peaked on December 22, and the situation began to turn in favor of the Allies. Although they were surrounded and short of supplies, the Americans continued to frustrate the enemy at Bastogne, and when the Germans demanded that he surrender, General Anthony McAuliffe gave his famous answer: "Nuts!"

On December 23, the defensive stage of the battle ended as the skies finally cleared, and the Allies were able to get supply and fighter planes into the air. Eisenhower also sent the newly arrived 11th Armored Division to attack west of Bastogne and support Patton's attack from the south, which broke the encirclement. Although the Germans would continue to attack Bastogne until January 3, their counteroffensive had failed, and the Allies would soon begin to overrun Germany.

Eisenhower's leadership during the Battle of the Bulge was one of his finest moments. He didn't panic, and he continued to stress resolve and optimism that the enemy's advance would be stopped. His reaction and composure during these intense days were not missed by those he led. Tedder, one of Eisenhower's staff members, wrote, "The fact that the Hun has stuck his neck out is, from the point of view of shortening the whole business, the best thing that could happen."[98] On the fourth day of the battle, "when the situation still looked dangerous...most Allied officers were cautiously optimistic about the short-range future and eagerly anticipated the long-range possibilities. The Germans had come out of their shell," and the allied armies "would make them pay the price."[99]

As was typical for Eisenhower, he dismissed any attempt to blame his subordinates for enabling the counteroffensive. "The responsibility for maintaining only four divisions on the Ardennes front and for running the risk of a large German penetration in that area was mine," Eisenhower wrote. "At any moment from November 1st onward I could have passed to the defensive along the whole front and made our lines absolutely secure from attack while we awaited reinforcements. My basic decision was to continue the offensive to the extreme limit of our ability and it was this decision that was responsible for the startling success of the first week of the German December attack."[100]

After the war, Eisenhower gave credit where it was due—to the soldiers.

> *From the start of OVERLORD, we knew that we would win...When the Nazis' situation was hopeless, by any rational standard, they could still explode into fitful snatches of energy and deadliness. With the Russians on the east, and the Western Allies driving in from the other side, only in the frenzied mind of Hitler and those hypnotized by him could there have been the expectation of lightning strokes that would liberate Germany from our tightening, encircling armies.*
>
> *The Bulge was a dangerous episode but at Bastogne, the most publicized (but possibly not the most critical) stand in our furious defense, encircled thousands of paratroopers, hemmed in, held out and wrecked the Nazis' time schedule. On a smaller*

scale, Bastogne was repeated in scores of little places, hamlets and bridge crossings and road bends, where handfuls of men might for hours hold up a Nazi column.

Our men responded gallantly. These were the times when the grand strategy and the high hopes of high command became a soldiers' war, sheer courage, and the instinct for survival. More than the constant threat of imminent death, our men had overcome all that the unbridled elements could inflict on them in the way of snow and ice and sleet, clammy fog and freezing rain; all the pain of arduous marches and sleepless watches. They had given up their wives and children, or set aside their hope of wives and children, overcome luxuries or poverty, fought down their own inclinations to rest their tired bodies, to play it safe, to search out a hiding place.[101]

- -

"This world of ours...must avoid becoming a community of dreadful fear and hate, and be, instead, a proud confederation of mutual trust and respect."

- -

"Our civil and social rights form a central part of the heritage we are striving to defend on all fronts and with all our strength," Eisenhower said before Congress in his first State of the Union address. "I believe with all my heart that our vigilant guarding of these rights is a sacred obligation binding upon every citizen. To be true to one's own freedom is, in essence, to honor and respect the freedom of all others." In the same address, Eisenhower also promised to "use whatever authority exists in the office of the President to end segregation in the District of Columbia, including the Federal Government, and any segregation in the Armed Forces."[102]

Today, it's fairly easy to take these statements for granted, since as a nation we've made some decent progress on race relations. However, in 1953, the subject of race relations was similar to Social Security today—extremely emotional and volatile—and most politicians wouldn't touch it. Eisenhower not only raised the issue, but promised to do something about it in his first major speech as president.

There continues to be much debate about Eisenhower's leadership regarding civil rights. Many believe he didn't do enough to rally the nation through a great moral issue, that he was too sympathetic to his friends in the South who wanted segregation to continue, and that he gave mixed signals in his communications, which only caused confusion.

However, Eisenhower's results speak for themselves. By the time he left office, the armed forces and most of Washington, DC were completely integrated; he was the first president to hire an African American to an executive level in the White House (E. Frederic Morrow, administrative officer for special projects); and he prohibited racial discrimination in the federal workforce and within businesses operating under federal contracts. He was also the first president since Reconstruction to meet with African American civil rights leaders in the White House, and he consistently appointed federal judges in southern districts who were committed to equal rights.

This last action probably did more to advance the cause of civil rights than anything else in his and subsequent administrations. Eisenhower's "appointments to the Fourth and Fifth Circuit Courts of Appeal played a major role in desegregating the South in the 1950s and 1960s. The judges Eisenhower appointed implemented the Supreme Court's decision of 1954 and began to turn the promise of racial equality into a reality."

On a personal level, Eisenhower was repulsed by any form of discrimination. In high school, he and his brother forced the reinstatement of an African American football player who had been harassed and ejected from the team by the high school coach. Once, Eisenhower was about to check into a hotel when he noticed a sign that said "Negroes and Jews not welcome." He turned around and left, telling Lucius Clay: "Let's go somewhere else. I would never stay in a place like that."[103]

One of the reasons for the ongoing debate is Eisenhower's insistence on working within the boundaries of his job. He believed one couldn't legislate morality, and he didn't agree with those who believed "coercion could cure all civil rights problems." He also refused to comment on civil rights decisions by the courts, believing strongly in the separation of powers. These beliefs led Eisenhower to remain silent or to communicate in vague terms at critical times, which led some people to believe he wasn't sincere in his commitment to civil rights.[104]

But he was committed, and there's nothing vague about the results above, and two other events—his sponsorship of the first civil rights bill in eighty years and his actions at Little Rock—also prove Eisenhower's commitment to equal rights for all. As on many issues, Eisenhower had a long horizon for civil rights, which ran counter to the justified impatience of minorities. In this cause, he chose to lead behind the scenes and by example.

On May 17, 1954, the Supreme Court ruled in favor of the plaintiffs in the Brown v. Board of Education Topeka case, stating that "separate but equal" classrooms in public education violated the Fourteenth amendment, which guarantees equal protection under the law to all citizens. This historic decision set the foundation to end segregation in schools and other public facilities. When asked about the decision at a May 19 press conference, Eisenhower responded, "The Supreme Court has spoken and I am sworn to uphold the constitutional processes in this country; and I will obey."[105]

Eisenhower would not give his opinion, because he didn't believe it was his place to judge the highest court in the land—his role was to execute the laws. However, in his memoirs, he said he did agree with the decision, and he understood its importance. A few weeks after the decision, he told the White House press secretary, James Hagerty, "You know Jim, I suppose nobody knows how they feel or how many pressures or insults they have to take. I guess the only way you can realize exactly how they feel is to have a black skin for a few weeks."[106]

Agreement was one thing—how to implement the ruling was the hard part. Eisenhower believed civil rights should evolve over time. "When emotions are deeply stirred," he wrote a friend, "logic and reason must operate gradually and with consideration for human feelings or we will have a resultant disaster rather than human advancement."

But regardless of what he personally thought, he said "there must be respect for the Constitution—which means the Supreme Court's interpretation of the Constitution—or we shall have chaos. We cannot possibly imagine a successful form of government in which every individual citizen would have the right to interpret the Constitution according to his own convictions, beliefs and prejudices. Chaos would develop. This I believe with all my heart—and shall always act accordingly." So he went to work to desegregate the areas under his direct control and worked with his administration to create a civil rights bill to begin moving the country towards equality.[107]

Within days of the decision, Eisenhower met with commissioners from the District of Columbia and told them to begin desegregation throughout the Capitol, which would set an example for the rest of the country. The policy of nonsegregation was quietly put into effect in September 1954, without any hostilities, and by 1956, segregation was being voluntarily eliminated in hotels, theaters, and restaurants.

In his State of the Union address in January 1956, Eisenhower highlighted the advances in civil rights by the administration, including Washington, DC, and the progress being made to eliminate discrimination throughout the executive branch and with government contractors. He also recommended the establishment of a bipartisan commission to assess the country's current racial situation and recommend legislation.

"The stature of our leadership in the free world has increased through the past three years because we have made more progress than ever before in a similar period to assure our citizens equality in justice, in opportunity and in civil rights," Eisenhower told Congress and America. "We must expand this effort on every front. We must strive to have every person judged and measured by what he is, rather than by his color, race or religion. There will soon be recommended to the Congress a program further to advance the efforts."[108]

The further advancement would be a civil rights bill crafted by Attorney General Brownell. As the bill was being finalized, 101 members of the House and Senate signed a manifesto stating their commitment to overturn the desegregation decision. When asked about it at a news conference on March 14, 1956, Eisenhower responded, "If ever there was a time when we must be patient without being complacent, when we must be understanding of other people's deep emotions as well as our own, this is it." Eisenhower was for making progress, without getting distracted by "extremists" who would not "help this situation, and we can only believe that the good sense, the common sense, of Americans will bring this thing along."

Eisenhower's entire cabinet vetted and approved the civil rights bill drafted by Brownell. The bill had four parts, including a call for a new bipartisan civil rights commission, the creation of a civil rights division within the Department of Justice, the empowerment of the attorney general to seek injunctions against any violation of civil rights and to intercede when rights were being violated, and laws to enforce voting rights. The bill passed in the House but never got out of the Senate judiciary committee, so there wouldn't be a civil rights bill in 1956.

As Eisenhower ran for reelection, he continued to push for the civil rights bill. In his January 1957 State of Union address, Eisenhower urged Congress to enact the bill submitted in 1956. The House took the bill up in the summer of 1957, and once again it passed. This time, the bill made it to the floor of the Senate, because the majority voted to bypass the Senate judiciary committee.

Pleased that the bill could now be debated, Eisenhower issued a statement requesting that the Senate "keep the measure an effective piece of legislation to carry out" the four components of the bill, "each one of which is consistent with simple justice and equality afforded to every citizen under the Constitution of the United States. I hope that Senate action on this measure will be accomplished at this session without undue delay."[109]

But the Senate wouldn't leave the bill as submitted. Discussion began on amending the third provision (enabling the attorney general to bring civil actions against violators). Eisenhower and

Brownell were extremely disappointed. Over the next month, negotiations would go back and forth between the administration and the Senate, with refinements and additional amendments.

On August 7, the Senate passed a bill that was essentially a "gun with no bullets." The watered-down bill had one amendment, which effectively added enough bureaucracy to kill the ability to prosecute discrimination. "This week has been a depressing one," Eisenhower wrote to a friend. "I think the country took an awful beating in the second defeat that the civil rights bill took in the Senate."[110]

Eisenhower received many calls from civil rights leaders and others urging him to veto the "phony" bill, and he considered doing so. But Eisenhower and his team began to work with the Senate leaders to give some teeth to the bill, and, by late August, they had a compromise that all parties could sign. It included the civil rights commission, the creation of a civil rights division in the Department of Justice, extended the jurisdiction of district courts to include civil rights violations, enabled the attorney general to seek injunctions when an individual's right to vote had been violated, and allowed district courts to determine when contempt cases required a jury.

It wasn't everything that Eisenhower and Brownell wanted, but it was a start. Eisenhower signed the bill into law on September 9, 1957, and the country had its first civil rights act in eighty-two years. Within two months, Eisenhower established the Civil Rights Commission, and, in the subsequent years of his administration, more than one hundred cases would be brought to court, and more than four thousand complaints of civil rights violations would be investigated.

"Only Americans can hurt America."

Eisenhower didn't have much time to reflect on events. On September 4, Orval Faubus, the governor of Arkansas, defied the court order for desegregation and called out the National Guard to prevent nine students from entering Central High School in Little Rock. The governor said the troops were required to maintain order, and peace would prevail only if the schools operated in the same manner as before the court order.

The next day several African American students were turned away, which Eisenhower believed was a direct and flagrant defiance of a federal court order. On September 9, an injunction against the governor's use of the National Guard was requested by the US Department of Justice, and a hearing was set for September 20.

On September 11, Faubus requested a meeting with Eisenhower in Rhode Island to defuse the crisis, and Eisenhower agreed, although Brownell warned nothing would come of it. On September 14, Eisenhower met with Faubus for about twenty minutes. Faubus kept repeating his insistence that he was a loyal citizen and that he respected federal law and the courts.

Eisenhower suggested that Faubus not withdraw the troops when he returned home, and instead have them maintain peace as the African American students attended Central High. Eisenhower stressed that if Faubus acted quickly enough, he could avoid going to court. "In any area where the federal government has assumed jurisdiction and this is upheld by the Supreme Court," Eisenhower warned Faubus, "there can only be one outcome: the state will lose."[111]

After the meeting Eisenhower issued a statement, approved by Faubus, indicating "the Governor stated his intention to respect the decisions of the United States District Court and to give his full cooperation in carrying out his responsibilities in respect to these decisions." Eisenhower had every reason to believe Faubus would take his advice and allow the students to enter school under the protection of the National Guard.[112]

Faubus returned home and did nothing. The troops stayed in place, under the same orders. Faubus had failed to keep his word to the president, which escalated tensions on both sides. On September 20, the injunction against the governor's use of troops was granted, and Faubus withdrew the troops, replacing them with local police.

By now, hundreds of angry parents of white students were congregating at the high school. On September 23, the police were able to get the nine students into school through a side door, unseen. When the mob learned that the students were inside, they erupted in a riot. As the protests grew, the outnumbered police escorted the nine students out of the building to the jeers and racial slurs of the mob.

Eisenhower called the situation at the school "disgraceful" and made it very clear that "federal law and orders...cannot be flouted with impunity by any individual or any mob of extremists." He said he hoped that common sense would prevail, but he was ready to use "the full power of the United States including whatever force may be necessary to prevent any obstruction of the law and to carry out the orders of the Federal Court."[113]

The next day, the mob swarmed the streets again. Eisenhower didn't expect the situation to improve and was reviewing his options for intervention when an urgent request to send troops arrived from the mayor of Little Rock, Woodrow Wilson Mann. Eisenhower immediately federalized the Arkansas National Guard and ordered the deployment of the 101st Airborne Division, and, by that afternoon, five hundred paratroopers arrived in Little Rock, with another five hundred arriving the next day. The following day, the nine students entered the school under the protection of the US Army, and Eisenhower went on national television to address the American people.

"As you know, the Supreme Court of the United States has decided that separate public educational facilities for the races are inherently unequal and therefore compulsory school segregation laws are unconstitutional," Eisenhower said as he sat in his White House office. "Our personal opinions about the decision have no bearing on the matter of enforcement; the responsibility and authority of the Supreme Court to interpret the Constitution are very clear."

Eisenhower noted that many public schools were aligned with the court order and were becoming integrated without any violence, proving "to the world that we are a nation in which laws, not men, are supreme." However, in Little Rock at Central High, "the cornerstone of our liberties was not observed," so it was his responsibility to enforce the laws. "The very basis of our individual rights and freedoms rests upon the certainty that the President and the Executive Branch of Government will support and insure the carrying out of the decisions of the Federal Courts, even, when necessary with all the means at the President's command. Unless the President did so, anarchy would result."

Eisenhower emphasized that the troops were not there for any reason other than "to enforce the orders of a Federal Court," which is only done in "extraordinary and compelling circumstances," such as the "extreme situation...in Little Rock." Eisenhower said he knew that the majority of people across the country were repulsed by the extremists and mob rule and realized "a foundation of our American way of life is our national respect for law."[114]

Throughout the fall the nine students attended classes, although they continued to be harassed both verbally and physically. By Thanksgiving, the 101st Airborne turned protection over to the National Guard, and by the end of the school year, the National Guard stood down. Meanwhile, Eisenhower's actions resulted in loud protests from all sides. At home, opponents questioned his judgment and his motives. Abroad, the Soviets used the event to point to racial terror in the United States.

Prior to the crisis, Eisenhower had said he couldn't imagine a situation where he'd have to send in troops to enforce federal laws, because the common sense of Americans would prevail. But emotions in Little Rock blinded people to common sense, and while Eisenhower had a deep respect for the Constitution and the rule of law, not everyone was so committed. Some people believe Eisenhower's comment on the deployment of troops may have exacerbated the situation in Little Rock, giving Faubus the impression that Eisenhower would never use force against him.

But Eisenhower never backed away from his responsibilities, regardless of the circumstances. Faubus and others underestimated Eisenhower's resolve and his willingness to do whatever was necessary to stop the obstruction of justice, even though he had told them he would do so. Eisenhower thought the whole affair was tragic and unnecessary, but he had no regrets for his actions. "If the day comes when we can obey the orders of our courts only when we personally approve of them," he wrote to a friend after the crisis, "the end of the American system, as we know it, will not be far off."[115]

"We cannot subscribe to one law for the weak, another law for the strong."

Adaptive leadership sometimes means having difficult confrontations with friends and allies. People will not agree to everything all the time. Taking a stand based on principles and beliefs is more important than maintaining a relationship under false pretenses, and if the friendship is strong enough, it will survive any crisis that happens to surface.

For three weeks beginning October 20, 1956, Eisenhower and his administration were tested with a number of challenges, all happening at once. Poland was resisting pressure from Khrushchev to keep a Russian marshal in its ministry of defense, freedom fighters were stirring in Hungary, the presidential election was in full swing, and the United States found itself in the unusual position of defending Egypt against three of its major allies — Israel, Britain, and France. With this last crisis, Eisenhower's leadership and guidance were needed once again to prevent events from spinning out of control toward a superpower conflict.

In December 1955, the United States joined with the World Bank and the United Kingdom in an agreement to provide financial assistance to Egypt to build the Aswan Dam, which was actually the common name for two dams on the Nile River in Aswan, Egypt. However, during the first six months of 1956, it became apparent that Egypt could not provide the appropriate resources for the project to succeed, and many issues involving the water rights of the surrounding states remained unresolved.

So on July 19, 1956, Foster Dulles informed the Egyptian ambassador of the United States' decision to withdraw from the project, although they did leave the door open for a future engagement if the issues were resolved. In hindsight, Eisenhower wondered if the exit from the agreement was a bit undiplomatic, but Dulles defended the approach, indicating that the Egyptians could not possibly be surprised by the decision.

Surprised or not, when Egypt's president Gamal Nasser received the news, he went into a rage, conducting a three-hour public speech aggressively attacking the United States. On July 26, 1956, Nasser announced the nationalization of all Suez Canal properties and assets, claiming the revenues would help to pay for the Aswan Dam. Nasser imposed military law in the Canal Zone, and he forced all canal employees, including foreigners, to stay on the job, threatening long-term prison sentences to anyone who tried to leave their job.

"The fat was now really in the fire," Eisenhower wrote. Western Europe depended heavily on oil and other goods coming through the canal, and it would be seriously crippled if the waterway was shut down. France and Britain were especially concerned about the seizure. Britain owned forty-four percent of the Suez Canal Company, but beyond the economic impact, both countries "considered the Suez as something of a symbol...of their position in the entire Middle East and Arab world."[116]

Britain and France wanted immediate discussions with the United States to consider how to respond. UK Prime Minister Anthony Eden said that Britain "must be ready, in the last resort, to use force to bring Nasser to his senses."[117] French Premier Guy Mollet was even more distressed. He wanted aggressive action to prevent the situation from deteriorating and to show a united front, in part to prevent any increase in Soviet influence in the region.

Eisenhower appreciated their candor but urged restraint. "Utmost calm is required in charting the course of the Western nations at this time," Eisenhower wrote to Eden. "I am convinced that the Western nations must show the world that every effective peaceful means to resolve this difficulty has been exhausted and I sincerely hope that precipitate action can be avoided."

Nevertheless, Eden gave orders to his military to begin mobilization for a potential conflict.[118]

Eisenhower sent Dulles to London to meet with France and Britain to find a solution. The talks ended with a proposal to conduct a twenty-four-nation conference to reach agreement on international control of the Suez Canal, while respecting Egypt's sovereignty and its right to a greater financial return for the use of the waterway. Although Egypt decided not to attend, the results of the conference on August 16, 1956, were promising.

While the conference events looked encouraging, Eisenhower began to question the sincerity of the British and French commitment to the Suez proposal. For example, just as a conference team was on its way to present the proposal to Nasser, the British and French ordered the evacuation of their citizens from Egypt, Jordan, Syria, and Lebanon, and the mobilization of their troops near the Middle East continued.

The British believed Nasser's actions were the first part of an elaborate plan with Russia to expand its power in Middle East and restrict the flow of oil and other goods to the West. Eden told Eisenhower that if the talks in Egypt weren't successful, "then it seems to us that our duty is plain. We have many times led Europe in the fight for freedom. It would be an ignoble end to our long history if we tamely accepted to perish by degrees."[119]

Eisenhower didn't agree, and he continued to call for restraint. He believed the fears about the loss of oil were exaggerated, and that the British and French had decided to get tough about the wrong issue. "To choose a situation in which Nasser had legal and sovereign rights and in which world opinion was largely on his side, was not in my opinion a good one on which to make a stand."[120]

Nasser was noncommittal on the proposal. He promised to keep the canal operating but wouldn't agree to international control of the canal. It was clear to everyone that Nasser was essentially rejecting the proposal. Britain and France decided to take the matter to the United Nations, asking them to conduct a study on Egypt's actions to end international control of the canal.

Egypt also filed a motion, asking the Security Council to help stop the aggressive behavior of Britain and France. Eisenhower welcomed these UN proposals, because at least both sides were seeking some kind of diplomatic solution. However, as the weeks went on, an ominous silence took hold between the United States, France, and Britain.

The Suez was not the only Middle Eastern issue Eisenhower had to contend with. Israel and Jordan were involved in frequent border skirmishes. Jordan's government was somewhat unstable, and Israel seemed intent on destabilizing it further and maybe capturing some additional land in the process.

On October 15, Dulles informed Eisenhower that the Jordan-Israel situation was deteriorating. France had recently provided Israel with sixty fighter planes, not the twelve that France had previously reported to the United States, which went against the 1950 Tripartite Agreement (where Britain, France, and the United States agreed to exchange information regarding military aid and force used to protect the Middle East borders as they existed in 1950).

"Obviously a blackout of communications had been imposed," Eisenhower wrote in his memoirs. "From about this time on, we had the uneasy feeling that we were cut off from our allies."[121] Adding to the tension, Jordan, Egypt, and Syria signed an agreement of military cooperation in the event of war with Israel.

Eisenhower suspected that Israel's Prime Minister Ben-Gurion was considering military action because of the upcoming US elections. But Eisenhower would never put votes above principles. "Ben-Gurion should not make any grave mistakes based upon his belief that winning a domestic election is as important to us as preserving and protecting the interests of the United Nations and other nations of the free world in that region."

Eisenhower told Dulles to "make very clear to the Israelis that they must stop these attacks against the borders of Jordan." Continued aggression would probably lead to a condemnation against Israel by the United Nations, which would give Russia an excuse to get involved, "the ultimate effect of which would be to Sovietize the whole region."[122] Putting the pieces together,

Eisenhower believed Israel was planning to attack Jordan, and France and Britain would use the instability as an excuse to seize control of the canal.

On October 28, Eisenhower learned that Israel had called for a general mobilization of its troops. Eisenhower sent messages publicly and privately to Ben-Gurion, urging him "to do nothing which would endanger the peace." Ben-Gurion responded that Nasser had joined alliances that circled Israel, and that he would be remiss if he didn't take action to protect Israel from destruction by its Arab neighbors.[123]

Eisenhower was puzzled and troubled by the entire Middle East situation, and he believed that a great mistake was about to be made. "I just can't figure out what the Israelis think they're up to...Maybe they're thinking they just can't survive without more land.... But I don't see how they can survive without coming to some honorable and peaceful terms with the whole Arab world that surrounds them."

Eisenhower became even more animated when discussing French and British behavior. "Damn it, the French, they're just egging the Israelis on—hoping somehow to get out of their own North African troubles," and he just couldn't believe the British "would be so stupid as to invite on themselves all the Arab hostility to Israel." Were the British actually "going to *dare* us—dare *us*—to defend the Tripartite declaration?"[124]

On October 29, an Israeli attack finally occurred, not against Jordan as everyone had suspected, but against Egypt. Eisenhower got the news in the late afternoon as he was on his way to Richmond for a campaign stop. By 7:00 p.m., he was back in the White House with his advisors. Some thought this was just another border skirmish; others thought Israel would quickly take over the canal and bring an end to the turmoil.

Dulles disagreed with all of them. "It is far more serious than that," he told the group. "The Canal is likely to be disrupted, and the oil pipelines through the Middle East broken. If these things happen, we must expect British and French intervention. In fact, they appear to be ready for it and may even have concerted their action with the Israelis."[125]

Everything was becoming clear. The lack of communication from Britain and France, the clandestine arms deal between France and Israel, and the needless escalation of tensions. Britain, France, and Israel had hatched a bizarre plot to justify armed intervention in the Middle East and taking back the Suez Canal, and they probably counted on the support from an old ally—the United States.

"I have one yardstick by which I test every major problem — and that yardstick is: Is it good for America?"

But they were badly mistaken. From the beginning, Eisenhower was determined to make sure this plan would not succeed. He didn't like to be surprised, he certainly didn't like to be lied to, but he was especially incensed about being double-crossed. As much as it pained Eisenhower to go against allies and friends, especially the British, he was not about to back down from an established agreement and what he considered the right thing to do.

In the 1950 Tripartite Agreement, the United States had pledged to support the victim of any aggression in the Middle East. "We cannot be bound by our traditional alliances, but must make good on our pledge," Eisenhower told his team. It was the only honorable thing to do. He didn't care if he got reelected or not. If the American people didn't want him in office, so be it. Eisenhower told his team to submit a resolution to the United Nations first thing in the morning, asking for an immediate end to the use of force in the Middle East. He was going to make it clear to the world that in this dispute, the United States would be on Egypt's side.[126]

On October 30, Eisenhower sent a note to Eden. "Without bothering here to discuss the military movements themselves and their possible grave consequences, I should like to ask your help in clearing up my understanding as to exactly what is happening between us and our European allies—especially between us, the French and yourselves," Eisenhower wrote his old friend. The United States was taken by surprise by the amount of equipment provided to Israel by the French, and the escalation of hostilities—potential and real—could lead to Egypt and the rest of the Arab world to turn to the Russians.

The current state of affairs "with its possible consequences, including the possible involvement of you and the French in a general Arab war, seems to me to leave your government and ours in a very sad state of confusion, so far as any possibility of unified understanding and action are concerned...for we may shortly find ourselves not only at odds concerning what we should do, but confronted with a de facto situation that would make all our present troubles look puny indeed." Eden responded that Egypt had brought this on itself, and Israel was justified in its actions, since decisive action was needed to stop the violence.[127]

At the United Nations, the US resolution was vetoed by the British and French but supported by the Soviet Union. Britain and France then issued a twelve-hour ultimatum that unless Egypt and Israel withdrew from the vicinity of the Suez, Britain and France would intervene and take control of the canal. Israel agreed at once, since it had already captured most of the Sinai, but Egypt remained silent. Eisenhower's plea to withdraw the ultimatum fell on deaf ears.

Believing the United Nations held the most promise to defuse the situation, Eisenhower had his team prepare another resolution. This one called for an immediate cease-fire between Israel and Egypt, for Israel to pull back to its original borders, and for all UN members to refrain from the use of force. It also called for the withholding of all military, economic, and financial aid to Israel until it complied with the resolution.

When it was announced that the United States would submit the resolution, the response was overwhelmingly positive. Many countries just couldn't believe the United States would go against its allies to support a third-world country, or that the United States would side with Egypt against Israel. Small countries around the world were amazed and thrilled. It was a shining moment for the United States and Eisenhower. Privately, Eisenhower said, "It is hard for me to see any good final result emerging from a scheme that seems to antagonize the entire Muslim world."[128]

But despite Eisenhower's warnings, plus the UN resolutions and the weight of world opinion, Eden gave the order to attack. Britain and France conducted bombing runs over Cairo, Alexandria, and other Egyptian cities, destroying airfields, ports, railways, and other infrastructure. While resistance was light, the Egyptians quickly sent thirty-three ships, some loaded with cement and rocks, to the bottom of the Suez Canal. The canal was now blocked.

That night, Eisenhower spoke to the American people. "The United States was not consulted in any way about any phase of these actions. Nor were we informed of them in advance. As it is the manifest right of any of these nations to take such decisions and actions, it is likewise our right — if our judgment so dictates — to dissent. We believe these actions to have been taken in error. For we do not accept the use of force as a wise or proper instrument for the settlement of international disputes...The peace we seek and need means much more than mere absence of war. It means the acceptance of law, and the fostering of justice, in all the world."[129]

The next day Eisenhower met with his NSC team. He didn't want to give the Soviets an opportunity to seize a leadership position in the Middle East with a resolution of their own, so he told Dulles to issue a statement about the sanctions against Israel and to go forward with the UN cease-fire resolution. He then left for his last campaign trip before the election.

"We cannot and we will not condone armed aggression — no matter who the attacker, and no matter who the victim," Eisenhower told his Philadelphia audience. "We cannot subscribe to one law for the weak, another law for the strong; one law for those opposing us, another for those allied with us. There can be only one law — or there will be no peace. We do not speak — let me emphasize — in any angry spirit of self-righteousness. We value — deeply and lastingly — the bonds with those great nations, those great friends, with whom we now so plainly disagree. And I, for one, am confident that those bonds will do more than survive.

They can, they must—grow to new and greater strength. But this we know above all: there are some firm principles that cannot bend—they can only break. And we shall not break ours."[130]

As he usually did during difficult times, Eisenhower expressed his thoughts and feelings in writing, this time to his friend Al Gruenther. "Life gets more difficult by the minute. I really could use a good bridge game...sleep has been a little slower to come than usual. I seem to go to bed later and wake up earlier—which bores me. I am not going to bore you with reciting all of our Mid East troubles...Strangely enough, I have seen some of my old British friends in the last few days and most of them are truly bitter about the action taken by their Government.... One man said, 'This is nothing except Eden trying to be bigger than he is.' I do not dismiss it that lightly. I believe that Eden and his associates have become convinced that this is the last straw and Britain simply *had* to react in the manner of the Victorian period. If one has to have a fight, then that is that. But I don't see the point in getting into a fight to which there can be no satisfactory end, and in which the whole world believes you are playing the part of the bully and you do not even have the firm backing of your entire people."[131]

Meanwhile, the United Nations had approved the US cease-fire resolution, and Canada introduced a proposal for a United Nations police force to help move toward a peaceful solution. While the Egyptian air force had been destroyed, and Israel had captured the Sinai and the Gaza strip, there was still a chance to avoid a British and French troop invasion. But Eden rejected the cease-fire proposal and another appeal from Eisenhower to not invade. "If we draw back now," Eden wrote to Eisenhower, "everything will go up in flames in the Middle East...We cannot have a military vacuum while a UN force is being constituted."[132]

The chaos continued the next day, November 5, 1956, the day before the presidential election. At 8:00 am, eleven hundred British and French paratroopers surrounded Port Said on the Suez Canal, and more troops continued to land throughout the day. By that evening, the Egyptian commander at the port had surrendered.

The Russians, who were feeling the heat of world opinion as they suppressed the Hungarian freedom fighters, had been quiet about the Middle East crisis, but they now sent messages to Britain, France, and Israel that Russia "was prepared to use force to crush the aggressors and restore the peace." Nikolai Bulganin, the Russian chairman of the Council of Ministers, wrote to Eisenhower suggesting that Russia and the United States join forces to stop the fighting. "If this war is not stopped," he told Eisenhower, "it is fraught with danger and can grow into a World War Three."[133]

Eisenhower pulled his team together to respond to Bulganin's note. While the mood was somber, Eisenhower was poised and relaxed. They immediately dismissed any notion of joining forces with the Soviets for military intervention in the Middle East. As mad as they were against their allies, they weren't about to align with the Soviets and viewed their rhetoric as a diversion from their own troubles.

They worried that the Soviets might become aggressive out of both hope and fear—hope that the Middle East crisis would divide the West and fear that the Hungarian crisis would spread throughout Eastern Europe. The Russian leaders "are both furious and scared...and might be ready for any wild adventure," Eisenhower told his team.

"Just as with Hitler, that makes for the most dangerous possible state of mind. And we better be damn sure that every intelligence point and every outpost of our Armed Forces is absolutely right on their toes." Eisenhower knew the Soviet reference to "World War Three" was a not-so-subtle threat to use nuclear weapons, especially if they thought they would lose control of Eastern Europe.

"You know," Eisenhower said calmly, "we may be dealing here with the opening gambit of an ultimatum. We have to be positive and clear in our every word, every step. And if those fellows start something, we may have to hit 'em and if necessary, with everything in the bucket." Eisenhower directed his team to issue a warning that if the Russians entered the conflict, the United States would respond with "effective countermeasures."[134]

The next day was November 6 — Election Day. As he arrived at his office, Eisenhower learned that the Soviets told Egypt that they would "do something" in the Middle East. Eisenhower told his team to be alert to Soviet intentions and directed U-2 flights over Syria to determine what the Soviets were up to. "If the Soviets should attack Britain or France directly," he said, "we would of course be in a major war." Eisenhower asked if American forces in the Middle East were equipped with atomic antisubmarine weapons, and he wanted the US military to mobilize "by degrees, in order to avoid creating a stir."[135]

But just as it seemed as if the world was on the brink of a catastrophe, events shifted. As he left the White House to vote, Eisenhower received word that there were no Soviet planes either in the Middle East or on the way there. Then there was word that the British government had ordered a cease-fire. Israel had also stopped fighting.

Eisenhower called Eden to tell him how pleased he was with the cease-fire decision. Eden wanted to know if American troops would be part of the peacekeeping force, but Eisenhower told him he didn't want any of the large nations to provide troops — it would only provide an opportunity for the Soviets to be in the Middle East and cause trouble. Eden asked how the election was going. "I don't give a damn about the election," Eisenhower told him.[136]

By that evening, it was clear that Eisenhower had won the election by a landslide. Despite his earlier indifference, Eisenhower was fiercely competitive, and he confessed he wanted to win as many states as possible. "When I get into battle, I just want to win the whole thing," he told Hughes. The next day the fighting ended in the Middle East. By the end of November, UN forces were moving into place and British and French troops were leaving — they would be completely out by Christmas — and the cleanup of the canal would begin. After initially refusing to withdraw from Egypt — which prompted a strong protest from Eisenhower to Ben-Gurion — Israel announced it would leave Egypt as soon as the UN forces were in place.[137]

Eisenhower had once again led the nation through a major crisis. He insisted on aligning with those who were right, regardless of past alliances or political consequences. The western alliances, while battered, held together. In the court of world opinion, the United States held the moral high ground and was viewed favorably for the first time since the end of World War II.

Eisenhower would use every diplomatic maneuver in his playbook to avoid a conflict, but he also made it clear the United States would respond, with frightening power, if required. Eisenhower wanted to take advantage of the aftermath and the fear of nuclear war to make progress on disarmament, but the Soviets would have none of it. Once again an opportunity was lost, but Eisenhower would continue to seek peace.

INNOVATION

"Rigidity inevitably defeats itself."

Today, in a world where the pace of change is accelerating, the ability to innovate and rapidly outmaneuver competitors on a consistent basis may be the most critical skill a leader can bring to an organization. Most successful leaders aren't satisfied with the status quo, because they know organizations that stand still will eventually get run over, and there is always room for improvement in any operation.

Ever since George Washington's victory at Trenton, the American military has favored strategies and tactics that emphasize offensive maneuvers. George Patton thought fixed defensive positions were so pointless he called them "monuments to man's stupidity."[138] Eisenhower wanted offensive plans that were simple, surprising (to the enemy), and strong, with a concentration of all available power to achieve the desired objective. But there were two other keys to success.

One was flexibility. Eisenhower believed there were three phases to a flexible battle plan: the minimum objectives to be achieved to avoid failure, the objectives of reasonable expecta-tions, and, lastly "the realm of hope—all that might happen" if everything went well. "These phases of a plan do not comprise rigid instructions, they are merely guideposts," Eisenhower wrote in his memoir.

"A sound battle plan provides flexibility...to meet the con-stantly changing factors of the battle problem in such a way as to achieve the final goal of commander. Rigidity inevitably defeats itself, and the analysts who point to a changed detail as evidence of a plan's weakness are completely unaware of the characteris-tics of the battlefield."[139]

The other key was fast execution. "Speed of movement often enables troops to minimize any advantage the enemy may tem-porarily gain but, more important, speed makes possible the full exploitation of every favorable opportunity and prevents the enemy from re-adjusting his forces to meet successive attack," Eisenhower continued.

"Through speed and determination each successive advantage is more easily and economically gained than the previous one. Continuation of the process finally results in the demoralization of the enemy. Relentless and speedy pursuit is the most profitable action in war. Long periods of inaction for regrouping are justi-fied only by sheer necessity. Speed requires training, fitness, con-fidence, morale, suitable transport, and skillful leadership."[140]

While Eisenhower and his staff developed detailed battle plans, he remained flexible in responding to situations as they developed and encouraged his generals to do the same. He wanted rapid exploitation of any opportunities or enemy weaknesses. "One of the most important characteristics of the successful officer today is his ability to continue changing his methods, almost even his mental processes, in order to keep abreast of the constant change that modern science...brings to the battlefield."[141]

In August 1944, the Allies were finally able to break out of the Cotentin Peninsula in France between Mortain and Avranches, unleash Patton's Third Army to secure the ports of Brittany, and move southward to destroy as much of the enemy's Seventh Army as possible before securing the Seine. However, "Hitler saw an opportunity to reverse the situation, cut Patton off, recapture the Cotentin ports, and possibly even drive the Allies back into the sea by counterattacking and moving out to Mortain and then the coast. If successful, the attack would isolate Patton."[142] Hitler ordered his commander Günther von Kluge to attack at Mortain and to not retreat under any circumstances. The US First Army's 30th infantry division was hit hard by the counteroffensive, and despite having some of its forces surrounded, it continued to hold its position.

Eisenhower had just arrived to assume command of the ground forces the day before the counteroffensive. With the enemy attacking directly westward toward Mortain, Eisenhower was at Bradley's headquarters and had an idea that would bring a devastating blow to the enemy. Patton's army was continuing southward toward the Seine. Rather than continue that path as originally planned, Eisenhower suggested that Patton's easternmost army under Haislip, which was nearing Le Mans, turn north. If Haislip could move fast enough, the Allies might be able to encircle the German forces at Falaise. Bradley had also seen the opportunity, and he and Eisenhower worked together through the pros and cons of the plan.

The biggest decision was how many divisions to leave defending Mortain. Leave too many, and the encirclement may not succeed. Leave too few, and von Kluge may be able to overrun the Allies and cut off Patton. This risk was substantial — if the enemy were able to reach Avranches, it would mean that Patton would have to backtrack to reopen the peninsula, and it would be seen as an Allied defeat.

But when Eisenhower noted he could still supply Patton through airlifts, Bradley "unhesitatingly determined to retain only minimum forces at Mortain, and to rush the other [armies] on south and east to begin envelopment of the German spearheads."[143] Bradley called Montgomery to explain the plan. Montgomery had some concern about the battle raging at Mortain, but after Eisenhower agreed to take full responsibility for any failures, he agreed and gave Bradley the go-ahead to execute the plan.

Within nine days, the encirclement of the Falaise Gap was completed — one of the major turning points of the war. By the time von Kluge realized what the Allies were up to, it was too late. He lost a significant amount of men and resources, and the Nazis would never really recover. The events leading to this major victory illustrates the ability of Eisenhower and his generals to respond rapidly to battlefield realities, think creatively, and outmaneuver an overextended enemy. The change to established plans was done quickly and informally, on the battlefield, without consulting the CCS.

The flexibility and ease in Eisenhower's leadership style comes from knowing your competition and knowing your team and its capabilities. Had Eisenhower adhered to the original plan, or took the conservative course and ordered a defensive stand at Mortain, one of the great victories of the war would have been lost. The Nazis would never think of acting independently — all orders came from Hitler. Eisenhower could never operate like that. He had to have the authority and flexibility to change and execute plans as needed.

"I instinctively dislike ever to uphold the conservative as opposed to the bold."

Many soldiers returned from World War II with scenes of devastation and destruction etched in their minds. The relentless battles and bombings had left Europe in rubble, which would take years to repair. Eisenhower was one of these soldiers. He didn't think war settled anything, and it left nothing but death and ruin in its wake. As the soldiers came home, many of them had a deep desire to create and build rather than destroy, in order to make life better for themselves and others. This led to a post-World War II demographic boom, which resulted in a surge in building — everything from housing, to cars, to corporations.

One of Eisenhower's major accomplishments during his presidency was his sponsorship and oversight of the Federal-Aid

Highway Act, commonly known as the Interstate Highway System. Eisenhower's interest in a modern highway system dates to a cross-country convoy trip he took in 1919. And during World War II, Eisenhower had also "seen the superlative system of the German Autobahn—national highways crossing that country and offering the possibility, often lacking in the United States, to drive with speed and safety at the same time." He thought the United States "was behind in highway construction," and by the mid-1950s, he did "not want us to fall still further behind."[144]

As president, Eisenhower championed the effort. In May 1954, he signed a bill to spend close to $2 billion over two years to begin modernizing America's highway system. On signing the bill, Eisenhower said, "I am very gratified that this important measure has now become law. I am especially glad that the scope and pace of our efforts to make up our highway deficiencies will be considerably increased. In recent years the nation has accumulated tremendous highway needs, which are becoming increasingly acute. Our highways badly need modernization and expansion to accommodate today's vastly increased motor traffic. Large-scale improvement is needed simply to remedy deficiencies not met in the past."[145]

Meanwhile, Eisenhower was thinking bolder. Just a few days after signing the first bill, Eisenhower asked his chief of staff Sherman Adams, "Where do we stand on our 'dramatic' plan to get $50 billion worth of...highways under construction?"[146] To move the effort forward, Eisenhower asked General Lucius Clay to lead a presidential commission to prepare a report to plan, fund, and execute the building of the interstate road system.

Eisenhower sent the report to Congress in February 1955, with a message: "Our unity as a nation is sustained by free communication of thought and by easy transportation of people and goods. The ceaseless flow of information throughout the Republic is matched by individual and commercial movement over a vast system of interconnected highways criss-crossing the Country and joining at our national borders with friendly neighbors to the north and south."

Eisenhower stressed the urgency to act. Thousands of accidents were occurring due to unsafe roads; the poor road conditions were adding to the cost of owning an automobile; in cases of emergencies, roads must enable rapid evacuation; and economic and population growth meant more people on the road. He stressed the interstate system needed to be a "top priority in construction planning."

The cost would be $101 billion over ten years, with 30 percent paid by the federal government and the rest paid by state and local units. The federal portion would be paid by issuing bonds, along with gas taxes and tolls. Eisenhower concluded that he hoped the report would "generate recognition of the urgency that presses upon us; approval of a general program that will give us a modern safe highway system; realization of the rewards for prompt and comprehensive action. They provide a solid foundation for a sound program."[147]

Based on the report, a highway bill was passed in the Senate, but failed in the House, primarily because of disagreements over the issuance of $20 billion worth of bonds. More than a year went by, and Eisenhower had grown tired over the financing debate. He wanted the job done. Finally, in June 1956, based on financing from various transportation taxes, the Federal Aid Highway Act was approved with strong bipartisan support. Eisenhower was thrilled.

Eisenhower and the interstate highway signage

Work could now begin on "the forty-one thousand-mile network of roads linking nearly all major cities with a population of fifty thousand or more." Over the next few decades, highways of up to fourteen lanes would be built, with enough concrete to "build eighty Hoover Dams or six sidewalks to the moon...bulldozers and shovels would move enough dirt and rock to bury Connecticut two feet deep." The positive impact on the American economy, including jobs created in construction, manufacturing, and transportation were incalculable.[148]

Today, the construction of the interstate highway system continues, and as of 2010, consists of 47,182 miles of road, serving almost all major cities.[149] It's the largest and greatest public works project ever, changing the American landscape and its society, enabling the expansion of the middle class through mobility and commerce. Taken for granted by many of us today, it was Eisenhower's enthusiastic sponsorship and leadership that made the large network of consistent highways a reality. It was his favorite piece of legislation. As Joel Garreau aptly put it, "Dwight D. Eisenhower changed America forever with the creation of the interstate highway program."[150]

- -

"The world moves, and ideas that were once good are not always good."

- -

Life was good for most Americans in the 1950s. The economy was booming after World War II, American science and industry was thriving and respected throughout the world, and most Americans felt safe and secure with Eisenhower in the White House. He continued to maintain the peace and manage the economy, and he was extremely intelligent and knowledgeable about world affairs.

Even those who didn't agree with Eisenhower would admit that he inspired trust and confidence, and when the inevitable crisis did occur (such as the Suez Canal or in Little Rock), most people were relieved that Eisenhower was president, leading the way to a solution. This was generally the climate throughout the Eisenhower years. Then, on October 4, 1957, everything changed.

On that night, Russia launched Sputnik, a twenty-three-inch orb, into space, which did nothing except coast and beep. It was powered by a battery that would die in three weeks, and after three months, it was pulled into Earth's atmosphere and disintegrated. However, the impact of this first successful satellite launch by the Soviet Union was significant.

Americans wanted and expected to be first in everything. That the Russians could achieve this feat before the United States initiated a severe crisis in confidence throughout much of the American public. The idea that the Russians could control the skies caused much fear and uncertainty. The stock market dropped 10 percent, and it led people to second-guess the direction the country was heading in under Eisenhower's leadership.

But Eisenhower was neither surprised nor worried about Sputnik. The real danger to him was a surprise nuclear attack on America. Having lived through Pearl Harbor, Eisenhower was determined to do everything possible to prevent a nuclear war, which he believed would destroy the planet. To avoid such a conflict, Eisenhower needed information about what the Russians were doing, and to get it, he had authorized U-2 surveillance flights over the Soviet Union.

A recent CIA report had warned Eisenhower that the Russians were probably capable of launching a satellite in the near future. Eisenhower believed that while the successful launch of Sputnik was an impressive scientific achievement, in the long run, it would be a minor success. Because of the secret intelligence he was receiving, he knew that Russia was not as big a threat that the rest of the world thought. However, since the rest of the world didn't have the information Eisenhower did, they thought he was out of touch.

While Eisenhower wasn't surprised by the Russians' achievement, he was stunned by the intensity of the public reaction. Many were worried that the country's defense and educational systems were inadequate. Suddenly, Eisenhower was being pressed to increase spending in every kind of military, scientific, and educational program. But Eisenhower refused. In 1957, the economy was weak, tax revenues were down, and Eisenhower was concerned about deficit spending to compete in a space race that wasn't real.

Eisenhower met with politicians, military personnel, and scientists to get their insights into whether the United States was really falling behind in its scientific and security capabilities. The belief was that America was still ahead on many fronts, but there was no doubt that the Russians had momentum on their side, which could propel them ahead.

Eisenhower wasn't so sure. He didn't think the Russians could sustain their momentum and that the United States would continue, if not increase, its lead in science and the military. Eisenhower didn't want to compete in a space race, and he was skeptical about a manned space program. What he wanted was a pragmatic, cost-effective program for producing spy satellites for national security, not a spectacular space program.

At a cabinet meeting in early November 1957, Eisenhower was bombarded with various spending proposals, everything from fallout shelters to missile programs, to increased federal aid to colleges. Eisenhower thought most of the suggested spending was unjustified, and at one point he had finally had enough.

"Look," Eisenhower said forcefully, "I'd like to see what's on the other side of the moon, but I won't pay to find out this year!"[151] He explained "we must remember that we are defending a way of life, not merely property, wealth, and even our homes.... Should we have to resort to anything resembling a garrison state, then all that we are striving to defend...could disappear."[152]

But contrary to the public's perception, Eisenhower did indeed have a vision for space. In the summer of 1955, Eisenhower had authorized a secret project for building and launching satellites to spy on the Soviet Union. The government awarded the project to the navy (called Vanguard) instead of Werner Von Braun's team, which was in Huntsville, Alabama, building the Redstone rocket to carry nuclear weapons under the direction of the army. But the Vanguard effort was floundering, and soon Eisenhower and others became aware that the Redstone program could have launched a satellite into space months earlier, beating the Russians into space.

The launch of Sputnik 2 on November 3 placed more pressure on Eisenhower to act. The administration told Von Braun's team to get their satellite ready for launch. Four months after Sputnik, on January 31, 1958, Explorer was launched on top of the Redstone rocket. The United States had its own satellite in orbit, which did more scientific work than any of the Soviet satellites, including the discovery of the Van Allen Radiation Belt. In March 1958, Vanguard was launched (which is still in orbit today), and in July, Eisenhower created NASA (the civilian agency to run the space program). During the next budget cycle, Eisenhower agreed to increase federal funding in math and science to compete with the Russians.

Eisenhower showed extraordinary leadership and courage in the days after Sputnik. He refused to give into the pressure of dramatic spending increases, and he stayed calm in the face of severe criticism. He would not expand military and nuclear programs based on unjustified fears, and in the process he saved the country billions of dollars and probably avoided numerous war scares.

Just before he left office in 1960, Eisenhower's dream of a spy satellite (named Corona) became a reality. The launching of Corona initiated a revolution in American intelligence gathering. The first twenty pounds of film had more information than all the U-2 flights combined. Just as Eisenhower had hoped, satellites proved to be a bonanza for him and every president after him, providing an amazing amount of information. When the United States went to treaty talks, American negotiators knew exactly what the Russians were up to because of the satellites — it was a huge advantage.

For the rest of his life, Eisenhower never disclosed his role in the creation of one of America's most valuable intelligence tools. Even in his memoirs, he never mentioned all the programs he created. We now know that he was very much in command of what was going on behind the scenes. He paid very close attention to secret intelligence, but he preferred to keep his hand hidden.[153]

- -

"We will bankrupt ourselves in the vain search for absolute security."

- -

In the 1950s, almost every political event in foreign affairs was amplified by the undercurrent of the Cold War. Alliances, rebellions, and politics were analyzed not only on their own, but also from the perspective of the strategies and rivalries of the two superpowers. During the Cold War, the paranoid survived, and an occasional show of strength could send a very clear message.

In January 1958, President Nasser of Egypt and President al-Quwatli of Syria announced that their two countries would unite to form the United Arab Republic (UAR). In response, King Faisal of Iraq and King Hussein of Jordan joined to form a federation, the Arab Union. As the two new unions competed for other countries to join their respective groups, Western nations became increasingly concerned about Communist influence within the UAR and the ramifications of Soviet control of Middle Eastern oil and the security of Israel.

Saudi Arabia was concerned that pro-Nasser support within his country could undermine its monarchy, and Lebanon's President Camille Chamoun was being confronted by rebels who resented his pro-Western government. Chamoun's troubles worsened with his support for a change to the country's constitution to allow him to serve an unprecedented second term, which triggered armed uprisings by the rebels in Beirut.

Eisenhower and Dulles were concerned about the small size of Lebanon's army and their ability to put down the rebellion, and they both continued to believe Communists were responsible for stirring up this trouble. In early May, Eisenhower began to consider how the United States could help the Lebanese, telling Dulles "it was much cheaper to try to hold the situation than to try to retrieve it," and he would do what was needed "to insure prompt action."[154]

In late May, Chamoun requested an urgent meeting of the United Nations Security Council to address his concerns that the UAR was inciting revolt and arming the rebels. The UN responded by sending an observation team, and in mid-June, an informal truce had been established, and the situation seemed to settle down.

Then, on July 14, 1958, the Iraq Hashemite monarchy was ousted in a coup by the Iraqi army and others who were sympathetic to Nasser. This reignited tensions and fears, especially in Lebanon. Saudi Arabia requested the deployment of United States troops in the Middle East, and Chamoun requested that the United States and Britain intervene within forty-eight hours. Eisenhower had decided — "the time had come to act."

That same day Eisenhower met with his top advisors to make sure nothing was overlooked. In the meeting, Eisenhower was the calmest person in the room, discussing the political ramifications both at home and abroad and the likely reaction of the Soviets. He was at ease and confident with the decisions he was about to make.

"Because of my long study of the problem, this was one meeting in which my mind was practically made up regarding the general line of action we should take, even before we met," Eisenhower wrote in his memoirs. "The time was rapidly approaching...when we had to move into the Middle East...to stop the trend toward chaos."[155]

After hearing from his team, including their confirmation with his view that the Soviets would probably make threatening gestures but not act militarily, Eisenhower moved rapidly. He wanted American troops in Lebanon as quickly as possible. He met with congressional leaders to inform them of his plans. Some congressmen were worried about getting immersed in a civil war and negative reaction from other countries.

Eisenhower emphasized that American troops would be there only until the UN could take over, and reminded them that the United States was not acting on its own — Lebanon was asking them to send troops. As that meeting ended, Eisenhower called British Prime Minister Harold Macmillan to discuss US plans and British participation. The prime minister agreed with the decision to deploy troops, and together they decided it was best if British troops were held in reserve while American troops conducted the landing. British troops would be deployed later as needed, and they agreed that should the situation grow, they "were in this together, all the way."[156]

Eisenhower then discussed logistics of the landing with General Nathan Twining. Three Marine battalions were in the region and could be deployed immediately. Eisenhower ordered that the landings take place the next day at 3:00 p.m. Lebanon time (9:00 a.m. eastern time). Other troops in Europe and elsewhere would get their orders for moving to Lebanon at about the same time as the landings took place.

Having concluded military discussions, Eisenhower directed Dulles to tell UN Ambassador Henry Cabot Lodge to request an emergency meeting of the UN Security Council the next morning to make the case that the United States was in Lebanon only to stabilize the country until the United Nations could take over. Lastly, Eisenhower knew he had to address the American people and the world to explain his actions. He wrote an announcement for the press secretary to issue the morning to coincide with the landings and prepared for a television address the next evening.

Within several hours Eisenhower made a number of critical decisions and managed to either communicate, or plan to communicate, his intentions to all. He moved with the cool decisiveness of a confident leader, who was comfortable as commander in chief. The next day, the 2,500 troops landed and secured their positions in the capital and the airport of Lebanon, and its citizens went about their business. The troops were given orders not to pursue rebels in the countryside—that action was the responsibility of the Lebanese army—and they met little resistance. At that same moment, Eisenhower's message went out to the United Nations, to Congress, and to the American people.

"Warned and alarmed by" recent developments, Eisenhower told the country, "President Chamoun of Lebanon sent me an urgent plea that the United States station some military units in Lebanon to evidence our concern for the independence of Lebanon, that little country, which itself has for about two months been subjected to civil strife. This has been actively fomented by

Soviet and Cairo broadcasts and abetted and aided by substantial amounts of arms, money and personnel infiltrated into Lebanon across the Syrian border."

Eisenhower had decided to comply with the request after taking "advice from leaders of both the Executive and Congressional branches of the government." He stressed that the America was not there to intervene in the internal affairs of Lebanon, and the troops were not there to fight. But they "will have a stabilizing effect which will preserve the independence and integrity of Lebanon." He expressed the hope that the United Nations would take over shortly and "that our forces can be promptly withdrawn."

Eisenhower did not make this decision lightly, explaining that he was "well aware of the fact that landing of United States troops in Lebanon could have some serious consequences." But having considered the situation and the options, he came "to the sober and clear conclusion that the action taken was essential to the welfare of the United States. It was required to support the principles of justice."[157]

Two days later, 2,200 British solders landed in Jordan. Within three weeks, fourteen thousand troops were in Lebanon. Reaction around the world ranged from being grateful (Turkey) to being worried (West Germany). Russia reacted as predicted, with diplomatic maneuvering and protests, but no military action. Nasser, who was in Yugoslavia when the landings occurred, headed to Moscow in a state of near panic, fearing his country would be next. Nasser had probably hoped that Russia would supply troops and arms to support Egypt, but he was disappointed — the Russians decided to sit this one out.

The troop deployment was a great success. American and British troops stabilized the region without initiating a general war. Within four months, the crisis was over, and all American troops were withdrawn from Lebanon by October 25, which went almost unnoticed by the American public.

But Eisenhower had accomplished much more than the stabilization of the Middle East in solving this crisis. For the first and only time during his presidency, Eisenhower had harnessed and displayed the power of the US military—it was impressive, and it was noticed.

Although Russia had known about the imposing strength of America's military, it had now seen it in action, and it was fast and effective. Nasser, who had felt free to do as he pleased in the region because he had doubted the capacity of the United States to take military action and believed he could rely on the Soviets to counter US actions, now had to rethink his assumptions.

Eisenhower had "demonstrated the ability of the United States to react swiftly with conventional armed forces to meet small-scale...situations," which quieted critics about a perceived overreliance on large plans and destructive bombs. He had also sent a message to the world that the United States had the will to act swiftly and decisively to protect its interests.[158]

Overall, it was an impressive display of leadership. Eisenhower was thoughtful and inclusive in his decision making: he weighed the possible scenarios, he communicated the rationale to all concerned parties, he acted quickly once the decisions were made, and he kept his word on the length of deployment. It was one of his finest leadership moments as president.

Eisenhower's Leadership: Achieving Results

1. Don't conduct affairs by committee.
2. Focus on the possible — doubts and criticisms discourage efforts.
3. Every project will astonish you in the way it's executed — expect the unexpected.
4. Ensure clarity of roles and responsibilities.
5. Weigh alternatives, but decide quickly.
6. Make sure the tactical plans support the overall strategy.
7. When required, have the courage to be patient.
8. Act aggressively and swiftly when negotiations and patience are at an end.
9. Look at problems holistically and analytically before deciding.
10. If you know you're right, don't give in to pressure.
11. Most of the anticipated calamities never occur.
12. Focus on the endgame.
13. Provide your teams with the resources they need to succeed.
14. Assess risks and results objectively, and learn from them.
15. Observe situations for yourself — get close to the action.
16. Use downtime to strengthen the team's capabilities.
17. Turn challenges into opportunities.
18. Be consistent in relationships and processes — no favoritism, even with friends.
19. Be bold rather than conservative.
20. Leverage technology to achieve results.
21. Don't ignore the competition — get ahead of them.

CHAPTER 6.

ON COMMUNICATION

"We succeed only as we identify in life, or in war, or in anything else, a single overriding objective, and make all other considerations bend to that one objective."

Eisenhower started speaking publicly as a cheerleader in West Point, and he improved over time. By the time he became president, public speaking was a natural skill—he knew when to be precise and when to intentionally obfuscate. When Eisenhower had an important presentation or speech to make, he would be sure to allow enough time to prepare and rehearse what he intended to say. He would think about the kinds of questions people were likely to ask and determine the proper responses. He always preferred using plain, simple language, so everyone understood what he was trying to say.

Eisenhower was also a prolific and exceptional writer. Anyone who does any research on the life and times of Eisenhower cannot help but be impressed with the amount of material he wrote over his lifetime. His papers, beginning with World War II, fill twenty-one volumes. He wrote letters to everyone—his wife and family, his superiors and subordinates, and presidents and prime ministers.

A few years after leaving the service, Eisenhower began writing his memoir on World War II, *Crusade in Europe*. In typical fashion, Eisenhower had already considered how to organize the effort and the vast amount of material at his disposal. He then set out "on a writing program, at a speed that a soldier would call a blitz," working about sixteen hours a day on the initiative.

He would rise at 6:00 a.m. every day, begin work at 7:00 a.m. "with a short breakfast conference about the work immediately ahead," and work until 11:00 at night with breaks for lunch and dinner. He recalled, "It was a tough grind for all of us, but in a way it was fun. The task was there to do. There were no delays for lack of material, my secretarial help was superb and at times my execrable handwriting provided the reason for a laugh."[1] The final copy needed very little help from editors.

Writing his three-thousand-page presidential memoirs, *The White House Years*, proved to be more difficult. The timeframe was longer but there were many more people involved, some of whom Eisenhower didn't particularly care for, and he hated to criticize anyone. He described how he made decisions regarding Korea, Vietnam, McCarthy, and managing the economy, but the results didn't always have the finality of the battles that led to success in World War II, so he labored to present his views as positively as possible. Regardless, the two-volume memoir is extremely detailed and reads a bit like an encyclopedia. However, it does provide a rich history of the political and international events of the 1950s.

Eisenhower's informal autobiography, *At Ease: Stories I Tell My Friends*, was more of a labor of love. In it he tells funny stories about his life, with rich anecdotes about Connor Fox, George Marshall, and Douglas McArthur. His writing style was very relaxed, as if he really was telling the reader a story of his life. It was received warmly by the public and had much higher sales than his presidential memoirs.

In general, there are three reasons to communicate — to direct, to influence, and to inform. Leaders direct when they give specific instructions on what to do and by when. Influencing is about persuading or collaborating with people to come up with the best solution to a problem. Informing is about sharing information and knowledge. Eisenhower was excellent at all three.

DIRECTING

"Positive results are obtained only through positive action."

Upon taking command as the supreme commander, Eisenhower wanted to set expectations of all those who worked on his team. There were a large number of American troops stationed in England in preparation for D-day, and Eisenhower knew this would bring challenges to his officers. He wanted his team to make a good impression on his British hosts, so he sent out a memo to all those under his command to set expectations.

The close understanding and mutual trust between officers and men that develop readily under field conditions are not easy to establish when the living conditions, distractions and diversionary interests of city existence intervene. This situation places an added burden upon all officers. Only leadership of a high order can solve the many problems involved, problems that are increased in complexity by reason of the fact that we are stationed in an Allied rather than in our own country. It is vital that we work with the people of Great Britain, both in the fighting services and in civil life, on the basis of mutual respect, consideration and cooperation. This means that we must earn and keep their respect as a great military machine, dedicated to the single task of doing our duty in the winning of the war.

Consequently, every officer must live, as well as teach, the things we all know to be necessary.

Every company commander must know all his men, their qualifications, their problems, their habits and their personalities. He must train them individually and collectively for present and future tasks. He must protect them and *insure to each a chance to serve intelligently and usefully in the cause for which our country is engaged in this war.*

Officers of all grades must strive to be examples to others. They must encourage their subordinates to understand that each is a representative of our country in Great Britain, and they must, themselves, serve as examples of how such representatives should act.

Eisenhower "recognized the need for proper recreation and entertainment," and he stressed that "Officers and men should have equal opportunity" to relax. However, he emphasized that "only a self-disciplined army can win battles," and he urged his officers to instill a sense of self-control and common courtesy while they were guests of Britain, which he felt would pay dividends as the troops moved through Europe.[2]

After returning from a visit to his troops in February 1944, Eisenhower felt compelled to send another memo out to everyone in the theater. He wanted to use the opportunity prior to the invasion to build teamwork. "Troops must train together, work together and live together in order to attain successful teamwork in campaign," he wrote. "The sharing of work opportunities and recreational facilities must be willingly accepted and utilized to unite more closely the troops of our several commands. All commanders are charged with exemplifying to their troops a generous attitude of respect for other troops and with planning with other commanders, especially their own subordinates, effective coordination not only of work and training but of recreation."

Eisenhower also wanted his commanders to be fair and respectful in dealing with their subordinates, most of whom were young and away from home for the first time. "Equal opportunities of service and of recreation are the right of every American soldier regardless of branch, race, color or creed," he wrote, and "all officers including NCOs will so treat their juniors as to preserve their self respect and to enhance their pride as members of their organization." He also used the memo to express his intolerance for slander against any of the Allies. "Any person subject to military law who makes statements derogatory to any troops of the United Nations will be severely punished for conduct prejudicial to good order and military discipline."[3]

On June 6, 1944, as the Allies prepared to invade Normandy, Eisenhower sent out an Order of the Day to all the troops:

Soldiers, Sailors and Airmen of the Allied Expeditionary Forces! You are about to embark upon a Great Crusade, toward which we have striven these many months. The eyes of the world are upon you. The hopes and prayers of liberty-loving people everywhere march with you. In company with our brave Allies and brothers-in-arms on other Fronts you will bring about the destruction of the German war machine, the elimination of Nazi tyranny over oppressed peoples of Europe, and security for ourselves in a free world.

Your task will not be an easy one. Your enemy is well trained, well equipped and battle-hardened. He will fight savagely.

But this is the year 1944! Much has happened since the Nazi triumphs of 1940-1941. The United Nations have inflicted upon the Germans great defeats, in open battle, man-to-man. Our air offensive has seriously reduced their strength in the air and their capacity to wage war on the ground. Our Home Fronts have given us an overwhelming superiority in weapons and munitions of war, and placed at our disposal great reserves of trained fighting men. The tide has turned! The free men of the world are marching together in Victory!

I have full confidence in your courage, devotion to duty and skill in battle. We will accept nothing less than full victory!

Good Luck! And let us all beseech the blessing of Almighty God upon this great and noble undertaking.[4]

The order provided inspiration to many of those brave men who participated in D-day. Many soldiers had their copies signed and put into plastic bags, and they carried the document throughout the war, from Normandy to the Elbe River.

In December 1944, as the Germans mounted their last, desperate offensive in the Battle of the Bulge, Eisenhower sent out another communication to encourage the troops to not only turn them away, but to use this as an opportunity to crush the opponent.

> The enemy is making his supreme effort to break out of the desperate plight into which you forced him by your brilliant victories of the summer and fall. He is fighting savagely to take back all that you have won and is using every treacherous trick to deceive and kill you. He is gambling everything, but already, in this battle, your unparalleled gallantry has done much to foil his plans. In the face of your proven bravery and fortitude he will completely *fail*.
>
> But we cannot be content with his mere repulse.
>
> By rushing out from his fixed defenses the enemy has given us the chance to turn his great gamble into his worst defeat. So I call upon every man, of all the Allies, to rise now to new heights of courage, of resolution and of effort. Let everyone hold before him a single thought — to destroy the enemy on the ground, in the air, everywhere — destroy him! United in this determination and with unshakable faith in the cause for which we fight, we will, with God's help, go forward to our greatest victory.[5]

After the war, when he took on the role of Chief of Staff in late 1945, Eisenhower held a meeting with his staff. After discussing a number of points, Eisenhower ended by acknowledging to his staff that, although he was ultimately accountable, he knew "that it's you people who have to do the job. The best I can do is to keep you acquainted with decisions that come down from above, to give you the interpretations that I place on them, and, when necessary, to make a decision within my province between differing views."

He promised to empower his staff by following "the only system I believe will work in a large command and a large degree of decentralization. I want every single one of you to feel a personal responsibility for what you do. There is no ducking behind anyone else. You do it. Follow your best judgment and take action as you see necessary if it's entirely within your section. There you are expected to be completely responsible. If coordination is necessary, you are expected to get it...In following this system, the only thing I can promise you is 100 percent support in your job. As long as you occupy a position of responsibility in any organization that I head, it means just this: That to the last minute you are there you have my confidence. If you don't have it, you won't be there."[6]

- -

"A foreign policy is the face and voice of a whole people. It is all that the world sees and hears and understands about a single nation. It expresses the character and the faith and the will of that nation. In this, a nation is like any individual of our personal acquaintance; the simplest gesture can betray hesitation or weakness, the merest inflection of voice can reveal doubt or fear."

- -

As Eisenhower began his campaign as the Republican presidential nominee, he knew that the major issue of the election was the Korean War and that there was no easy solution. By the time Eisenhower was elected in 1952, 21,000 soldiers had been killed, 91,000 were wounded, and 13,000 were missing. The majority of American people wanted the conflict to end. Eisenhower had told a few people that if there wasn't some kind of agreement to end the conflict before he became president that he would go to Korea. During a campaign speech in October 1952, Eisenhower talked about the endless fighting and the inability of the current administration to end the conflict.

"When the enemy struck, on that June day of 1950, what did America do? It did what it always has done in all its times of peril. It appealed to the heroism of its youth. This appeal was utterly right and utterly inescapable. It was inescapable not only because this was the only way to defend the idea of collective freedom against savage aggression. That appeal was inescapable because there was now in the plight into which we had stumbled no other way to save honor and self-respect. The answer to that appeal has been what any American knew it would be. It has been sheer valor — valor on all the Korean mountainsides that, each day, bear fresh scars of new graves.

"Now — in this anxious autumn — from these heroic men there comes back an answering appeal. It is no whine, no whimpering plea. It is a question that addresses itself to simple reason. It asks: Where do we go from here? When comes the end? Is there an end? These questions touch all of us. They demand truthful answers. Neither glib promises nor glib excuses will serve. They would be no better than the glib prophecies that brought us to this pass.

"To these questions there are two false answers. The first would be any answer that dishonestly pledged an end to war in Korea by any imminent, exact date. Such a pledge would brand its speaker as a deceiver. The second and equally false answer dares that nothing can be done to speed a secure peace. It dares to tell us that we, the strongest nation in the history of freedom, can only wait — and wait — and wait. Such a statement brands its speaker as a defeatist.

"My answer — candid and complete — is this: The first task of a new Administration will be to review and re-examine every course of action open to us with one goal in view: To bring the Korean War to an early and honorable end. This is my pledge to the American people. For this task a wholly new Administration is necessary. The reason for this is simple. The old Administration cannot be expected to repair what it failed to prevent. Where will a new Administration begin? It will begin with its President taking a simple, firm resolution. The resolution will be: To forego the diversions of politics and to concentrate on the job of ending the

Korean war—until that job is honorably done. That job requires a personal trip to Korea. I shall make that trip. Only in that way could I learn how best to serve the American people in the cause of peace. I shall go to Korea. That is my second pledge to the American people."[7]

Eisenhower had always been leading in the polls, but this dramatic moment, just two weeks before the election, helped put him over the top. Even though he didn't say what he expected to do when he got to Korea or promise any results, just the idea that the nation's favorite World War II hero was taking action against the country's most critical problem gave comfort to many Americans.

While politics surely played a role in Eisenhower's decision to announce the trip, as many of the opposition claimed, he was actually doing what he had always done—communicating what the nation could expect from him. He was going to Korea to get unfiltered information to help him determine a way forward.

- -

"I hate war as only a soldier who has lived it can, and as one who has seen its brutality, its futility, its stupidity."

- -

Eisenhower left for Korea after the election on November 29 with several of his cabinet designees and General Bradley, who was now chairman of the Joint Chiefs of Staff. In the three days he was there, Eisenhower met with South Korean President Dr. Syngman Rhee and Mark Clark, the commander of UN forces. He shared a mess kit meal and chatted with the troops in freezing weather, bundled up to do a reconnaissance mission on the front, and had several briefings with the military leadership. Both Rhee and Clark wanted to present plans for a full-scale offensive attack, but Eisenhower didn't give them the opportunity.

Instinctively Eisenhower had thought for some time that the war needed to end, and, after reviewing the situation for himself, he believed any plans for an all-out offensive were borderline insane. "In view of the strength of the positions the enemy had developed it was obvious that any frontal attack would present great difficulties," Eisenhower wrote. "My conclusion as I left Korea was that we could not stand forever on a static front and continue to accept casualties without any visible results. Small attacks on small hills would not end this war."[8] He wanted an armistice and to find an honorable way for both sides to end the fighting.

Eisenhower in Korea

Once in office, Eisenhower was now responsible for finding "an acceptable solution to a problem that almost defied...any solutions."[9] With his team, Eisenhower considered his options, while they continued to negotiate for an armistice. One option would be to let the war continue as it was, but since casualties were heavy with little to show for them, Eisenhower thought this option was unacceptable. Another option would be to mount an all-out attack by conventional methods.

But given that the Chinese and Koreans had held their front line for a year and a half, and during that time had reinforced their position with an impressive build out of an underground network, stocked with ammunition and weapons, this alternative was the least attractive, since it would be extremely costly and without any guarantee of success.

Since the status quo and the use of conventional means weren't attractive alternatives, Eisenhower moved toward the unconventional. He increased the amount of military aid to South Korea, which enabled them to increase their troops by 65,000 to 525,000. He also would make more US troops available if they were needed. Eisenhower then increased the psychological pressure on the Chinese and North Koreans, by implying the potential use of atomic weapons.

Through back channels, Eisenhower let the Communists know that "in the absence of satisfactory progress, we intended to move decisively without inhibition in our use of weapons, and would no longer be responsible for confining activities to the Korean Peninsula. We would not be limited by any world-wide gentlemen's agreement."[10] Eisenhower also used every opportunity he could to call the current stalemated situation in Korea intolerable.

These words were clearly understood by the Chinese, primarily because of Eisenhower's reputation. They were well aware that Eisenhower had used every possible weapon and method at his disposal to obtain an unconditional surrender from the Nazis just seven years earlier. The Chinese also knew the United States had atomic weapons readily available in the region, and if Eisenhower said the status quo was unacceptable, they believed him. Suddenly, there was progress being made in the armistice talks, especially with a breakthrough regarding the repatriation of prisoners — a major hurdle in the negotiations.

Despite some last-minute attempts by Syngman Rhee to undermine the armistice agreement, the peace treaty was signed on July 27, 1953. This was one of Eisenhower's finest accomplishments, and it was achieved because of his clear communication, prestige, and reputation.

He did what he said he would do — go to Korea and find a way forward. He achieved the peace within six months of taking office. Eisenhower realized that it would probably be a long time before Korea was reunited, and he cautioned the American people that "we have won an armistice on a single battlefield — not peace in the world." But it was still significant that "three years of heroism, frustration and bloodshed were over."[11]

INFLUENCING

- -

"I would rather try to persuade a man to go along, because once I have persuaded him, he will stick. If I scare him, he will stay just as long as he is scared, and then he is gone."

- -

In the fall of 1943, as the Italian campaign and the massive buildup for Overlord continued, the Allies decided to meet in Cairo and then in Tehran with the Russians to discuss the strategy for 1944 and the command structure going forward. There were critical decisions to be made, and Walter "Beetle" Smith, Eisenhower's chief of staff, thought it would be the "hottest one yet," since Churchill and many on his team were "still unconvinced as to the wisdom of OVERLORD" and were "persistent in their desire to pursue" Allied "advantages in the Mediterranean."[12]

While Eisenhower "never at any time heard Mr. Churchill urge or suggest complete abandonment of" the invasion of France, he did feel that the prime minister and "his chief military advisors...looked upon the OVERLORD plan with scarcely concealed misgivings; their attitude seemed to be that we could avoid the additional and grave risks implicit in a new amphibious operation by merely pouring into the Mediterranean all the air, ground, and naval resources available."[13]

Eisenhower had heard Churchill caution often that "we must take care that the tides do not run red with the blood of American and British youth, or the beaches be choked with their bodies." A strong reminder of what was at stake. Meanwhile, the decision on who would lead Overlord was still open, and Stalin was pressing hard for the appointment.

Prior to the Cairo conference, Eisenhower met with Churchill and his military advisors in Malta, to "spend the day going over a number of subjects of interest to current and future operations." Eisenhower always found Churchill to be "entertaining and interesting...capable of keeping a dinner gathering on its toes."[14] Discussing strategy and command options, Churchill continued to present arguments for keeping the momentum going in attacking Germany through Italy.

Churchill also told Eisenhower that "originally it was intended that General Brooke should command in England and the Mediterranean command should remain undisturbed. However, when the Americans insisted upon American command in England" since they would be providing most of the resources, Churchill relented and left the decision to the US president.

Churchill told Eisenhower he felt the original proposal would probably be approved, which was "that General Marshall would take command of Overlord in England" and Eisenhower "would possibly go to Washington." This meant a change of command would be required in the Mediterranean, and Churchill "expressed a great desire to have General Smith remain" in the region "to assist the new Commander." But Eisenhower protested, insisting that Smith follow him, telling Churchill "this was one point on which I would not yield, except under directions from the President."

Of course Churchill could influence the supreme commander decision, and the prime minster told Eisenhower that "there were only two Americans that he would willingly accept in London as Commander of OVERLORD" — Marshall or him. However, he also felt strongly that agreements on the amount of authority and overall command structure in Europe needed to be reached first, regardless of who was to command.

As the debate on the supreme commander gained momentum, and with his own future in question, Eisenhower traveled to Cairo on November 24, 1943, to consult with the CCS on operations in his theater. His presentation was crisp and concise. He told them that from his perspective, "the most important land objective in the Mediterranean, from a strategic standpoint is the Po Valley [in northern Italy] because of the fact that land forces based there are extremely threatening to the German structure in the Balkans, in France and in the Reich itself. Next, from that position, landing operation either to the east or to the west can be more readily supported. Third, a position in that area brings our Air Forces closer and closer to the vitals of the German industries."

However, Eisenhower noted that the capture of this region would require more resources than he currently had at his disposal, and he calculated that a redeployment of assets to his theater would cause a sixty to ninety day delay in Overlord. It was up to the Chiefs to decide on the priority. Eisenhower then brought up one of Churchill's main concerns — a possible campaign in the Aegean Sea. Churchill continued to argue for expanded operations in the Mediterranean, which could potentially delay any cross-channel operation — something the Americans and some British were strongly against.

Eisenhower was one of those strongly in favor of moving forward with Overlord in the spring of 1944, and he was personally opposed to any activity that might distract from that effort. But his current role required him to focus on his own theater and present realistic alternatives for leveraging potential opportunities.

"If a campaign toward taking of the Po Valley began to develop favorably," he reported, "there would at a certain point become available landing craft and forces that could be used for rapid descent upon the Dodecanese and destruction of the German position in the Aegean Sea, but only if Turkey should come into the war." But he declined to get into a discussion about the "advisability of Turkey's entering the war" because he knew nothing about it.

Eisenhower concluded his presentation by stating that if the Chiefs decided to maintain the current level of resources in his theater, then the operation would be constrained to primarily a defensive operation in Italy. Although once established, "forces would be disposed to carry on active minor operations against the enemy, the general attitude would from thereafter be defensive, unless there came about a considerable weakening of the German forces."[15]

When Eisenhower finished, the Chiefs asked him a number of questions regarding the Italian operation. His answers were always direct, and he again refused to get into the political debate on Turkey's entry into the war. "In response to a question from Brooke, Eisenhower stressed the vital importance of continuing the maximum possible operation in an established theater. Much valuable time was invariably lost, he said, when the scene of action was changed, for it necessitated the arduous task of building up from a fresh base. He also constantly emphasized that what AFHQ needed was landing craft, not more men. He could barely maintain the number of divisions he had now in Italy... but he did need landing craft, both to bring in supplies on open beaches and to mount amphibious operations."[16]

Eisenhower had impressed the Chiefs with his presentation. Even the normally critical Brooke found that Eisenhower had clearly articulated the situation and provided realistic strategic options for going forward. It was actually rather easy for Eisenhower to provide such a winning presentation. He was deeply involved in his operation, so he could speak of it without much preparation. He also always spoke the truth, and he insisted on presenting facts as there were, rather than what he thought people would want to hear.

He kept his sentences precise and on topic. He had grown in confidence as the Mediterranean campaign continued, and he had little concern for his own future, trusting that as long as he performed well and stayed true to his principles that things would work out. That attitude allowed him to always "tell it like it is," so that his superiors could make the proper decisions regarding strategies and the allocations of valuable resources, regardless of what it meant to his career.

After the Cairo conference, Eisenhower returned to his headquarters to await "crucial decisions on the Mediterranean, OVERLORD buildup, and command arrangements." Churchill, Roosevelt, and their staffs traveled to Tehran to meet with Stalin, who quickly "settled the U.S.-British argument on the Mediterranean versus OVERLORD by insisting on a cross-Channel attack no later than May, 1944."[17]

Returning to Cairo after the meetings in Tehran, the British and Americans spent three days discussing the war in Southeast Asia and various details of Overlord. On the last day of the meeting, Roosevelt announced that Eisenhower would be supreme commander of Overlord. Roosevelt "was convinced that Eisenhower could handle the European command successfully. Not only had he proved his ability to command Allied forces in the Mediterranean theater, but his appearance before the CCS at Cairo had demonstrated a firm grasp of the military situation and added to the good impression he had previously made."[18]

One can only speculate what would have happened had Eisenhower not presented his views so well at the Cairo conference. His entire future may have been very different. Roosevelt may have made Marshall supreme commander, with Eisenhower leading an army group under Marshall, or Eisenhower may have returned to Washington to assume the assignment as Army Chief of Staff (which was what many people believed would happen, even though this would have made Eisenhower Marshall's superior, which didn't make much sense). Certainly the presidency would have been a long shot had Eisenhower not had the opportunity to succeed as supreme commander.

- -

"Atomic war could mean the end of all civilization, including our own."

- -

Early in his presidency, Eisenhower became deeply concerned about the escalating arms race between the United States and Russia and the horrific devastation and human suffering that atomic weapons could cause. "The only way to win World War III is to prevent it," he would repeat often, adding, "we must put effort, skill and faith in our diplomacy...for upon it ultimately will depend the prevention of World War III."[19]

Eisenhower believed that "much of the world is trapped in the same vicious circle. Weakness in arms often invites aggression or subversion, or externally manipulated revolutions. Fear inspired in others by the increasing military strength of one nation spurs them to concentrate still more of their resources on weapons and warlike measures. The arms race becomes more universal. Doubt as to the true purpose of these weapons intensifies tension. Peoples are robbed of opportunity for their own peaceful development. The hunger for a peace of justice and good will inevitably become more intense. Controlled, universal disarmament is the imperative of our time. The demand for it by the hundreds of millions whose chief concern is the long future of themselves and their children will, I hope, become so universal and so insistent that no man, no government anywhere, can withstand it."[20]

In an effort to put the brakes on a world racing towards catastrophe, Eisenhower wanted to "awaken the American people and the world to the incredible destruction power of the United States' stockpile of nuclear weapons," and establish a framework that would enable mutual trust between the United States and Russia.[21] This was a delicate balancing act — he needed to convey the urgency of the situation without causing alarm. He wanted the speech to emphasize awareness and caution, not panic.

He asked his advisor C. D. Jackson to work with him and others in his administration to develop a speech that would be candid in describing current realities, but also express a way forward and optimism for the future. Several iterations were developed, but there was division within his team.

Some harbored a deep distrust of the Russians and wanted to build even more bombs. Others wanted bomb production to stop and disarmament to begin immediately, regardless of what the Russians did. The drafts "left the listener with only a new terror, not a new hope," and provided no new ideas to build trust among the nuclear power nations and the world.

Eisenhower would have to come up with his own disarmament idea. "I began to search around for any kind of idea that could bring the world to look at the atomic problem in a broad intelligent and still escape the impasse to action created by Russian intransigence in the matter of mutual or neutral inspection of resources," he wrote to a friend. "I wanted...to give our people and the world some faint idea of the distance already traveled by this new science—but to do it in such a way as not to create new alarm."[22]

Soon Eisenhower came up with an idea. Russia, the United States, and Britain would donate nuclear isotopes to a common, neutral party, which could then use the material for peaceful purposes, such as creating nuclear power plants. This idea had many benefits. It eased the anxiety around atomic weapons; it allowed the program to start small and grow over time; it would be attractive to small nations, since they could participate in the constructive use of atomic sciences; it enabled the United States to reduce its stockpile of weapons even more than the Russians and still maintain security; and the American people would feel that "they had not poured their substance into this whole development with the sole purpose and possibility of its being used for destruction."[23]

As Eisenhower and his team worked through the details, he received an invitation to speak at the United Nations on December 8, 1953. Eisenhower and his team worked relentlessly in developing his "Atoms for Peace" speech, which was refined up until the last minute.

After thanking the United Nations and its members for the opportunity to speak, he provided a candid assessment of the current atomic situation. "I feel impelled to speak today in a language that in a sense is new," he said. "That new language is the language of atomic warfare," and it was "of the utmost significance to every one of us. Clearly, if the peoples of the world are to conduct an intelligent search for peace, they must be armed with the significant facts of today's existence."

He told the assembly that "the United States of America has conducted forty-two test explosions" since the first atomic bomb tests, and that the current "atomic bombs are more than twenty-five times as powerful as the weapons with which the atomic age dawned, while hydrogen weapons are in the ranges of millions of tons of TNT equivalent."

"Today," he continued, "the United States stockpile of atomic weapons, which, of course, increases daily, exceeds by many times the total equivalent of the total of all bombs and all shells that came from every plane and every gun in every theatre of war in all the years of the Second World War. A single air group whether afloat or land based, can now deliver to any reachable target a destructive cargo exceeding in power all the bombs that fell on Britain in all the Second World War."

Eisenhower then emphasized that the United States was not alone in knowing the secrets of atomic weaponry. The United Kingdom, Canada, and Russia also had nuclear capabilities, and "the knowledge now possessed by several nations will eventually be shared by others, possibly all others." Because of the spread of this knowledge, countries were building defensive systems, but, Eisenhower warned, "The awful arithmetic of the atomic bomb does not permit any such easy solution," since there was no defense against a surprise attack.

"Should such an atomic attack be launched against the United States," Eisenhower went on, "our reactions would be swift and resolute." But being able to completely destroy an enemy was not what the United States wanted. It did not want a future where the two superpowers would be "doomed malevolently to eye each other indefinitely across a trembling world," or to "accept helplessly the probability of civilization destroyed, the annihilation of the irreplaceable heritage of mankind handed down to us from generation to generation, and the condemnation of mankind to begin all over again the age-old struggle upward from savagery towards decency, and right, and justice. Surely no sane member of the human race could discover victory in such desolation. Could anyone wish his name to be coupled by history with such human degradation and destruction?"

Eisenhower explained that the United States wanted to be "constructive, not destructive" and wanted "agreements, not wars. It wants itself to live in freedom and in the confidence that the peoples of every other nation enjoy equally the right of choosing their own way of life. So my country's purpose is to help us to move out of the dark chamber of horrors into the light, to find a way by which the minds of men, the hopes of men, the souls of men everywhere, can move forward towards peace and happiness and well-being."

"In a world divided," Eisenhower said, "one dramatic act" would not create mutual trust or reduce atomic weapons. It would be a long process, requiring patience and compromise. Many steps would be needed to realize the benefits, but the process needed to start now in order to "hasten the day when fear of the atom will begin to disappear from the minds the people."

Eisenhower then communicated his vision. "The United States would seek more than the mere reduction or elimination of atomic materials for military purposes. It is not enough to take this weapon out of the hands of the soldiers. It must be put into the hands of those who will know how to strip its military casing and adapt it to the arts of peace."

Eisenhower proposed that counties make "joint contributions of their nuclear material" to "an international atomic energy agency (IAEC)," which would be managed by the United Nations. The exact process and ratios would need to be established, but the United States was ready to participate in "good faith" and to be a generous partner with any nation willing to participate. Even small contributions would be beneficial to eliminate "mutual suspicions."

Eisenhower explained that the new IAEC would be responsible for the housing and safeguarding of the nuclear material, but more importantly, it would "devise methods whereby this fissionable material would be allocated to serve the peaceful pursuits of mankind. Experts would be mobilized to apply atomic energy to the needs of agriculture, medicine and other peaceful activities. A special purpose would be to provide abundant electrical energy in the power-starved areas of the world. Thus the contributing powers would be dedicating some of their strength to serve the needs rather than the fears of mankind."

The United States would be a willing and proud participant in developing these plans, Eisenhower told the silent audience, and he was committed to submitting any such plans to Congress, with "every expectation of approval." The development of such a disarmament plan would show the world that the atomic nations were willing to take the lead, to be a model, and to prove they were "interested in human aspirations first rather than in building up the armaments of war." These "private and public conversations" were needed "if the world is to shake off the inertia imposed by fear and is to make positive progress towards peace."

"Against the dark background of the atomic bomb, the United States does not wish merely to present strength, but also the desire and the hope for peace," Eisenhower said. He concluded with the pledge that the United States was determined "to help solve the fearful atomic dilemma — to devote its entire heart and mind to finding the way by which the miraculous inventiveness of man shall not be dedicated to his death, but consecrated to his life."[24]

Throughout the speech, the audience had sat silently, without applauding. When Eisenhower finished, it was silent. After a slight pause, the thirty-five hundred assembly members erupted. Even the Russians were cheering and applauding. This kind of response had never occurred at the United Nations before. The reaction there and throughout the world was extremely positive. Eisenhower had devised and communicated a vision and laid the foundation for a plan that would replace terror with hope.

Eisenhower wasn't naïve enough to believe that his speech alone would achieve results, but he did think "ideas expressed in words must certainly have a function in getting people here and elsewhere thinking along these lines and helping to devise ways and means by which the possible disaster of the future can be avoided."[25] Eisenhower had succeeded in developing and effectively communicating a plan to solve one of the most difficult problems facing the world. His words and delivery had mesmerized and energized the audience.

Unfortunately, the follow-up required to realize the Atoms for Peace plan never happened. The Russians stalled, never formally responding to the proposal, and both sides continued the atomic weapons buildup. The IEAC was eventually created, but it never took on the role Eisenhower envisioned. Eisenhower was saddened and depressed that one of his greatest ideas and major goals was not accomplished. He always believed a great opportunity had been lost.

INFORMING

"There is nothing wrong with America that the faith, love of freedom, intelligence, and energy of her citizens can not cure."

Writing can be used for communication, but it was also cathartic for Eisenhower. Leaders cannot always openly express what is actually on their minds about people or situations. They need outlets to convey their personal beliefs and concerns in private, in a way that won't disrupt the activities and morale of those around them. Even if no one ever sees what is written, just putting the words on paper can be a relief, and sometimes it brings a new perspective to a problem. Eisenhower would often use writing as a release mechanism to vent his worries or frustrations. It also helped him think through various solutions.

In the dark, damp halls of Gibraltar before the Allied landings in North Africa in 1942, there was not much Eisenhower could do except wait. The plans were set. Six hundred and fifty ships were crossing the Atlantic with thousands of troops and tons of equipment on board to execute the plans. It was hard enough to go through what Eisenhower called "one of those interminable waiting periods" between launching a campaign and receiving status reports on progress, but he also had to deal with a French general, Henri Giraud, who had the notion that he (not Eisenhower) would be the one to command the Allied forces.

Eisenhower spent many hours trying to persuade Giraud to take the role as governor and chief of all French forces in North Africa. Finally, Giraud agreed to take the role, but he continued to press Eisenhower for additional equipment and wanted to discuss a landing in the South of France. After calming Giraud down and getting him refocused on the North African campaign, Eisenhower sat down, alone at his desk, and wrote on a blank sheet of paper:

Worries of a Commander:

1. Spain is ominously quiet that Governor of Gibraltar reports himself uneasy. No word from any agent or ambassador.
2. No news from task forces. Reports few and unsatisfactory.
3. Defensive fighting, which seemed halfhearted and spiritless this morning, has blazed up, and in many places resistance is stubborn.
4. No Frenchman immediately available, no matter how friendly toward us, seems able to stop the fighting.
5. Giraud is in Gibraltar, manifestly unwilling to enter the theater so long as fighting is going on.
6. Giraud is difficult to deal with—temperamental, wants much in power, equipment, etc., but seems little disposed to do his part to stop fighting.
7. Giraud wants planes, radios.
8. We are slowed up in eastern sector when we should be getting toward Bone-Bizerte at once.
9. We don't know whereabouts or conditions of airborne force.
10. We cannot find out anything.[26]

Although he could not control all the events swirling around him, he could find some sense of relief in articulating his thoughts at the moment. As the campaign in North Africa continued, Eisenhower had to cope with the uproar surrounding the Darlan deal, the exasperating delays caused by the lack of sufficient strength and poor weather in moving the offensive forward, and a quagmire of political intrigue. This was Eisenhower's first command, and he was anxious to succeed and prove himself worthy of the assignment—something he had worked his entire career for. Yet he was also humble enough to be aware that he had some things to learn in this enormous responsibility.

After the second delay in the offensive and finalizing the Darlan deal, Eisenhower wrote in his diary, "Through all this, I am learning many things: One, that waiting for other people to produce is one of the hardest things a commander has to do.

Two, that in the higher positions of a modern Army, Navy and Air Force, rich organizational experience and an orderly, logical mind are absolutely essential to success. The flashy, publicity-seeking type of adventurer can grab the headlines and be a hero in the eyes of the public, but he simply can't deliver the goods in high command.

"There must be a fine balance — that is exceedingly difficult to find. In addition to the above, a person in such a position must have an inexhaustible fund of nervous energy. He is called upon day and night to absorb the disappointments, the discouragements and the doubts of his subordinates and to force them on to accomplishments, which they regard as impossible. The odd thing about it is that most of these subordinates don't even realize that they are simply pouring their burdens upon the next superior."[27]

Immediately after World War II ended in May 1945, Eisenhower was besieged with invitations to celebration ceremonies throughout Europe. Eisenhower wanted to avoid any events that glorified his own contribution above the thousands of others who worked just as hard as he did and those who paid the ultimate sacrifice.

However, Churchill insisted that Eisenhower make the trip from his headquarters in Frankfurt to Britain on June 12 for a ceremony at the six-hundred-year-old Guildhall where he would be made a Freeman of the City of London and receive the Duke of Wellington Sword. There would be a large audience at the historic hall, including almost every politician and senior military official in the United Kingdom.

"The honor at the Guildhall would require a speech and for a good many days in advance, I worked on a text," Eisenhower wrote. "I knew what I wanted to say, but as usual, I wondered whether I could say it well." For weeks before the ceremony, Eisenhower would go to his quarters after an intense day of work and write until he fell asleep, adding new paragraphs and tweaking others repeatedly. "Although I had spent many hours preparing drafts of reports and speeches for my seniors at the war department, this was the first formal address of any length that

I had to give on my own. I labored at it mightily, never satisfied with a single paragraph."

Eisenhower went over the speech so many times that to his own surprise he committed it to memory. He decided that whether it was good or not, "...it's done. As long as I can do this without notes, I'm ready." But just in case, Eisenhower wrote the first words of each paragraph a small card. Despite his presence for nearly four years on the world's stage, carrying enormous responsibilities, Eisenhower was anxious and somewhat nervous prior to the speech. He decided to take a walk alone in Hyde Park to clear his mind and relax, but he soon had to be rescued by the police from a growing crowd of admirers who wanted to say thanks.

The ceremony was full of British pomp and circumstance. Eisenhower arrived at the famous hall in a horse and carriage, received the Wellington Sword from the mayor of London, and as the crowd sat in absolute silence, he began.

"The high sense of distinction I feel in receiving this great honor from the City of London is inescapably mingled with feelings of profound sadness. All of us must always regret that your great country and mine were ever faced with the tragic situation that compelled the appointment of an Allied Commander-in-Chief, the capacity in which I have just been so extravagantly commended.

"Humility must always be the portion of any man who receives acclaim earned in the blood of his followers and sacrifices of his friends." Eisenhower noted how the extraordinary effort required to achieve success and the feelings of accomplishment could not "soothe the anguish of the widow or the orphan whose husband or father will not return. The only attitude in which a commander may with satisfaction receive the tributes of his friends is in the humble acknowledgment that no matter how unworthy he may be, his position is the symbol of great human forces that have labored arduously and successfully for a righteous cause.... If all the Allied men and women that have served with me in this war can only know that it is they whom this august body is really honoring today, then indeed I will be content.

"I come from the very heart of America," Eisenhower said. The towns where he grew up— Denison, Texas and Abilene, Kansas—were small and young when compared to the grandeur and size of London. Somewhat amazed at the turn of events that found him in his current circumstance, Eisenhower still thought of himself as an ordinary person, unworthy of the attention. Thousands of miles from his roots, "Hardly would it seem possible for the London Council to have gone further afield to find a man to honor with its priceless gift of token citizenship.

"Yet kinship among nations is not determined in such measurements as proximity, size and age," Eisenhower went on. "Rather we should turn to those inner things—call them what you will—I mean those intangibles that are the real treasures free men possess. To preserve his freedom of worship, his equality before law, his liberty to speak and act as he sees fit, subject only to provisions that he trespass not upon similar rights of others—a Londoner will fight. So will a citizen of Abilene. When we consider these things, the valley of the Thames draws closer to the farms of Kansas and the plains of Texas. To my mind it is clear that when two peoples will face the tragedies of war to defend the same spiritual values, the same treasured rights, then in the deepest sense those two are truly related."

Eisenhower spoke of the admiration he and his countrymen had for the British people in standing "alone but unconquered" against Hitler. When United States soldiers began to arrive in England, they saw for themselves the British perseverance through relentless raids and the determination of its citizens to serve "quietly and efficiently in almost every kind of war effort," and the Americans were in awe. "Gradually we drew closer together until we became true partners in war."

Over the last few years, Eisenhower had found himself in London twice to prepare for the greatest military campaigns of their time, and possibly ever—the invasions of the Africa and Europe. That required consistent teamwork and flexibility for all nations involved.

"London's hospitality to the Americans, her good-humored acceptance of the added inconvenience we brought, her example of fortitude and quiet confidence in the final outcome — all these helped to make the Supreme Headquarters of the two Allied expeditions the smooth-working organizations they became." His team included "chosen representatives of two proud and independent peoples, each noted for its imitative and for its satisfaction with its own customs, manners, and methods. Many feared that those representatives could never combine together in an efficient fashion to solve the complex problems presented by modern war.

"I hope you believe we proved the doubters wrong. And, moreover, I hold that we proved this point not only for war — we proved it can always be done by our two peoples, provided only that both show the same good-will, the same forbearance, the same objective attitude that the British and Americans so amply demonstrated in the nearly three years of bitter campaigning."

Eisenhower continued, expressing his belief in that the victory was the result of the efforts of many beyond himself. "No man alone could have brought about this result. Had I possessed the military skill of a Marlborough, the wisdom of Solomon, the understanding of Lincoln, I still would have been helpless without the loyalty, vision, and generosity of thousands upon thousands of British and Americans.

"Some of them were my companions in the High Command. Many were enlisted men and junior officers carrying the fierce brunt of battle, and many others were back in the United States and here in Great Britain, in London.

"Moreover, in back of us always were our great national leaders and their civil and military staffs that supported and encouraged us through every trial, every test. The whole was one great team. I know that on this special occasion three million American men and women serving the Allied Expeditionary Force would want me to pay tribute of admiration, respect, and affection to their British comrades of this war.

"My most cherished hope is that after Japan joins the Nazis in utter defeat, neither my country nor yours need ever again summon its sons and daughters from their peaceful pursuits to face the tragedies of battle. But—a fact important for both of us to remember—neither London nor Abilene, sisters under the skin, will sell her birthright for physical safety, her liberty for mere existence.

"No petty differences in the world of trade, traditions, or national pride should ever blind us to our identities in priceless values.

"If we keep our eyes on this guidepost, then no difficulties along our path of mutual co-operation can ever be insurmountable. Moreover, when this truth has permeated to the remotest hamlet and heart of all peoples, then indeed may we beat our swords into plowshares and all nations can enjoy the fruitfulness of the earth.

"My Lord Mayor, I thank you once again for an honor to me and to the American forces that will remain one of the proudest in my memories."[28]

Eisenhower spoke from his heart, and his sincere expression and thoughtful words moved people to tears. The London press printed the address under the headline of "General Eisenhower Speaks in Immortal Words of His Men and the Meaning of Their Work: The Humility of a Great Soldier" and compared it to the Gettysburg Address. In typical fashion, Eisenhower thought that was "an excess of friendly misjudgment."[29]

"Good judgment seeks balance and progress; lack of it eventually finds imbalance and frustration."

As his presidency was nearing an end, Eisenhower had some things he wanted to say to the American people. He also wanted to express his hopes for the future. Eisenhower worked closely with his team, refining the speech until it hit the right tone. On January 17, 1961, Eisenhower gave his farewell address.

"Three days from now," Eisenhower began, "after half a century in the service of our country, I shall lay down the responsibilities of office as, in traditional and solemn ceremony, the authority of the Presidency is vested in my successor."

Eisenhower wished the new president well and thanked the Congress for working with him to achieve results. Sixty years into the century, the country had been tested by war three wars and had emerged as the strongest and most productive country in the world. While the country was proud of its accomplishments, it also realized that "America's leadership and prestige depend, not merely upon our unmatched material progress, riches and military strength, but on how we use our power in the interests of world peace and human betterment."

However, America's desire "to foster progress in human achievement, and to enhance liberty, dignity and integrity among people and among nations" was under attack, by "a hostile ideology – global in scope, atheistic in character, ruthless in purpose, and insidious in method." Unfortunately, this struggle would continue for decades, requiring vigilance and sacrifice. For each crisis, the allure of more spending to find "the miraculous solution to all current difficulties" would be compelling, but what was needed was balance.

Throughout his presidency, Eisenhower had pursued the "middle way," a path between the extremes, which would enable progress without too much sacrifice. When faced with choices, Eisenhower urged Americans to seek "balance between the private and the public economy, balance between cost and hoped for advantage – balance between the clearly necessary and the comfortably desirable, balance between our essential requirements as a nation and the duties imposed by the nation upon the individual; balance between actions of the moment and the national welfare of the future. Good judgment seeks balance and progress," Eisenhower explained, "lack of it eventually finds imbalance and frustration."

Eisenhower now touched on a topic which he had become increasingly uneasy about as his presidency progressed – the level of funding allocated to defend the nation during times of peace. Although he believed peacetime spending was necessary to discourage aggression from enemies of the country, he thought the government could become susceptible to special interests.

"A vital element in keeping the peace is our military establishment," Eisenhower said. Given the security risks to the country, "we can no longer risk emergency improvisation of national defense; we have been compelled to create a permanent armaments industry of vast proportion." This was "new in the American experience," and the impact was broad. "The total influence — economic, political, even spiritual — is felt in every city, every State house, every office of the Federal government. We recognize the imperative need for this development. Yet we must not fail to comprehend its grave implications. Our toil, resources and livelihood are all involved; so is the very structure of our society."

He warned that the country "must guard against the acquisition of unwarranted influence, whether sought or unsought, by the military-industrial complex. The potential for the disastrous rise of misplaced power exists and will persist. We must never let the weight of this combination endanger our liberties or democratic processes. We should take nothing for granted. Only an alert and knowledgeable citizenry can compel the proper meshing of the huge industrial and military machinery of defense with our peaceful methods and goals, so that security and liberty may prosper together."

Eisenhower then stressed the need to sometimes defer gratification and take a longer view to maintain the promise of America. "As we peer into society's future," Eisenhower continued, "we must avoid the impulse to live only for today, plundering, for our own ease and convenience, the precious resources of tomorrow. We cannot mortgage the material assets of our grandchildren without risking the loss also of their political and spiritual heritage," so future generations could also live and thrive within our democracy.

Throughout his presidency, Eisenhower had strived for arms reductions, and his biggest disappointment when leaving office was that he wasn't able to end the Cold War, which would help to replace "fear and hate" with "mutual trust" and "respect."

Eisenhower confessed "as one who has witnessed the horror and the lingering sadness of war — as one who knows that another war could utterly destroy this civilization which has been so slowly and painfully built over thousands of years — I wish I could say tonight that a lasting peace is in sight." And although "war has been avoided...much remains to be done," and Eisenhower pledged to do everything he could as a private citizen to achieve world peace.

Eisenhower, never a deeply religious man, ended with a prayer. "We pray that peoples of all faiths, all races, all nations, may have their great human needs satisfied; that those now denied opportunity shall come to enjoy it to the full; that all who yearn for freedom may experience its spiritual blessings; that those who have freedom will understand, also, its heavy responsibilities; that all who are insensitive to the needs of others will learn charity; that the scourges of poverty, disease and ignorance will be made to disappear from the earth, and that, in the goodness of time, all peoples will come to live together in a peace guaranteed by the binding force of mutual respect and love."[30]

The address was well received, and it is considered by many to be among the most important speeches ever made by a United States president. His vision of powerful military contractors exerting influence over the government was prescient, and his hopes for an America that would lead the world toward peace and human progress were heartfelt. Although his speech was soon forgotten as the Kennedy administration took office with the promise of closing a fictitious "missile gap," Americans couldn't say they weren't warned about the dangers of the military-industrial complex.

Eisenhower's Leadership Lessons: Communicating

1. Look for opportunities to sharpen your communication skills.
2. Set aside the proper time needed for thinking and writing.
3. Write in an informal style whenever possible.
4. Clearly communicate your assumptions, plans, and expectations.
5. Use communication to build teamwork, morale, and motivation.
6. Frame arguments with questioning.
7. Be crisp and concise in presentations.
8. Answer questions directly and stay on topic.
9. Influence through rational, reasoned communications.
10. Keep a diary to express personal thoughts and ideas.
11. Practice speeches until you've internalized them.
12. Use the power of your position to communicate powerful ideas.

NOTES

DE = Dwight Eisenhower
EL = Eisenhower Library
EP = Eisenhower's Papers
PP = Presidential Papers
MEMCON = Memorandum of Conversation

Chapter 1: Principles

1   Dwight D. Eisenhower, *At Ease: Stories I Tell To Friends* (New York: Doubleday, 1967), 4-5

2   Viscount Montgomery of Alamein, *The Memoirs of Field Marshal Montgomery* (South Yorkshire, England: Pen & Sword Military, 2005), 484

3   Dwight D. Eisenhower, *The Papers of Dwight David Eisenhower*, ed. Alfred D. Chandler, Jr. (Baltimore: The Johns Hopkins Press, 1970), No. 723

4   Dwight D. Eisenhower, *Crusade in Europe* (Baltimore: The Johns Hopkins University Press, 1997), 113-114

5   EP, No. 745

6   EP, No. 745, including footnote 2

7   EP, No. 1564

8   Eisenhower, *At Ease*, 17-18

9   Jack Beatty, Pols: Great Writers on American Politicians from Bryan to Reagan (Cambridge: Public Affairs, 2004)

10   Harry C. Butcher, *My Three Years with Eisenhower: The personal diary of Captain Harry C. Butcher, USNR, naval aide to General Eisenhower, 1942 to 1945* (New York: Simon and Schuster. 1946), 452

11   Eisenhower, *Crusade in Europe*, 453

12   EP, No. 545

13   Steve Neal, *The Eisenhowers* (Lawrence, KS: University Press of Kansas, 1984), 184

14   Dwight D. Eisenhower, *Letters to Mamie*, ed. John S. D. Eisenhower (New York: Doubleday, 1978), 190

15   Dwight D. Eisenhower to Edgar Eisenhower, 9/26/44, Eisenhower Library

16   Ann Whitman to James Hagerty, 6/10/58, James C. Hagerty Papers, EL

17   EP, No 1248

18   DE to Henry Luce, 8/8/60, EL

19   EP, No. 599

20   Dwight D. Eisenhower, *The Eisenhower Diaries*, ed. Robert H. Ferrell (New York: W.W. Norton & Company, 1981), 99-100

21   EP, No. 1734, and footnote 1

22   EP, No. 566

23   Eisenhower, *At Ease,* 354

24   EP, No. 29

25   Eisenhower, *At Ease,* 241

26   DE to Milton S. Eisenhower, 1/3/39, EL

27   Butcher, *My Three Years,* 189

28   Fred I. Greenstein, *The Hidden-Hand Presidency: Eisenhower as Leader* (Baltimore: The John Hopkins University Press, 1994), 45

29   Greenstein, *The Hidden-Hand Presidency,* 43-44

30   Butcher, *My Three Years,* 48

Chapter 2: Learning to Lead

1   Eisenhower, *At Ease*, 7
2   Eisenhower, *At Ease*, 14
3   Stephen E. Ambrose, *Eisenhower, Soldier and President* (New York: Simon and Schuster, 1990), 27
4   Kenneth S. Davis, *Soldier of Democracy – A Biography of Dwight Eisenhower* (Garden City, NY: Doubleday, Doran & Company, 1945), 177-78
5   Dwight D. Eisenhower, *Eisenhower: The Prewar Diaries*, eds. Daniel D. Holt and James Leyerzapf (Baltimore: The Johns Hopkins University Press, 1998), 59
6   Pershing to DE, 8/15/27, EL; Ambrose, *Eisenhower, Soldier and President*, 43
7   Eisenhower, *At Ease*, 213
8   Holt and Leyerzapf, *Eisenhower: The Prewar Diaries*, 44, footnote 1
9   Eisenhower, *At Ease*, 169-172
10 Eisenhower, *At Ease*, 173
11 Eisenhower, *Crusade*, 18
12 Eisenhower, *At Ease*, 187
13 Holt and Leyerzapf, *Eisenhower: The Prewar Diaries*, 60, footnote 1
14 "Dwight D. Eisenhower: Douglas MacArthur's Aide in the 1930s," accessed 10/5/10, http://www.historynet.com/dwight-d-eisenhower-douglas-macarthurs-aide-in-the-1930s.htm
15 Eisenhower, *At Ease*, 214
16 Eisenhower, *At Ease*, 220
17 Holt and Leyerzapf, *Eisenhower: The Prewar Diaries*, 311
18 Holt and Leyerzapf, *Eisenhower: The Prewar Diaries*, 111
19 Holt and Leyerzapf, *Eisenhower: The Prewar Diaries*, 364
20 Geoffrey Perret, *Eisenhower* (Holbrook, MA: Adams Media, 1999), 129-130
21 Eisenhower, *At Ease*, 226
22 DE to John S.D. Eisenhower, 3/2/67, EL
23 Ambrose, *Eisenhower, Soldier and President*, 47

24 Eisenhower, *Crusade in Europe,* 21-22
25 Mark Perry, *Partners in Command: George Marshall and Dwight Eisenhower in War and Peace* (New York: Penguin Books, 2007), 10
26 Eisenhower, *At Ease,* 249-250
27 Butcher, *My Three Years,* 247
28 Eisenhower, *Crusade in Europe,* 141
29 EP, No. 808
30 Eisenhower, *Crusade in Europe,* 142
31 Carlo D'Este, *Eisenhower: A Soldier's Life* (New York: Henry Holt and Company, 2002), 393
32 Martin Blumenson, *Kasserine Pass* (New York: Cooper Square Press, 2000), 142
33 Eisenhower, *Crusade in Europe,* 144
34 Stephen E. Ambrose, *The Supreme Commander: The War Years of General Dwight D. Eisenhower* (New York: Anchor Books, 1969), 174
35 EP, No. 819
36 Eisenhower, *Crusade in Europe,* 150
37 Butcher, *My Three Years,* 287-88
38 Arthur Tedder, *With Prejudice: The World War II Memoirs of Marshal of the Royal Air Force Lord Tedder* (New York: Little, Brown and Company, 1967), 590-591
39 Eisenhower, *Crusade,* 279
40 Ambrose, *Eisenhower: Soldier and President,* 216

Chapter 3. People

1 EP, No. 1062
2 Eisenhower, *At Ease,* 16
3 Hastings Lionel Ismay, *The Memoirs of General Lord Ismay* (New York: Viking Press, 1960) 258-59
4 EP, No. 899
5 EP, No. 1565
6 William L. Shirer, *The Rise and Fall of the Third Reich* (New York: Touchstone, 1959), 1091-92

7   Forest C. Pogue, *Supreme Command: United States Army in World War II European Theater of Operations* (Washington D.C.: Office of the Chief of Military History, Dept. of the Army, 1954), 289

8   Bradley, *A Soldier's Story* (New York: Holt, 1951), 63

9   EP, No. 854

10   EP, No. 927

11   Bradley, *A Soldier's Story*, 62

12   Tedder, *With Prejudice*, 411

13   Bradley, *A Soldier's Story*, 63

14   EP, No. 928

15   EP, No. 915

16   Davis, *Soldier of Democracy*, 177-178

17   Eisenhower, *Crusade in Europe*, 210

18   EP, No. 164

19   Eisenhower, *Crusade in Europe*, 238

20   EP, No. 1377

21   Perret, *Eisenhower*, 324

22   D' Este, *Eisenhower: A Soldier's Life*, 607

23   Eisenhower, *Crusade in Europe*, 210

24   Eisenhower, *At Ease*, 243

25   D' Este, *Eisenhower: A Soldier's Life*, 514

26   Pogue, *Supreme Command*, 166

27   Eisenhower, *Crusade in Europe*, 389

28   Pogue, *Supreme Command*, 289

29   Max Hastings, *Overlord: D-Day and the Battle for Normandy* (New York: Simon & Schuster, 1984), 69

30   D'Este, *Eisenhower: A Soldier's Life*, 511

31   Eisenhower, *Crusade in Europe*, 286

32   Eisenhower, *Crusade in Europe*, 285

33   Montgomery, *Memoirs*, 240

34   D' Este, *Eisenhower: A Soldier's Life*, 553-554

35   EP, No. 1909, footnote 1

36   EP, No. 1934

37   EP, No. 1935

38   Eisenhower, *Crusade in Europe*, 305

39   EP, No.1935

40 EP, No.1936

41 Perret, *Eisenhower,* 320

42 Cornelius Ryan, *A Bridge Too Far: The Classic History of the Greatest Battle of World War II* (New York: Touchstone, 1974), 85-86

43 Kay Summersby, *Eisenhower Was My Boss,* ed. Michael Kearns (New York: Prentice-Hall, 1948), 170

44 EP, No.1957

45 EP, No. 1975, footnote 3

46 EP, No. 1979, footnote 3

47 EP, No. 1193

48 EP, No. 2031, footnotes 3 and 4

49 EP, No. 2032, footnote 2;

50 EP, No. 2032, footnote 2

51 Arthur Bryant, *Triumph of the West* (New York: Doubleday, 1959), 219

52 D' Este, *Eisenhower: A Soldier's Life,* 623

53 EP, No. 2038, also footnote 6

54 Eisenhower, *Crusade in Europe,* 323

55 Bryant, *Triumph in the West,* 252-259

56 Bryant, *Triumph in the West,* 257

57 EP, No. 2145; Bryant, *Triumph in the West,* 260-261

58 Bryant, *Triumph in the West,* 264-265

59 D' Este, *Eisenhower: A Soldier's Life,* 635

60 EP, No. 2163, footnote 1

61 Eisenhower, *Crusade in Europe,* 338, 340

62 D' Este, *Eisenhower: A Soldier's Life,* 641

63 Eisenhower, *Crusade in Europe,* 361

64 EP, No. 2206, footnote 2

65 Butcher, *My Three Years,* 737

66 Eisenhower, *Crusade in Europe,* 286

67 Ambrose, *The Supreme Commander,* 573

68 EP, No. 2210, footnote 2

69 Butcher, *My Three Years,* 737

70 EP, No. 2211

71 EP, No. 2210

72   Sir Francis Wilfred De Guingand, *Generals at War* (London: Hodder and Stoughton, 1964), 108-111
73   Eisenhower, *Crusade in Europe*, 61
74   Winston S. Churchill, *The Second World War Volume 6: Triumph and Tragedy* (New York: Houghton Miffin, 1953), 468
75   "Senator Joseph McCarthy: The History of George Catlett Marshall, 1951," accessed 11/7/10, http://www.fordham.edu/halsall/mod/1951mccarthy-marshall.html
76   Dwight D. Eisenhower, *Mandate for Change, 1953-1956* (Garden City, NY: Doubleday, 1963), 318-319
77   Eisenhower, *Mandate for Change*, 320
78   PP, "104—Remarks at the Dartmouth College Commencement Exercises, Hanover, New Hampshire. June 14, 1953," http://www.presidency.ucsb.edu
79   Haggerty Diary, 3/24/54, EL; Ambrose, *Eisenhower, Soldier and President*, 348
80   EP, No. 757
81   Ambrose, *Eisenhower, Soldier and President*, 364
82   Haggerty Diary, 3/17/54, EL
83   EP, No. 879
84   PP, "128—Address at the Columbia University National Bicentennial Dinner, New York City. May 31, 1954," http://www.presidency.ucsb.edu
85   Holt, *Eisenhower: The Prewar Diaries*, 224
86   Ferrell, *Eisenhower Diaries*, June 11, 1943
87   EP, No. 807
88   Pogue, *Supreme Command*, 164-165
89   Patton to DE, 8/11/45, EP
90   EP, No. 325
91   Ladislas Farago, *Patton: Ordeal and Triumph* (Yardley, PA: Westholme Publishing, 1964), 812-13
92   EP, No. 345
93   EP, No. 358
94   Summersby, *Eisenhower Was My Boss*, 278
95   Ambrose, *Eisenhower, Soldier and President*, 215
96   Eisenhower, *At Ease*, 308

97   PP, "182—Statement by the President on the Death of Chief Justice Vinson, September 8,1953," http://www.presidency.ucsb.edu
98   PP, "198—The President's News Conference of September 30, 1953," http://www.presidency.ucsb.edu
99   Eisenhower, *Mandate for Change*, 228; EP No. 457
100 EP, No. 417
101 EP, No. 414
102 EP, No. 444
103 EP, No. 460

Chapter 4: On Planning and Organizing

1   Pogue, *Supreme Command*, Preface, xii
2   EP, No. 207
3   EP, No. 162
4   EP, No. 207
5   EP, No. 162
6   EP, No. 254
7   Eisenhower, *Crusade in Europe*, 69
8   EP, No. 379
9   EP, No. 387
10   Butcher, *My Three Years*, 29
11   Butcher, *My Three Years*, 30
12   Marshall to King, memorandum, 15 July 1942, WDCSA 381 War Plans, Folder 1, Record Group 165, National Archives, Washington, DC; Robert E. Sherwood, *Roosevelt and Hopkins: An Intimate History* (New York: Harper, 1948), 602-12
13   Butcher, *My Three Years*, 50
14   Eisenhower, *Crusade in Europe*, 71
15   Hastings, *Overlord*, 34
16   Ambrose, *Supreme Commander*, 338-339
17   Eisenhower, *Crusade in Europe*, 449
18   Eisenhower, *Crusade in Europe*, 225
19   Eisenhower, *Crusade in Europe*, 228-229
20   Pogue, *The Supreme Command*, 30
21   EP, No. 89

22 Ambrose, *The Supreme Commander*, 31
23 EP, No. 1536
24 EP, No. 1531, also footnote 3
25 EP, No. 1538
26 EP, No. 1531, footnote 3
27 EP, No. 1547, footnote 1
28 D'Este, *Eisenhower: A Soldier's Life,* 501, Endnote #28, 778
29 EP, Volume 14, Introduction, xvii
30 PP, "53—The President's News Conference of March 11, 1959", http://www.presidency.ucsb.edu
31 Ambrose, *Eisenhower: Solider and President,* 484
32 Ambrose, *Eisenhower: Solider and President,* 484
33 Ambrose, *Eisenhower: Solider and President,* 487
34 EP, No. 1285
35 EP, No. 1145
36 EP, No. 1154, footnote 1
37 EP, No. 1154
38 EP, No. 1189
39 Tedder, *With Prejudice,* 458
40 EP, No. 1198
41 Perret, *Eisenhower,* 236
42 EP, No. 1248
43 EP, No. 1249
44 EP, No. 1255
45 Eisenhower, *Crusade in Europe,* 188
46 EP, No. 1254
47 Eisenhower, *Crusade in Europe,* 188
48 EP, No. 1258, footnote 2
49 EP, No. 1257, footnote 2
50 EP, No. 1283, footnote 1
51 EP, No. 1289, footnotes 1 and 2
52 Eisenhower, *Crusade in Europe,* 194
53 EP, No. 1289
54 Tedder, *With Prejudice,* 473
55 Tedder, *With Prejudice,* 478
56 Eisenhower, *Crusade in Europe,* 191; Tedder, *With Prejudice,* 478

57 EP, No. 1315
58 EP, No. 1318 and footnote 1; Tedder, *With Prejudice*, 476-77
59 EP, No. 1319 and footnote 1
60 EP, No. 1323, footnotes 1 and 3
61 Butcher, *My Three Years*, 430
62 EP, No. 1323 and footnote 3
63 "Gang of Four," accessed 7/7/12, http://www.cfr.org/publication/19583/gang_of_four.html
64 EP, No. 1323 footnote 3
65 Eisenhower, *Crusade in Europe*, 191
66 EP, No. 1329 and footnote 3
67 PP, "31—The President's News Conference of March 19, 1953," http://www.presidency.ucsb.edu
68 Eisenhower, *Mandate for Change*, 446
69 Eisenhower, *Mandate for Change*, 451
70 PP, "54—The President's News Conference of April 23rd, 1953," http://www.presidency.ucsb.edu
71 Emmet John Hughes, *The Ordeal of Power: A Political Memoir of the Eisenhower Years* (New York: Dell Publishing, 1962), 91-92
72 PP, "50—Address "The Chance for Peace," delivered before the American Society of Newspaper Editors, April 16, 1953," http://www.presidency.ucsb.edu
73 Holt, *Eisenhower: The Prewar Diaries*, 54
74 Holt, *Eisenhower: The Prewar Diaries*, 45-46
75 Holt, *Eisenhower: The Prewar Diaries*, 49
76 Holt, *Eisenhower: The Prewar Diaries*, 51
77 DE, Draft Introduction to *Crusade in Europe*, EL
78 Winston S. Churchill, *The Second World War, Volume 4: The Hinge of Fate* (New York: Houghton Miffin, 1950), 610
79 Pogue, *Supreme Command*, 145
80 SHAEF Office Diary, 8/29/44, EL
81 Ambrose, *Eisenhower, Soldier and President*, 331
82 Ambrose, *Supreme Commander*, 510
83 Butcher, *My Three Years*, 645
84 Eisenhower, *Letters to Mamie*, 204, 210
85 Butcher, *My Three Years*, 646

86   EP, No. 533

87   EP, Introduction, xiv

88   EP, Introduction, xv

89   EP, No. 533

90   EP, No. 842

91   EP, No. 718, footnote 1; Hagerty Diary, Feb. 8, 1954, Hagerty Papers, EL

92   EP, No. 842

93   PP, "73 — The President's News Conference, April 7, 1954," http://www.presidency.ucsb.edu

94   Ambrose, *Eisenhower, Soldier and President*, 359;

95   Ambrose, *Eisenhower, Soldier and President*, 363

96   PP, "73 — The President's News Conference, April 7, 1954," http://www.presidency.ucsb.edu

97   Eisenhower, *Mandate for Change*, 374

98   EP, No. 1278

99   Dwight D. Eisenhower, *Waging Peace, 1956-1961* (New York: Doubleday, 1965), 630

100   Eisenhower, *Waging Peace*, 631

101   EP, Introduction, xiv

102   EP, No. 278

103   EP, No. 280

104   EP, No. 292

105   Eisenhower, *Crusade in Europe*, 49

106   EP, No. 313

107   Eisenhower, *Crusade in Europe*, 49

108   Eisenhower, *Crusade in Europe*, 50

109   EP, No. 318

110   EP, No. 320

111   EP, No. 327

112   EP, No. 325

113   EP, No. 329

114   Forrest C. Pogue, *George C. Marshall, Vol. 2: Ordeal and Hope, 1939-1942* (New York: Viking Press, 1966), 330-335

115   Ambrose, *The Supreme Commander*, 55-56

116   Butcher, *My Three Years*, 6-7

117   Butcher, *My Three Years*, 47

118 EP, No. 995
119 Eisenhower, *Mandate for Change*, 83
120 Eisenhower, *Mandate for Change*, 86
121 EP, No. 995
122 Eisenhower, *Mandate for Change*, 87
123 Eisenhower, *Mandate for Change*, 99
124 Greenstein, *The Hidden-Hand Presidency*, 108
125 EP, No. 23
126 Richardson, *Presidency of Eisenhower*, 25
127 EP, No. 1
128 Eisenhower to Captain Evertt ("Swede") Hazlett, January 23, 1956; Greenstein, *The Hidden-Hand Presidency*, 41
129 Eisenhower, *Mandate for Change*, 114
130 Andrew J. Goodpaster interview, EL; Perret, *Eisenhower*, 437
131 Greenstein, *The Hidden-Hand Presidency*, 127
132 Greenstein, *The Hidden-Hand Presidency*, 128

Chapter 5: Achieving Results

1   Eisenhower, *Crusade in Europe*, 222
2   EP, No. 1472
3   Ambrose, *Supreme Commander*, 367
4   EP, No. 1539
5   EP, No. 1539, footnote 2
6   Pogue, *Supreme Command*, 128
7   EP, No. 1539, footnote 2
8   D' Este, *Eisenhower*, 496
9   Perret, *Eisenhower*, 265
10 Eisenhower, *Crusade in Europe*, 222
11 EP, No. 1575, footnote 1; Tedder, *With Prejudice*, 508-512; Butcher, *My Three Years*, 498
12 EP, No. 1577
13 EP, No. 1599
14 David John Cawdell Irving, *War Between the Generals* (New York: Congdon and Weed, 1981), 81
15 EP, No. 1601
16 Tedder, *With Prejudice*, 519

17   Pogue, *Supreme Command*, 129
18   EP, No. 1601, footnote 9
19   EP, No. 1584
20   Ambrose, *The Supreme Commander*, 373
21   EP, No. 1630
22   EP, No. 1662, footnote 1
23   P, No. 1630, footnote 3
24   EP, No. 1658
25   EP, No. 1662; Churchill, *The Second World War, Volume 5: Closing the Ring* (New York: Houghton and Miffin, 1951), 529-530
26   Williamson Murray and Alan R. Millett, *A War To Be Won: Fighting the Second World War* (Cambridge, MA: Belknap Press, 2000), 327; Pogue, *Supreme Command*, 132
27   Ambrose, *Eisenhower: Soldier and President*, 127
28   Ambrose, *Eisenhower, Soldier and President*, 202
29   Eisenhower, *Crusade in Europe*, 246
30   Pogue, *Supreme Command*, 170
31   Tedder, *With Prejudice*, 546
32   Ambrose, *Supreme Commander*, 417
33   PP, "200—The President's News Conference of August 17, 1954," http://www.presidency.ucsb.edu/
34   Eisenhower, *Mandate for Change*, 464
35   PP, "No. 192—The President's News Conference of August 11, 1954," http://www.presidency.ucsb.edu/
36   PP, "No. 345—The President's News Conference of December 2, 1954," http://www.presidency.ucsb.edu/
37   PP, "No. 56—The President's News Conference of March 16, 1955," http://www.presidency.ucsb.edu/
38   PP, "No. 59—The President's News Conference of March 23, 1955," http://www.presidency.ucsb.edu/
39   EP, No. 1363
40   EP, No. 599
41   EP, No. 435
42   EP, No. 593
43   EP, No. 292
44   Eisenhower, *Crusade in Europe*, 105

45 EP, No. 615
46 EP, No. 616
47 Ambrose, *Supreme Commander*, 127
48 Butcher, *My Three Years*, 226
49 Butcher, *My Three Years*, 178
50 Eisenhower, *Crusade in Europe*, 105
51 EP, No. 622
52 U.S. Department of State, *Foreign Relations, 1942*, II, 445-46
53 Sherwood, *Roosevelt and Hopkins*, 655
54 EP, No. 641
55 EP. No. 731
56 EP, No. 673
57 EP, No. 675
58 Eisenhower, *Crusade in Europe*, 121
59 EP, No. 673
60 Eisenhower, *Crusade in Europe*, 121
61 EP, No. 685, footnote 1
62 EP, No. 685, footnote 5
63 EP, No. 698
64 EP, No. 702
65 EP, No. 705
66 Eisenhower, *Crusade in Europe*, 124
67 EP, No. 738
68 Eisenhower, *Crusade in Europe*, 124
69 EP, No. 742
70 EP, No. 741
71 EP, No. 738
72 EP, No. 743
73 EP, No. 756
74 EP, No. 751
75 EP, No. 770
76 Eisenhower, *Crusade in Europe*, 136
77 EP, No. 771, footnote 1
78 D' Este, *Eisenhower: A Soldier's Life*, 383; Sherwood, *Roosevelt and Hopkins*, vol. 2, 667
79 Eisenhower, *Crusade in Europe*, 137
80 EP, No. 783, footnote 2

81   EP, No. 796
82   Eisenhower, *Crusade in Europe,* 139
83   Sir Arthur Bryant, The *Turn of the Tide: a history of the war years based on the diaries of Field-Marshal Lord Alanbrooke, chief of the Imperial General Staff* (New York: Doubleday, 1957), 452-455
84   Sherwood, *Roosevelt and Hopkins,* 677
85   EP, No. 811 and footnote 2
86   Ambrose, *Supreme Commander,* 552; Chester Wilmot, *The Struggle for Europe,* (Old Saybrook, CT: Konecky & Konecky, 1952), 573-74
87   Eisenhower, *Crusade in Europe,* 344-345
88   John S.D. Eisenhower, *The Bitter Woods: The Battle of the Bulge* (New York: G. P. Putnam's Sons, 1969), 215
89   Eisenhower, *Crusade in Europe,* 354
90   EP, No. 2177
91   EP, No. 2178
92   Eisenhower, *Crusade in Europe,* 350
93   EP, No. 2184
94   Eisenhower, *Crusade in Europe,* 355
95   D' Este, *Eisenhower: A Soldier's Life,* 648; Bradley, *A General's Life,* 363; Ambrose, *Eisenhower,* Soldier and President, 368, based on an interview with Strong
96   EP, No. 2191
97   EP, No. 2193
98   Tedder, *With Prejudice,* 629
99   EP, No. 2198, footnote 4
100 Eisenhower, *Crusade in Europe,* 340
101 Eisenhower, *At Ease,* 291
102 PP, "6 – Annual Message to the Congress on the State of the Union, February 2, 1953," http://www.presidency.ucsb.edu
103 Michael S. Mayer, *President Dwight D. Eisenhower and Civil Rights,* Introduction. Eisenhower World Affairs Institute, Washington, DC, accessed 7/7/11, http://www.eisenhowermemorial.org/DDEandCivil%20Rights-screen.pdf
104 Dwight D. Eisenhower, *Waging Peace,* 149

105 PP, "115 – The President's News Conference of *May 19, 1954,*" http://www.presidency.ucsb.edu
106 Robert H. Ferrell, *The Diary of James Hagerty* (Bloomington: Indiana University Press, 1983), 66
107 Eisenhower, *Waging Peace*, 153
108 PP, "2 – Annual Message to the Congress on the State of the Union, January 5, 1956," http://www.presidency.ucsb.edu
109 PP, "133 – Statement by the President on the Objectives of the Civil Rights Bill, July 16, 1957," http://www.presidency.ucsb.edu
110 Eisenhower, *Waging Peace*, 159
111 Eisenhower, *Waging Peace*, 166
112 PP, "189 – Statement by the President Following a Meeting with the Governor of Arkansas,September 14, 1957," http://www.presidency.ucsb.edu
113 PP, "197 – Statement by the President Regarding Occurrences at Central High School in Little Rock,September 23, 1957," http://www.presidency.ucsb.edu
114 PP, "198 – Radio and Television Address to the American People on the Situation in Little Rock,September 24, 1957," http://www.presidency.ucsb.edu
115 Eisenhower, *Waging Peace*, 175
116 Eisenhower, *Waging Peace*, 34
117 EP, No. 1032, footnote 2
118 EP, No 1933, footnote 1
119 EP, No. 1981, footnote 1
120 Eisenhower, *Waging Peace*, 50
121 Eisenhower, *Waging Peace*, 56
122 EP, No. 2038
123 EP, No. 2048
124 Hughes, *The Ordeal of Power*, 185-186
125 Eisenhower, *Waging Peace*, 73
126 Memcon, 10/29/56, EL
127 EP, No. 2051
128 Eisenhower, *Waging Peace*, 80
129 PP, "282 – Radio and Television Report to the American People on the Developments in Eastern Europe and the

Middle East, October 31, 1956," http://www.presidency.ucsb.edu

130 PP, "283—Address in Convention Hall, Philadelphia, Pennsylvania, November 1, 1956" http://www.presidency.ucsb.edu

131 EP, No. 2064

132 Eisenhower, *Waging Peace,* 88

133 Eisenhower, *Waging Peace,* 89

134 Eisenhower, *Waging Peace,* 90; Hughes, *The Ordeal of Power,* 194

135 Eisenhower, *Waging Peace,* 91

136 Eisenhower, *Waging Peace,* 92

137 Hughes, *The Ordeal of Power,* 198

138 James F. Dunnigan. *The World War II Bookshelf: 50 Must Read Books* (New York: Citadel Press, 2004), 110

139 Eisenhower, Crusade in Europe, 256

140 Eisenhower, *Crusade in Europe,* 176

141 Eisenhower, *Crusade in Europe,* 75

142 EP, No. 1886

143 Eisenhower, *Crusade in Europe,* 275

144 Eisenhower, *Mandate for Change,* 548

145 PP, "102—Statement by the President Upon Signing the Federal-Aid Highway Act of 1954, May 6, 1954" http://www.presidency.ucsb.edu

146 EP, No. 871

147 PP, "39—Special Message to the Congress Regarding a National Highway Program, February 22, 1955," http://www.presidency.ucsb.edu

148 Eisenhower, *Mandate for Change,* 544-548

149 Office of Highway Policy Information (December 2011), Table HM-20: Public Road Length - 2010 (Report), Federal Highway Administration, accessed 8/10/10, http://www.fhwa.dot.gov/policyinformation/statistics/2010/hm20.cfm

150 Joel Garreau, *Edge City: Life on the New Frontier* (New York: Doubleday, 1991),14

151 Ambrose, *Eisenhower: Soldier and President,* 453

152 Ambrose, *Eisenhower: Soldier and President*, 453
153 Rushmore DeNooyer, *Sputnik Declassified, Top-secret documents rewrite the history of the famous satellite and the early space race*, aired November 6, 2007 on PBS, accessed 10/6/10, http://www.pbs.org/wgbh/nova/sputnik/
154 EP, No. 683, footnote 1
155 Eisenhower, *Waging Peace*, 270
156 Eisenhower, *Waging Peace*, 273
157 PP, "173 — Statement by the President following the Landing of United States Marines at Beirut, July 15, 1958," http://www.presidency.ucsb.edu
158 Eisenhower, *Waging Peace*, 290

Chapter 6: On Communication

1 Eisenhower, *At Ease*, 326-327
2 EP, No. 1559
3 EP, No. 1567
4 EP, No. 1735
5 EP, No. 2195
6 EP, No. 533
7 "Documents of American History II, 1950s: Dwight D. Eisenhower's 'I Shall Go to Korea" Speech, 1952' Speech, 1952," accessed 9/8/2010, http://tucnak.fsv.cuni.cz/~calda/Documents/1950s/Ike_Korea_52.html
8 Eisenhower, *Mandate for Change*, 95
9 Eisenhower, *Mandate for Change*, 190
10 Eisenhower, *Mandate for Change*, 181
11 Eisenhower, *Mandate for Change*, 191
12 Butcher, *My Three Years*, 442
13 Eisenhower, *Crusade in Europe*, 198-199
14 Eisenhower, *Crusade in Europe*, 194
15 EP, No. 1408
16 Ambrose, *The Supreme Commander*, 304-05
17 EP, No. 1408, footnote 1
18 Pogue, *Supreme Command*, 31

19   PP, "210—Radio and Television Address Opening the President's Campaign for Re-Election, September 19, 1956," http://www.presidency.ucsb.edu

20   PP, "311—Address Delivered Before a Joint Session of the Parliament of India, December 10, 1959," http://www.presidency.ucsb.edu

21   Eisenhower, *Mandate for Change*, 252

22   Eisenhower, *Mandate for Change*, 252

23   EP, No. 598

24   PP, "256—Address Before the General Assembly of the United Nations on Peaceful Uses of Atomic Energy, New York City, December 8, 1953," http://www.presidency.ucsb.edu

25   EP, No. 598

26   EP, No. 589

27   EP, No. 705

28   Eisenhower, *At Ease*, 388-390

29   Butcher, *My Three Years*, 862

30   PP, "421—Farewell Radio and Television Address to the American People, January 17, 1961," http://www.presidency.ucsb.edu

INDEX